Contemporary Appellate Advocacy

Contemporary Appellate Advocacy

Ann Ching
CLINICAL PROFESSOR OF LAW
ARIZONA STATE UNIVERSITY
SANDRA DAY O'CONNOR COLLEGE OF LAW

David B. Gass
CHIEF JUDGE
ARIZONA COURT OF APPEALS
DIVISION ONE

CAROLINA ACADEMIC PRESS
Durham, North Carolina

Library of Congress Cataloging-in-Publication Data
Names: Ching, Ann author | Gass, David B. author
Title: Contemporary appellate advocacy / Ann Ching, David B. Gass.
Description: Durham, North Carolina : Carolina Academic Press, 2025. | Includes bibliographical references and index.
Identifiers: LCCN 2025005486 | ISBN 9781531026523 paperback | ISBN 9781531026530 ebook
Subjects: LCSH: Appellate procedure—United States | Trial practice—United States | Appellate procedure | Legal composition
Classification: LCC KF9050 .C49 2025 | DDC 347.73/8—dc23/eng/20250207
LC record available at https://lccn.loc.gov/2025005486

Carolina Academic Press
700 Kent Street
Durham, North Carolina 27701
(919) 489-7486
www.cap-press.com

Printed in the United States of America

Contents

Acknowledgments

Contemporary Appellate Advocacy is the culmination of my appellate practice experience as both a lawyer and educator. I am grateful for the support and contributions of numerous individuals who have guided and inspired me throughout the journey of writing this book.

I would like to express my sincere appreciation to my appellate advocacy students at the Pepperdine Caruso School of Law and the Arizona State University Sandra Day O'Connor College of Law. Their thoughtful feedback has significantly influenced the development of this book. I also wish to thank my research assistants, Kenneth Misajet and Mira Eissa, for their outstanding contributions.

I am fortunate to have worked alongside exceptional legal writing colleagues at Pepperdine and Arizona State University. Their encouragement and willingness to share teaching materials and practical insights has been invaluable.

To my family and friends, I offer heartfelt thanks for their unwavering support throughout the writing process. My husband deserves special recognition for his patience and partnership. I also wish to honor the memory of my parents, Nancy Ann Ching and Anthony B. Ching, whose enduring influence continues to inspire me. My father, Arizona's first Solicitor General, has been a lasting role model for me and many others in the appellate practice community, and his legacy motivates me to strive for excellence.

Finally, I extend my deepest gratitude to the editors at Carolina Academic Press, particularly David Herzig, for believing in this project. As an educator who has long relied on CAP's publications, I am honored to contribute to their collection of high-quality legal writing texts.

Ann Ching

I will be brief, otherwise the acknowledgment would be longer than the book. I start with my husband Donald Karl, who believed in me before I did. I advance to my mother, Betty Gass, who endured so much and who found her options limited because of others. My options came because of her. Then

I move on to my granny, Velma Jean Moser, who taught me love and kindness and acceptance. I cannot end without mentioning my co-author, Ann Ching, who envisioned a book to help students in an ever changing world. It truly is her book. And lastly, I have Ann's husband Al to thank, who adores Ann and encourages her to live her dreams, like writing this book. His love for Ann is inspiring and endearing. He makes us both laugh.

David B. Gass

Introduction

Appellate advocacy is often viewed through an aura of nobility and intellectual challenge. Think of the movies and television shows that depict a lone advocate standing before a panel of esteemed judges, passionately arguing on behalf of a deserving client. In popular culture, appellate practice is typically portrayed as a high-stakes, dramatic showdown between advocates and jurists.

However, the reality of appellate practice is more nuanced. While it can be a noble pursuit, it can also be routine, even unappreciated. Yet appellate practice remains both a vital component of the U.S. legal system and a laudable career goal. Effective appellate advocates play a crucial role in representing clients while ensuring adherence to high ethical standards and the rule of law.

For law students, studying appellate advocacy offers a unique opportunity to hone written and oral advocacy skills. Developing expertise in appellate advocacy can enhance your ability to analyze complex legal issues, craft persuasive arguments, and communicate effectively with judges, clients, and colleagues.

For practicing lawyers, appellate advocacy presents a chance to refine skills, expand knowledge, and make a meaningful impact. Even those who practice appellate law only on a pro bono basis want to deliver their best performance. Career appellate practitioners can also benefit from exploring new perspectives and best practices.

This textbook aims to demystify the appellate process by providing a comprehensive guide to the art and practice of appellate advocacy. Through a combination of theoretical foundations and practical advice, this book explores the intricacies of appellate practice and empowers you to become a more effective advocate.

Why choose this book?

Contemporary Appellate Advocacy is a comprehensive textbook designed to teach the fundamentals of appellate advocacy to law students and lawyers. This book aims to be a practical, relatable, and engaging guide to the art and science of appellate advocacy.

Contemporary Appellate Advocacy stands out from other textbooks due to its:

- Practical approach, making complex concepts accessible and easy to understand
- Emphasis on ethics and technology, reflecting the evolving nature of appellate practice
- Direct discussions of professionalism and bias, promoting self-awareness and effective advocacy
- Reliance on disciplines outside the law, such as psychology, economics, and social science, to teach concepts relating to persuasion
- Modern approach to writing style and grammar, eschewing old-fashioned rules in favor of a more conversational style

Based on these qualities, *Contemporary Appellate Advocacy* is a suitable text for a wide variety of audiences. You'll find this book to be useful, whether you are:

- New to appellate practice and seeking a comprehensive introduction
- Looking to sharpen your writing skills and improve your advocacy
- Interested in understanding the psychology of persuasion and effective legal writing
- Teaching appellate advocacy and seeking a valuable resource for your students
- Participating in a moot court program or clerking for a judge

The practical nature of this text extends beyond these pages. For one, both authors bring a wealth of real-world expertise and practical wisdom to these pages. Ann Ching is an experienced lawyer and a full-time law professor. Even throughout her teaching career, Professor Ching has continued to serve as a part-time judge, a volunteer appellate attorney for veterans, and a volunteer ethics lawyer for the State Bar of Arizona. David Gass is a seasoned judge, having served on the trial bench of the Arizona Superior Court and as an appellate judge for the Arizona Court of Appeals, Division One. Judge Gass is nationally recognized for his excellence in teaching judges and lawyers the finer points of written and oral advocacy.

Using *Contemporary Appellate Advocacy* to enhance your skills

This book is designed to support your goals and enhance your skills in appellate advocacy. It can be used as a:

- Primary textbook for appellate advocacy courses
- Supplemental resource for moot court programs or clerkships
- Reference guide for practicing lawyers seeking to improve their skills

The way you approach this book will be guided by your purpose in using it. In terms of structure, this book is divided into five parts:

1. Introduction to Appellate Advocacy
2. Constructing Appellate Briefs
3. A Contemporary Advocate's Guide to Persuasive Writing
4. Oral Argument: Strategies for Success
5. Special Considerations (including legal technology, moot court, and clerkships)

If you're a teacher adopting this book as a primary text, then you'll want to assign chapters of the book in a way that best fits your lesson plans. For example, you may want students to draft only the appellate argument before turning in a full brief. If so, then you'll want to skip the chapter on other parts of the appellate brief early in the semester, returning to that material after the first draft. Or perhaps you'd prefer to discuss the ethics of appellate practice at the midpoint of the semester, rather than at the beginning. Although the ethics chapter is in Part 1, you could easily assign it later in the semester without sacrificing meaning or context. The Teacher's Manual provides a sample syllabus in addition to exercises and other materials.

If you're a student using this book as either a primary or supplementary textbook for an appellate advocacy class, you have several options. You can certainly follow your teacher's syllabus, reading the material as assigned. But given the manageable length and readability of this text, you could also choose to read ahead and focus on parts that interest you most. So, for example, if you'd like to start your semester reading about the psychology of persuasion, you could skip to Part 3.

Practicing lawyers, even those with significant experience, can also benefit from this text. If you're an experienced appellate lawyer, then perhaps you can skim or skip some of the foundational chapters on the appellate process or the different parts of an appellate brief. However, you'll likely learn something new in the other chapters, especially with regard to technology-related topics like formatting briefs for text-to-speech, using legal analytics and generative artificial intelligence tools, and the ethical considerations for lawyers seeking to adopt new legal technology.

Regardless of your purpose in using *Contemporary Appellate Advocacy*, thank you for taking the time to read and engage with this text. We're confident it will help you gain a deeper understanding of the complexities of appellate practice, enabling you to become a more effective and persuasive advocate.

Ann Ching
Clinical Professor of Law
Arizona State University
Sandra Day O'Connor College of Law

David B. Gass
Chief Judge
Arizona Court of Appeals
Division One

Part 1

Introduction to Contemporary Appellate Advocacy

Chapter 1

Overview of Appellate Practice in the United States

In this chapter, you will become familiar with:

- The skills required in appellate practice
- The appellate court structure in the federal system
- Appellate practice in state courts and tribal courts
- Appeals from administrative agency decisions

I. Introduction

Appellate advocacy is a specialized area of practice with its own courts, rules, and legal doctrines. Moreover, successful appellate practice requires developing skills that differ from those employed by trial advocates and other lawyers. This chapter introduces you to some of the fundamental skills required for a successful appellate practice. You'll also become familiar with the general structure of appellate courts within the federal, state, tribal, and administrative systems. By the end of this chapter, you'll see that many opportunities exist for lawyers to engage in appellate advocacy within the federal, state, and tribal systems. The next chapter takes a closer look at the procedural steps within the life cycle of a typical appeal.

II. How to be a successful appellate advocate

At a fundamental level, appellate advocates must develop the skills that are required in all areas of legal practice:

- Communicating professionally, whether in writing or orally
- Researching the law
- Critically analyzing legal precedent and applying it to a client's facts
- Paying attention to details, big and small
- Balancing workload
- Planning for contingencies
- Meeting deadlines
- Staying abreast of developments in your area of practice
- Maintaining emotional and physical well-being

Take a close look at this list. If you feel that you're deficient in any of these areas, then addressing the deficiency should be the first priority. In the long run, a productive and healthy legal career requires a strong command of these fundamentals.

Beyond these foundational skills, appellate practice requires both specialized legal knowledge and a deep understanding of how to persuade. Appellate advocates must develop expertise not only in their substantive practice area but also in the legal concepts that are essential to appellate practice:

- Appellate jurisdiction
- Standards of review
- Preservation of error
- Doctrines like justiciability, collateral estoppel, law of the case, res judicata, and abstention
- Federalism and the relationship between state and federal courts

You can acquire this knowledge in many ways. Lawyers usually develop their expertise through a combination of law school classes, continuing education courses, self-study, and on-the-job training. Many lawyers also join groups geared toward appellate practitioners, whether through the American Bar Association, a state bar association, or a legal nonprofit organization.

Although this book touches on some of the legal concepts above, it focuses on the technical skills possessed by the best appellate practitioners. Writing a persuasive appellate brief is the sine qua non of appellate practice. Doing so requires these skills:

- Identifying appellate issues
- Structuring appellate arguments
- Learning how to effectively persuade judges
- Employing persuasive writing techniques
- Drafting all components of an appellate brief
- Consulting the rules of appellate procedure and an appellate court's local rules
- Formatting a brief for electronic filing and screen reading
- Developing confidence and competence in oral advocacy
- Using legal technology effectively
- Understanding the ethical and professional issues arising in appellate practice

If this list seems daunting, do not despair. This book provides a solid foundation for each of the skills described above. But of course, a book can only do so much. The practice of law requires, well, practice. The rest of this chapter provides a starting point with a high-level overview of appellate practice in the United States.

III. Appellate practice in federal courts

In the federal system, appellate practice begins at the district courts, which are the federal trial courts. The United States currently has ninety-four district courts, divided among twelve federal circuits—the eleven numbered circuits plus the D.C. Circuit. Broadly speaking, district courts have jurisdiction over actions involving federal law, both civil and criminal. Title 28 of the U.S. Code, Chapter 85, sets forth the civil jurisdiction of district courts. You're likely most familiar with civil actions that present a question under federal law (statutes, treaties, and the U.S. Constitution) and civil actions where the amount in question exceeds $75,000 and the parties have diversity of citizenship. The district courts also exercise jurisdiction in a number of other areas, such as actions against foreign states, admiralty and maritime cases, election disputes, postal matters, and patent law. On the criminal side, district courts have jurisdiction over "all offenses against the laws of the United States."

Once a case is litigated to a final judgment in a district court, a non-prevailing party may file an appeal. (In criminal cases, however, the United States cannot appeal an acquittal.) Sometimes, a party can file an appeal before the court renders its final judgment or order. Interlocutory appeals are appeals from a court order that decides some issue(s) in a case before the case is litigated to a final judgment. The most common example is an appeal of a district court's injunction.

An appeal from a district court will go to an intermediate appellate court. The federal system has thirteen intermediate courts of appeals—one for each of the eleven numbered circuits plus the D.C. Circuit and the Federal Circuit. (Although the Federal Circuit does not have any district courts, it exercises appellate jurisdiction over certain types of claims such as patents, trademarks, international trade, and veterans' benefits.)[1]

Once an appeal reaches a federal court of appeals, it will be assigned randomly to a panel of three judges. In the majority of cases, the panel will decide the appeal based on the briefs filed by the parties, which are accompanied by the record of what occurred in the court below. In some cases, the court will also hear oral argument from the parties. Sometimes, a nonparty will file a brief as an amicus curiae, or friend of the court. An amicus brief may educate the court on relevant issues or explain the consequences of any potential decision.

Federal appellate courts are limited in what they can consider. When it comes to facts, the court must consider only what's contained in the record; the parties cannot submit new evidence. If additional evidence is material to resolving an issue, the court may remand the case to the district court for further proceedings. In addition, the appellate court will typically only consider issues that are properly preserved at trial and adequately argued by the parties in their briefs. Under some circumstances, such as avoiding manifest injustice, the court will exercise its discretion to consider issues outside of the briefs.

Within the federal system, the court of appeals is bound to follow mandatory authority, sometimes called binding precedent. Stare decisis dictates that a federal court of appeals must follow precedent from the U.S. Supreme Court. In addition, a federal circuit court will ordinarily follow its own precedent. Put another way, a federal circuit court will not depart from its prior decisions absent a compelling reason such as:

- The prior decision was poorly reasoned.
- Intervening circumstances have made the prior decision unworkable or impractical.
- Following the prior decision would be unjust.

---

1. 28 U.S.C. § 1295.

Notably, there's no horizontal stare decisis among the federal circuit courts of appeals. For example, the U.S. Court of Appeals for the Ninth Circuit does not have to follow a prior decision from any other circuit, even when the prior decision deals with the same area of law and similar facts. This lack of horizontal stare decisis means that, over time, the law could develop in very different ways in one circuit as compared to another. When circuits diverge in this manner, a circuit split can develop.[2] The split will remain unless one court switches direction or the U.S. Supreme Court decides to take up a case that will resolve the split.

The three-judge panel will make a decision either unanimously or with a two-to-one decision, where one judge dissents. The court's decision may resolve the case altogether, or the court may remand the case to the lower court for additional proceedings. At that point, the parties have several options. They could petition the panel for a rehearing per Federal Rule of Appellate Procedure (FRAP) Rule 40. The party filing the petition "must state with particularity each point of law or fact that the petitioner believes the court has overlooked or misapprehended and must argue in support of the petition."[3]

In addition, FRAP Rule 35 allows the parties to petition for a rehearing en banc, which takes place before all of the judges for that court. (For circuits with more than fifteen judges, the court can decide per its local rules how many judges will hear a case en banc.) Rule 35 states: "An en banc hearing or rehearing is not favored and ordinarily will not be ordered unless: (1) en banc consideration is necessary to secure or maintain uniformity of the court's decisions; or (2) the proceeding involves a question of exceptional importance."

A party could also request that the U.S. Supreme Court review the appellate court's decision. Doing so requires filing a petition for a writ of certiorari within ninety days of the appellate court's decision or denial of a rehearing. The U.S. Supreme Court has the discretion to grant or deny certiorari, and a grant of certiorari requires four of the nine justices. Because Supreme Court review is discretionary, the Court will typically grant certiorari only when a case is of nationwide importance. For example, the Court may grant certiorari to resolve a circuit split or to address a precedent that has become untenable. Out of approximately 7,000 to 8,000 petitions received, the Court grants certi-

---

2. If you'd like to learn more, every year the Congressional Research Service publishes a report that documents circuit splits. To access Congressional Research Service reports on circuit splits, you can visit https://crsreports.congress.gov/ and type "circuit splits" in the search bar.

3. Fed. R. App. P. 40(a)(2).

orari in about eighty cases per term.[4] The Court hears oral argument in every case for which it grants certiorari.

When the Court grants certiorari, the case is docketed and undergoes a full briefing cycle. The Court hears oral argument in every case. The Court issues written decisions requiring a majority of justices (usually five out of nine) to agree on the outcome to create a majority opinion. When justices agree on the outcome but not the reasoning, they may file concurring opinions. Justices who dissent do not agree on the outcome, and they may file a dissenting opinion to explain their reasoning. Only the majority opinion creates binding precedent. Sometimes, a majority of justices agree on the outcome but not on the reasoning. This creates a plurality opinion. As with the circuit courts of appeal, a U.S. Supreme Court decision may resolve a case, or it may send the case back to a lower court for further proceedings.

The U.S. Supreme Court, unlike other federal courts, has no binding precedent to follow from a higher court. But as with the federal circuit courts, the U.S. Supreme Court will ordinarily follow its own precedents under the principle of stare decisis. Of course, this means that the Court is also free to depart from its own precedents, and the Court has done so in notable fashion in the last few years.[5]

In addition to its ordinary appellate jurisdiction (and its occasional exercise of original jurisdiction),[6] the U.S. Supreme Court also has certain responsibilities regarding death penalty cases. State or federal inmates sentenced to death may contest their imprisonment or death sentence by filing a writ of habeas corpus in any federal court, including the U.S. Supreme Court. A state inmate must exhaust the state's process for direct appeal and post-conviction review before filing a writ of habeas corpus in federal court. A writ of habeas corpus must allege a violation of federal law, such as a deprivation of the right to a public trial under the Sixth Amendment. In addition, a death-row inmate can petition the Court for an emergency stay of execution pending resolution of litigation in a lower court or grant of a writ of certiorari by the Court.

---

4. *Frequently Asked Questions — General Information*, Supreme Court of the United States, https://www.supremecourt.gov/about/faq_general.aspx (last visited Aug. 14, 2024).

5. *E.g.*, Dobbs v. Jackson Women's Health Org., 597 U.S. 215 (2022), *overruling* Roe v. Wade, 410 U.S. 113 (1973); Loper Bright Enters. v. Raimondo, 603 U.S. 369 (2024) (overruling the doctrine of *Chevron* deference established in Chevron U.S.A., Inc. v. Nat. Res. Def. Council, Inc., 467 U.S. 837 (1984)).

6. The U.S. Supreme Court exercises original jurisdiction in "all cases affecting ambassadors, other public ministers and consuls, and those in which a state shall be party." U.S. Const. art. III, § 2, cl. 2.

Although the section above describes the typical process for cases originating in district courts, the federal system also has specialty courts with their own procedures. The U.S. Court of International Trade, like the U.S. Supreme Court, federal appellate courts, and district courts, is a court constituted under Article III of the U.S. Constitution. As the name implies, this court has jurisdiction over international trade matters. Appeals from the U.S. Court of International Trade are heard by the U.S. Court of Appeals for the Federal Circuit.

Other specialty courts are constituted under Article I of the U.S. Constitution, meaning that they are created by an act of Congress and exercise less than full judicial power. For example, the military justice system has its own court system with jurisdiction over criminal cases arising from violations of the Uniform Code of Military Justice. A trial takes place at a court-martial, and each branch of service has its own court of appeals (e.g., the Army Court of Criminal Appeals). Decisions of these service courts can be appealed to the U.S. Court of Appeals for the Armed Forces, which grants discretionary review. In turn, final decisions of the U.S. Court of Appeals for the Armed Forces can be reviewed in the U.S. Supreme Court upon a grant of certiorari. Other examples of Article I courts are the U.S. Court of Federal Claims; the U.S. Military Commissions at Guantanamo Bay, Cuba; the U.S. Court of Appeals for Veterans Claims; and the U.S. Bankruptcy Courts.

Article IV of the U.S. Constitution empowers Congress to create courts in the U.S. territories. The federal territorial courts currently in existence are the district courts in Guam, the U.S. Virgin Islands, and the Northern Mariana Islands, which are included in the total number of federal district courts (ninety-four). Also included in that count is the U.S. District Court for the District of Puerto Rico, which is an Article III court by statute even though Puerto Rico is not a state.

You may have noticed that of the five inhabited U.S. territories, American Samoa is the only one without a federal district court. Instead, American Samoa has its own court system consisting of a local district court and the High Court of American Samoa. Still, the federal government has a role in American Samoa's judicial system; the Secretary of the Interior appoints two of the High Court's justices.

You may be most familiar with the standard appellate process in federal courts: district court, to a circuit court of appeals, to the U.S. Supreme Court (if certiorari is granted). Although less familiar, practicing in the specialty courts described above can also allow for a robust, challenging, and meaningful appellate practice. As the next section explained, state courts offer even more opportunities for appellate advocacy.

IV. Appellate practice in state courts

The court structure in the fifty U.S. states usually mirrors that of the federal system, with trial courts, intermediate appellate courts, and courts of last resort (i.e., the court having the highest appellate jurisdiction in the state). A handful of states (e.g., Montana, Delaware, and Vermont) and the District of Columbia do not have intermediate appellate courts. Beyond that general structure, state courts can differ widely from federal courts in terms of jurisdiction, lower court structure, appellate review, and types of opinions issued.

State constitutions and statutes set forth the structure of state judicial systems. At the trial level, many states divide their courts into those of general jurisdiction and those of limited jurisdiction.[7] A general jurisdiction court can hear any type of case arising under state law. A court of limited jurisdiction may be limited by the type of case it can hear (e.g., only criminal misdemeanors or only tax cases) or by the amount in controversy (e.g., a small claims court that is limited to $3,500 or less). For example, Wyoming has trial courts of general jurisdiction, called district courts,[8] and trial courts of limited jurisdiction, called circuit courts.[9] The Wyoming district courts serve as the appellate courts for decisions of the circuit courts. This system—general jurisdiction trial courts having appellate review of limited jurisdiction courts—is typical for states with limited jurisdiction courts.

States handle appeals in a variety of ways. For states without an intermediate appellate court, the state court of last resort (often called the supreme court) typically has mandatory review of certain appeals and discretionary review over other actions. For example, in Delaware the supreme court has mandatory review of final civil and criminal actions, but discretionary review of certified questions from federal courts.[10] In states with intermediate appellate courts, those courts typically have mandatory review, and the court of last resort exercises discretionary review.

State courts can depart from federal courts in terms of justiciability doctrines. For example, some state supreme courts issue advisory opinions.[11] In

---

7. *State Court Organization Data*, Nat'l Ctr. for State Courts, https://www.ncsc.org/sco (last visited Sept. 14, 2024).

8. *About the District Courts*, Wyo. Jud. Branch, https://www.courts.state.wy.us/district-courts/about-the-district-courts/ (last visited Sept. 14, 2024).

9. *Circuit Courts*, Wyo. Jud. Branch, https://www.courts.state.wy.us/circuit-courts/ (last visited Sept. 14, 2024).

10. Del. R. Sup. Ct. 41(b).

11. Alicia Bannon, *Judicial Advisory Opinions Explained*, State Court Report (Nov. 17, 2023), https://statecourtreport.org/our-work/analysis-opinion/judicial-advisory-opinions-explained.

contrast, the U.S. Supreme Court does not issue advisory opinions; it decides issues of law related only to actual cases and controversies before the court.

Although state and federal judicial systems run parallel, they do intersect and overlap. In general, state courts can hear cases that a federal court would also have jurisdiction over.[12] In those cases, a civil defendant in state court can file a motion to remove the case to federal court.[13] To do so, the federal court must have jurisdiction over the claim (e.g., federal question jurisdiction). Removing a state case to the federal district court terminates the state proceedings. At other times, a state court and the district court may be hearing cases involving the same area of law and/or the same parties. This may trigger doctrines that will preclude the federal court from deciding a case, such as the Rooker-Feldman doctrine[14] or various other abstention doctrines.[15]

When issues in a state case involve the U.S. Constitution, the parties could petition the U.S. Supreme Court to review the final decision from the state court of last resort in the form of a direct appeal. Although the federal circuit courts do not have jurisdiction over direct appeals from state courts, they may engage in collateral review of state court decisions, as with writs of habeas corpus.

Keep in mind that this section provides a fairly limited and high-level overview of the interplay between state and federal courts. Lawyers who handle state court appeals must be knowledgeable not only in their state's laws, court structure, and procedure but also in the federal law governing removal, abstention, and appellate jurisdiction.

But even this limited overview demonstrates the many opportunities for appellate practice within state courts. In states where trial courts of general jurisdiction review decisions from courts of limited jurisdiction, an advocate can engage in appellate practice entirely within the trial courts. When a case involves issues of federal constitutional law, an advocate may have the opportunity to argue in both state and federal appellate courts.

---

12. *E.g.*, Claflin v. Houseman, 93 U.S. 130, 136 (1876).

13. 28 U.S.C. § 1446.

14. This judicial abstention doctrine derives its name from two cases: *Rooker v. Fidelity Trust Co.*, 263 U.S. 413 (1923), and *District of Columbia Court of Appeals v. Feldman*, 460 U.S. 462 (1983). Generally speaking, this doctrine prevents federal courts from "attack[ing] state court judgments" and "claims that are 'inextricably intertwined' with those state court judgments." Michael R. Dezsi, *Obstacles to Federal Jurisdiction*: Rooker-Feldman *and Other Abstention Doctrines*, MICH. BAR J. 36, 36 (Feb. 2007) (quoting Pennzoil Co. v. Texaco Inc., 481 U.S. 1, 25 (1987) (Marshall, J., concurring)).

15. *See, e.g.*, Dezsi, *supra* note 24, at 38–39.

V. Appellate practice in tribal courts

According to the U.S. Department of the Interior, 574 tribal nations exist within the geographic boundaries of the United States.[16] These tribes are self-governing sovereign nations with their own systems of law. The 1934 Indian Reorganization Act authorized tribes to establish their own court systems.[17] As with any sovereign, tribes are free to design their judiciary as they desire, but the general structure of trial courts and appellate courts is common among tribes. In addition, many tribes use traditional dispute resolution practices either as part of the judicial system or adjacent to it.

The Navajo Nation's court system, the largest tribal judiciary in the United States, provides an example of tribal court structure. The Navajo Nation has a two-tier system consisting of district (trial) courts and a supreme court.[18] Patterned after the American court system, the district courts have civil and limited criminal jurisdiction.[19] The supreme court has appellate jurisdiction over final decisions of the district courts, appellate jurisdiction over agency decisions, and the authority to issue special writs.[20]

Per the Navajo Nation Code, the courts are authorized to apply the Navajo Nation's statutory law, Navajo traditional or customary law, federal law, and even state law, when appropriate.[21] Outside of the formal judicial system, parties may also engage in peacemaking as a form of alternative dispute resolution.[22] The Navajo Nation Peacemaking Program, although rooted in Navajo tradition, operates formally within the Navajo Nation with its own program staff and specialists.[23]

Thus, appellate practitioners in the Navajo Nation must understand the court system, including the Nation's code and rules of appellate procedure. In large part, the system's structure and rules mirror those of the U.S. federal

---

16. *Tribal Leaders Directory*, U.S. Dep't of Interior, Bureau of Indian Affairs (last updated Jan. 8, 2024), https://www.bia.gov/service/tribal-leaders-directory.

17. Indian Reorganization Act of 1934, 25 U.S.C. §§ 5101–5103, 5107–5113, 5115, 5116, 5118, 5120, 5121, 5123–5125, 5129; *Tribal Courts*, U.S. Dep't of Justice, Bureau of Justice Statistics, https://bjs.ojp.gov/topics/tribal-crime-and-justice/tribal-courts (last visited Aug. 14, 2024).

18. Jud. Branch of the Navajo Nation, https://courts.navajo-nsn.gov/ (last visited Aug 14, 2024).

19. Navajo Nation Code Ann. tit. 7, § 253.

20. Navajo Nation Code Ann. tit. 7, § 302.

21. Navajo Nation Code Ann. tit. 7, § 204(a)–(d).

22. *Courts & Peacemaking in the Navajo Nation*, Jud. Branch of the Navajo Nation (last updated Feb. 23, 2021), https://courts.navajo-nsn.gov (follow "Public Guide to the Courts" in the left-hand navigation menu).

23. *The Peacemaking Program of the Navajo Nation*, Jud. Branch of the Navajo Nation, https://courts.navajo-nsn.gov/indexpeacemaking.htm (last visited Aug. 14, 2024).

system. But in the Navajo Nation, as in other tribal court systems, practitioners must understand the interplay between codified law and tribal traditions and customs.[24] In smaller tribes, the appellate courts may lack opportunities to develop legal precedent, further complicating appellate practice.[25] Thus, the complex nature of tribal practice presents rewarding opportunities for appellate advocates.

VI. Appeals of administrative agency decisions

In federal, state, and tribal jurisdictions, opportunities abound for appellate practice in administrative law. Although this section examines only the structure of administrative agencies and appeals in the federal system, the state and tribal systems are often analogous.

The numerous administrative agencies in the federal government fall under the executive branch. Over the years, many commentators have described administrative agencies as "hydra-headed," based on their sheer number and size. Currently, the Federal Register lists 439 administrative agencies, ranging from those many Americans have heard of (Central Intelligence Agency, Defense Department) to those less familiar (Marine Mammal Commission, Susquehanna River Basin Commission).[26] Within their statutory authority, these agencies regulate numerous aspects of American life—the foods we eat, the drugs we take, and the delivery of mail, to name just a few.

Many agencies also perform adjudicatory functions, such as issuing licenses, determining immigration status, and awarding veterans benefits. Thus, the Administrative Procedure Act sets forth procedures for administrative agency hearings.[27] Formal hearings (and some informal hearings) are presided over by administrative law judges appointed pursuant to federal law.[28] Parties who are aggrieved by an agency decision may seek judicial review of the agency's final action in the matter.[29]

---

24. *See, e.g.*, Todd R. Matha, *An Unexpected Challenge: The Consequence of a Limited Tribal Appellate Caseload*, 23 J. App. Practice & Process 1–2 (Winter 2023).

25. *Id.*

26. Fed. Register: The Daily Journal of the United States Government, https://www.federalregister.gov/agencies (last visited Sept. 8, 2024).

27. 5 U.S.C. §§ 556–559.

28. 5 U.S.C. § 3105; *see also* Exec. Order No. 13843; Lucia v. Sec. & Exch. Comm'n, 585 U.S. 237 (2018).

29. 5 U.S.C. § 704.

In some federal agencies, obtaining a final action requires going through an appellate process within the agency itself. For example, the U.S. Social Security Administration administers many types of monetary benefits, including SSDI (Social Security Disability Insurance) and SSI (Supplemental Security Income). A person seeking these benefits initiates the process by submitting an application to the agency. If denied, a party may request a hearing before an administrative law judge. Similar to a trial, a party may request evidence, submit evidence, and appear with a representative. If the party is denied benefits in part or in full, the party may seek appellate review from the agency's Appeals Council. A party who disagrees with the Appeals Council's decision, which is the agency's final action, may then file a suit in the appropriate federal district court. The suit would then follow the typical federal litigation and appeals process.

For certain agency actions, federal statutes provide that final decisions are reviewed by a federal court of appeals rather than through a suit brought in a federal district court.[30] For example, final decisions from the U.S. Patent Trial and Appeal Board go directly to the Federal Circuit for judicial review. In a few instances, an Article I court is part of the appellate process. Final agency decisions by the Veterans Administration, for example, first undergo judicial review in the U.S. Court of Appeals for Veterans Claims; those decisions can then be appealed to the Federal Circuit.

Appellate practice in the administrative agency context is ideal for advocates with specialized subject-matter expertise. If you are well-versed in SSI/SSDI claims, veterans' benefits, or patent applications, for example, you can handle appeals in those areas from the agency appeals process all the way through appellate judicial review. Or you could focus on one aspect of that process, such as appeals only within the agency. Whichever path you choose, administrative agency appeals provide numerous opportunities to exercise appellate advocacy skills outside of the traditional judicial system.

---

30. *See* 5 U.S.C. § 703.

VII. Conclusion

Appellate advocacy is a challenging and rewarding area of practice. Although appellate practice requires specialized skills, any lawyer can become a competent appellate advocate through study and practice. As this chapter has demonstrated, opportunities for appellate practice abound within the U.S. legal system. This book provides a solid foundation upon which to develop the fundamental skills required of appellate advocates, regardless of practice area or jurisdiction.

Discussion Questions

1. Why are you studying appellate advocacy? How do you see appellate practice fitting into your career path?
2. Other than what's already been discussed in this chapter, what skills do you believe an appellate advocate must develop that are different from those of a trial advocate?
3. Look up the state court appellate structure for the state you practice in (or plan to practice in).
   a. Does your state have an intermediate appellate court?
   b. Which court has jurisdiction over appeals from municipal courts? Small claims courts? Agency decisions dealing with workers' compensation issues?
   c. Can the court of last resort in your jurisdiction issue advisory opinions?
4. What role should appellate courts play in addressing social justice issues?
5. How can appellate courts ensure accountability and transparency in their decision-making processes?

Chapter 2

Navigating the Appellate Process

In this chapter, you will learn about:

- The rules governing appeals
- The different types of appeals: of right, discretionary, and interlocutory
- Appellate jurisdiction
- Appellate motion practice

I. Introduction

Put simply, the appellate process is the means litigants use to challenge a lower court's or an agency's ruling in their cases. The appellate process is the lawyer's roadmap. It differs from court to court. And it can differ depending on the case type within the same court. The details matter, and failing to pay attention to those details can have devastating results. But nothing in this chapter, or indeed this book, is a substitute for learning the appellate process in the specific appellate jurisdiction in which you practice. The process can differ, even among courts at the same level. No two federal circuit courts have identical procedures. The same can be said of state appellate courts. And different courts use different terms to refer to similar concepts, such as referring to special actions instead of interlocutory appeals. This chapter thus gives a generalized overview of the appellate processes and discusses some common themes the appellate lawyer will find.

This chapter begins by offering suggestions on how to become competent to handle an appeal in the relevant jurisdiction. A lawyer must focus on the details of the relevant jurisdiction's process and not rely on generalizations. At no point during the appellate process should a lawyer cast caution to the wind. Details matter.

The chapter then offers an overview of how appellate processes work. It begins with the mechanics of initiating an appeal. It then offers some generalizations applicable to most courts sitting in an appellate role, but appeals may also lie in other settings, such as to an administrative law judge or administrative panel. Indeed, many lawyers work on appeals regularly but never file anything with a court. Regardless of the level of appeal, the process matters, and there are some general commonalities.

As a last point about the importance of the appellate process, new lawyers need to worry about it. Imagine how this associate felt until New Mexico's Supreme Court ruled that:

> Plaintiffs' lead trial counsel was on vacation when the notice of appeal was filed. He instructed an associate to supervise the progress of the appeal in his absence and instructed his secretary to make sure the notice of appeal was timely filed. It was standard office practice for his secretary to serve all pleadings and notices on opposing counsel. Counsel served notice of appeal on defendants' counsel as soon as the matter was brought to his attention. Although we do not condone the oversight in this case, we consider the importance of the case, which involves a personal injury claim involving serious injuries. Also, we consider the fact that defendants demonstrated no actual prejudice as a result of the untimely notice. [New Mexico courts] held that a showing of prejudice was necessary to deprive the district court of jurisdiction. We conclude that there was a sufficient showing of accident or excusable mistake and that such a showing permits us to allow plaintiffs' appeal to proceed. We are not persuaded that the burden of showing prejudice should be placed on plaintiffs.[1]

1. Russell v. Univ. of New Mexico Hosp./Bernalillo Cnty. Med. Ctr., 740 P.2d 1174, 1178 (N.M. 1987).

Almost forty years later, this case is likely that now-senior lawyer's war story of choice.

II. Understanding the rules governing appeals

As the above suggests, understanding all aspects of the appellate process is job one, but it is not an easy task. There is no shortcut to reading the applicable rules and cases addressing those rules. But where to begin? This section offers suggestions on how to begin the process of becoming competent to handle an appeal in the relevant jurisdiction. To begin, a good mentor can play a critical role in a new appellate lawyer's development. A good mentor can be hard to find, but it is worth the effort. But as the above example shows, sometimes mentors take vacations. The new lawyer still must be competent to handle the appeal before taking it on.

To that end, many courts and state bars publish materials for practitioners. They also publish materials for self-represented litigants. These online and widely available materials are invaluable and often provide a global overview of the relevant appellate process. The courts and agencies publish the handbooks in the hope of ensuring compliance. To the extent the rules are unclear, often these resources provide answers.

The Ninth Circuit is a prime example. The Ninth Circuit publishes a practice guide for lawyers, with explanations on how to work with PDFs, a video on how to handle a record, a shell brief, and more.[2] The Ninth Circuit also has a separate set of materials for self-represented litigants.[3] Materials like the Ninth Circuit's materials are available online for many jurisdictions, including

2. U.S. Courts for the Ninth Circuit, The Appellate Lawyer Representatives' Guide to Practice in the United States Court of Appeals for the Ninth Circuit (May 2021 ed.), https://cdn.ca9.uscourts.gov/datastore/uploads/guides/AppellatePracticeGuide.pdf.

3. *Pro Se and Self-Represented Litigants: Information, Links, and Forms*, U.S. Courts for the Ninth Circuit, https://www.ca9.uscourts.gov/forms/pro-se-litigants/ (last visited Aug. 14, 2024).

Arizona,[4] California,[5] Florida,[6] Illinois,[7] and Texas.[8] Agencies with appellate processes often will do the same thing. Almost all federal agencies provide this type of resource.[9] State agencies as well.[10]

It is important to focus on the rules and materials for the specific jurisdiction. Looking at online materials is a good point to start, but it is just that, a starting point. For example, unemployment benefits cases are filed daily across the nation. Each state has its own provisions, but similarities exist. Generally, the party must file a claim for unemployment benefits. An agency employee reviews the claim and decides whether the applicant qualifies for benefits. Depending on the employee's decision, either the applicant or the

---

4. *See, e.g.*, Arizona Courts, Guide for Self-Represented ("Pro Se" or "Pro Per") Appellants and Appellees (rev. ed. 2017), https://www.azcourts.gov/Portals/89/PDFs/GuideForSelfRep/ENGLISH2019UPDATEDCMS.pdf?ver=2019-04-19-142001-673.

5. The California Court of Appeal, Step by Step: Civil Appellate Practices and Procedures For the Self-Represented in the Fourth Appellate District Division One (Feb. 2021), https://selfhelp.appellate.courts.ca.gov/ (last visited Jan. 26, 2025).

6. The Appellate Practice Section of the Florida Bar, Pro Se Handbook: Representing Yourself on Appeal (2023 ed.), https://prose.flabarappellate.org/ (last visited Jan. 26, 2025).

7. Illinois Supreme Court Commission on Access to Justice, Guide for Appeals to the Illinois Appellate Court (June 2024), https://ilcourtsaudio.blob.core.windows.net/antilles-resources/resources/bb0c84c1-8696-4d36-890e-6f200d7135cb/Guide_for_Appeals_to_the_IL_Appellate_Court.pdf (last visited Jan. 26, 2025).

8. Texas Young Lawyers Association, Pro Se Appeals Guide for Texas Courts (2024), https://tyla.org/resource/pro-se-appeals-guide-for-texas-courts/ (last visited Jan. 26, 2025).

9. *See, e.g.*, *Appeals Process*, U.S. Equal Emp. Opportunity Commission, https://www.eeoc.gov/federal-sector/appeals-process; *Appeal a Decision We Made*, Soc. Security Admin., https://www.ssa.gov/benefits/disability/appeal.html; *VA Decision Reviews and Appeals*, U.S. Dep't of Veterans Affairs, https://www.va.gov/decision-reviews/; *Administrative Appeals*, U.S. Citizenship & Immigr. Servs. (USCIS), https://www.uscis.gov/administrative-appeals (all last visited Jan. 26, 2025).

10. *See, e.g.*, *Division of Workers' Compensation (DWC) Information and Assistance Unit*, Cal. Dep't of Indus. Rels., https://www.dir.ca.gov/dwc/IandA.html; Cal. Unemployment Ins. Appeals Board, https://www.cuiab.ca.gov/ (discussing appeal process at the appeal information tab); *Appealing to the Board of Review*, Ill. Dep't of Emp. Security, https://ides.illinois.gov/content/dam/soi/en/web/ides/ides_forms_and_publications/bor-appeal.pdf (discussing appeal process including administrative appeal at page 13); *Unemployment Insurance Appeal Board*, N.Y. State Dep't of Labor, https://industrialappeals.ny.gov/hearings (discussing appeal to New York State Supreme Court); N.Y. State Office of Temporary & Disability Assistance, https://otda.ny.gov/hearings/; *File an Unemployment Appeal*, Tex. Workforce Commission, https://www.twc.texas.gov/services/file-unemployment-appeal; *Hearing Requests*, Wash. State Office of Admin. Hearings, https://oah.wa.gov; *Benefit Denials and Appeals*, Wash. State Emp. Security Dep't, https://esd.wa.gov/get-financial-help/unemployment-benefits/appeal-unemployment-benefits-decision (all last visited Jan. 26, 2025).

employer may seek review before an administrative law judge or someone serving in a similar capacity. A party who is dissatisfied with that review generally can seek additional administrative review before an agency board. Anyone dissatisfied with a board's decision generally can look to the courts for further review.

The above discussion leads to an interesting question: Should a lawyer look at materials created for self-represented litigants? Yes. Should a lawyer stop there? No. The available online resources vary widely depending on the jurisdiction. For example, in Pennsylvania, the party has 30 days to seek review of the board's decision by filing an appeal as of right with the Commonwealth Court of Pennsylvania in Harrisburg.[11] The online resources provide the address and related information. In contrast, in Arizona, the party seeking review has 30 days to file an application for appeal with the Arizona Department of Economic Security, which then sends the application to the Arizona Court of Appeals, Division One, which then has discretionary review.[12] The online materials provide no guidance on this aspect of the appeal process.

That said, self-representation guides generally outline solid and easily understood frameworks and guardrails for the uninitiated. These materials also can provide useful information to help a new lawyer set a client's expectations about the process. One of the most common ethical complaints about lawyers is they fail to communicate with their clients. Explaining the process and setting expectations early is critical, especially with appeals that may take years to resolve. Clients with vast litigation experience, especially appellate experience, are not the norm. The lawyer needs to prepare the client for the realities of how long an appeal can take and the risks associated with an appeal.

State bar associations or other state-based organizations also often publish appellate procedure manuals.[13] These handbooks are comprehensive and written for professionals, not self-represented litigants. They provide an overview of the appellate process and detailed explanations of the steps in the process. For example, the Arizona Appellate Handbook covers the appellate process before Arizona's appellate courts, specifically the Arizona Court of

---

11. *Benefit Appeals: Important Information for Scheduling UC Appeal Hearings*, Dep't of Labor & Industry, Commonwealth of Penn., https://www.pa.gov/en/agencies/dli/programs-services/unemployment/appeals.html (last visited Jan. 26, 2025).

12. *Unemployment Insurance Benefit Appeals*, Ariz. Dep't of Economic Security, https://des.az.gov/services/employment/unemployment-individual/unemployment-insurance-benefits-appeals (last visited Jan. 26, 2025).

13. *See, e.g.*, Arizona Appellate Handbook (2020); Delaware Appellate Handbook (2d ed. 1996); Kentucky Basic Appellate Practice Handbook (2023); Idaho Appellate Handbook (4th ed. 2015), Michigan Appellate Handbook (Shannon & Gerville-Réache eds., 3d ed., Jan. 2018 update).

Appeals and the Arizona Supreme Court. It also provides information on the numerous other types of appeals in Arizona, including appeals from Arizona's limited jurisdiction courts and agencies. But it cannot stand alone. For example, the Arizona handbook does not address unemployment benefit appeals, which uniquely involve a discretionary review by the Arizona Court of Appeals.

In short, when looking for insight in the appellate process, a lawyer should look to an available handbook. And it's not just the authors of this book who suggest lawyers use these resources. In a case where the parties disputed how to interpret Arizona's civil appellate procedural rules, the Arizona Supreme Court stated, "[W]e suggest that in absence of contrary authority, it would be prudent for Arizona practitioners to follow the Arizona Appellate Handbook."[14] More recently, a dissenting opinion of the Kentucky Supreme Court said lawyers "should consult... pertinent resources, including 'West's Rules & Procedures,' 'Appellant Checklist,' 'Appellee Checklist,' and 'Basic Appellate Handbook.'"[15] In unpublished orders, Montana courts have directed clerks of court to send a copy of the Montana Appellate Handbook along with its order in certain cases.

Despite their being valuable resources, however, such handbooks and guides cannot be the end of a lawyer's research. As an Arizona court said, a handbook provides guidance, but it is not binding on the courts.[16] At bottom, a lawyer must know the procedural rules. Read them. Study them. Read the cases interpreting them. Study those cases.

If a lawyer does not know the rules of appellate procedure for a particular court, the lawyer is sure to break them. Unfortunately, it happens too often. For example, in *Riggs Oil & Gas Corporation v. Jonah Energy LLC*,[17] the Colo-

---

14. Barassi v. Matison, 636 P.2d 1200, 1202 (Ariz. 1981).

15. Hamburger v. Plemmons, 654 S.W.3d 99, 106 (Ky. Ct. App. 2022) (Thompson, J. dissenting).

16. Barassi, 636 P.2d at 1202 n.4 (noting that the court "cannot gainsay its future decisions on matters in the Handbook not yet judicially construed").

17. 555 P.3d 90 (Col. Ct. App 2024), cert. granted sub nom. Jonah Energy LLC, v. Riggs Oil & Gas Corporation; Gasconade Oil Co.; Helm Energy, LLC; McLish Res., L.P., LLLP; W. Clifton Arbuckle Tr. Dated 1/1/1996; Los Feliz Oil Co., LLC; Samis Oil Co., Inc.; MKB Energy, L.L.C.; Westar Oil & Gas, Inc.; JJB Energy Ventures, LC; Callaway Oil, L.L.C.; Anadarko Partners II, L.P.; Cartel Petroleum, Inc.; Castlebay Energy LLC; Coyote Energy LLC; S.N.S. Oil & Gas Properties, Inc.; Winchester Energy, LLC; El Dorado Corporation; & Ridgeview Expl., Inc., 2025 WL 242431 (Colo. Jan. 13, 2025). The Colorado Supreme Court granted certiorari on the following: "Whether the division erred in adopting a 'hard line' approach to 'excusable neglect' under C.A.R. 4(a)(4), despite acknowledging that excusable neglect requires an equitable balancing test under other rules." 2025 WL 242431, at *1 (Colo. Jan. 13, 2025).

rado Court of Appeals dismissed an appeal because the lawyer's assistant filed the notice of appeal with the trial court instead of the appellate court, though this ruling is subject to a grant of certiorari before the Colorado Supreme Court.[18] In *Johnson v. Arizona Registrar of Contractors*,[19] the Arizona Court of Appeals dismissed an appeal from an agency decision because the lawyer filed the notice of appeal with the agency instead of the state trial court. Other examples abound, and no lawyer wants to be an example on that list. Even so, lawyers lose appeals every year because of wholly avoidable procedural mistakes. Do not join that club. An appellate lawyer's power is in the details. At no point during the appellate process should a lawyer cast caution to the wind.

III. The mechanics of an appeal

Back in the day, which was not that long ago, lawyers often did not type their own briefs. Assistants, paralegals, and runners handled most filings. Clients did not want to pay lawyers to hunt and peck at the keyboard and then drive to the courthouse to stand in filing lines. Today's lawyers need to be competent in all aspects. Even the most senior partners generally do their own work at the computer. Many 21st century lawyers are working remotely and cannot rely on an assistant to handle the mechanics of the appeal, including filing. Because of technology, lawyers are enmeshed in the mechanics of an appeal, from electronic filing to processing fee payments. Today's lawyers must be self-sufficient and know how to leverage technology. Law firms expect it. Clients require it. And the economic realities of the practice of law demand it.

Even so, jurisdictions adopt technology at different paces. Many jurisdictions rely solely on physical filings, so many a young lawyer will still need to make a mad dash to the filing window to make sure the notice is filed timely. The days of standing in line at a filing counter are neither gone nor forgotten. At least one author remembers standing in line at the after-hours-filing counter for the state trial court and date-stamping and filing documents at the federal district court's after-hours-filing drop box. But today and in the future, lawyers are much more likely to need to know how to electronically file all the necessary documents.

---

18. As an example of how each case and each level of appeal differ, to appeal a decision to the Arizona Court of Appeals from the trial court, the parties must file the notice of appeal with the trial court under Rule 8(a), Arizona Rules of Civil Appellate Procedure.

19. 396 P.3d 645 (Ariz. Ct. App. 2017).

For a new lawyer, learning the mechanics is important. A mistake here can be costly. The more the new lawyer knows, the more the new lawyer can use the process to that lawyer's advantage. Appellate motion practice is rife with motions to dismiss because a lawyer did not follow the mechanics. For example, in jurisdictions where an appeal is not perfected until a filing fee is paid, the self-reliant lawyer needs to know how to process those payments or risk having an appeal dismissed.

A lawyer is responsible for dotting every i and crossing every t in this process. The lawyer must review and proofread every document. The simplest mistake, such as checking the wrong box on a form notice of appeal, may cost the lawyer's client an appeal. The lawyer ultimately is responsible for any mistake. In short, when playing in the appellate arena, a lawyer can face harsh consequences for a relatively minor mistake, even when someone else made it.

A. Initiating an appeal

The process for initiating an appeal generally is governed by statutes and court rules, though occasionally state constitutional provisions and administrative orders may come into play. They direct when a lawyer must file an appeal, what to file, where to file, how to file, and what fees must be paid. Any misstep could result in an ineffective appeal because the appellate court will not have jurisdiction.

Though many think of an appellate practice as slower paced than trial practice, the initial stages of an appeal move quickly, especially if the lawyer did not handle the case at the trial level. For most appeals as of right and discretionary reviews, strict deadlines apply, generally 30 days or less after the trial or lower appellate court enters the judgment or decision. In those appeals, missing the deadline by even a few minutes can cost the litigant their appeal. During that time, the lawyer must assess the appellate issues, consult with the client, and ensure everything is in order. There is little time for learning during this time. Strict deadlines might not attach to discretionary interlocutory appeals, but delay generally does not bode well for the party seeking review. To avoid costly mistakes, a lawyer who wants to handle an appeal must understand the mechanics before the time comes to file one.

Chapter 4, Appellate Foundations, will cover jurisdiction more broadly. For example, common missteps at the notice of appeal stage can create case-dispositive jurisdictional issues. Chapter 4 discusses common mistakes and suggests approaches for the lawyer to cure jurisdictional issues arising from notice of appeal issues. The important takeaway at this point is the notice of appeal is a critical jurisdictional document and could be case dispositive for the unwary.

B. Formatting the brief

Courts impose varying requirements on briefs. Most address margins, and font type and size. Courts vary on how they set the length of briefs, but generally it is either by word count or page count. They also often establish required sections. Though courts may overlook an occasional and minor mistake here, they do not always. And the sanctions imposed vary from striking noncompliant portions[20] to striking the entire brief.[21] And courts have considered imposing the ultimate sanction of dismissing the appeal.[22] The Tenth Circuit had some pithy thoughts for those who would use their word processing prowess to get around the limits:

> Using a favorite undergraduate gambit, defendants have visibly shrunk the type face and spacing of the footnotes and re-started the numbering several times....
>
> ....
>
> It appears that defendants have simply taken nine pages of material out of the double-spaced text and moved them into an excessive number of legitimately single-spaced, but illegitimately shrunken footnotes.
>
> ....
>
> While we appreciate the savings in time and labor made possible by such technological innovations as word processing, we regret the temptation they pose to the wordy to compress, rather than edit. Our rule requiring pica type and 10-pitch spacing applies to footnotes as well as text. Defendants will have to find some way of abridging their arguments, other than toying with their computers, to meet these requirements.[23]

---

20. *See, e.g.*, Mazzio's Corp. v. Bright, 46 P.3d 201, 204–05 (Okla. Ct. App. 2002) ("In this instance, we are not inclined to impose the ultimate sanction of dismissal as urged by Mazzio's. However, for the following reasons, we do find it appropriate to strike and deny consideration of portions of Bright's brief.").

21. *See, e.g.*, State of Oklahoma ex rel. Oklahoma Bar Ass'n v. Minter, 37 P.3d 763 (2001) (declining to strike sua sponte the opening brief for exceeding the page limits but granting appellee's motion to strike the reply brief for that reason); Kagy v. Toledo-Lucas Cnty. Port Auth., 699 N.E.2d 566 (Ohio Ct. App. 1997) (striking over brief because it exceeded the page limit).

22. Abner v. Scott Mem'l Hosp., 634 F.3d 962 (7th Cir. 2011) ("The flagrancy of the violation in this case might well justify the dismissal of the appeal: let this be a warning.").

23. TK-7 Corp. v. Estate of Barbouti, 966 F.2d 578, 579 (10th Cir. 1992).

The message is simple and plain: Follow the rules.

In most jurisdictions, the brief must include the following sections, though each jurisdiction may use slightly different terms:

- Case caption page
- Table of contents[24]
- Table of authorities
- Jurisdictional statement
- Statement of the issues
- Statement of the case
- Summary of the argument
- Argument
- Conclusion
- Certificate of compliance
- Certificate of service
- Request for attorney fees and costs

Chapter 5 explains best practices for structuring the Argument. Chapter 6 provides additional guidance for the other parts of the brief.

Some jurisdictions have additional requirements. For example, in a federal appellate court matter, each nongovernmental corporate party "must file a statement identifying all its parent corporations and listing any publicly held company that owns 10% or more of the party's stock."[25] Even when the party has filed the statement as part of a pre-briefing "motion, response, petition, or answer," the party must include the statement before the table of contents in the principal brief.[26]

Following the prescribed format is critical for reasons beyond just following the rules. Judges and their staff expect to find what they need where it is supposed to be. The prescribed format gives them predictability. If a lawyer steps outside that framework, the lawyer starts off on the wrong foot and could throw the court off track. Part of staying on message is following the rules. The court will not award creativity points to a lawyer who chooses to color outside the lines on this point.

---

24. Increasingly, courts are abandoning the Table of Contents and the Table of Authorities because technology has made them somewhat obsolete.

25. Fed. R. App. P. 26.1(a).

26. Fed. R. App. P. 26.1(b).

C. Jurisdiction over appeals

When discussing jurisdiction in the context of appeals, the focus is subject matter jurisdiction. True enough, personal jurisdiction issues can arise within an appeal, but the first step is establishing that the appellate court has subject matter jurisdiction over the case. Chapter 4 goes into greater detail on jurisdiction, but one basic rule applies: Appellate courts independently will determine subject matter jurisdiction, even if the parties do not raise an issue. And for good reason. If the court issues a decision in a case over which it lacks subject matter jurisdiction, the ruling is a nullity. And the consequences can be dramatic.

State v. Nix,[27] provides a good example. In *Nix*, the issue of appellate jurisdiction arose several years into the appeal process. The appellate process was nearly complete. The Oregon Supreme Court had issued an opinion affirming the Oregon intermediate appellate court's opinion. At that point, the State, the prevailing party, filed a motion saying the State "had lacked authority to file an appeal in the first place, because no statute authorizes it to appeal a judgment of conviction for a misdemeanor." The defendant agreed and moved "to vacate both opinions and dismiss the appeal." The Oregon Supreme Court ultimately agreed, saying, "[B]ecause the issues before us implicate our jurisdiction, we have an independent duty to determine whether the state's appeal was statutorily authorized, regardless of the state's concession that it was not. Likewise, we have an obligation to acknowledge the existence of jurisdiction if our review reveals it."[28] In short, no matter which side the lawyer represents, the lawyer wants to be sure the appellate court has the authority to hear the appeal.

At bottom, jurisdiction can be dispositive, but it is not intuitive. Appellate jurisdiction generally turns on four things: (1) what type of case it is, (2) where the case originated, (3) what order the appellant is appealing, and (4) when the order became appealable. An appellant can lose a case simply by filing a notice of appeal in the wrong court. In determining whether an appellate court has jurisdiction, other factors come into play, including whether the notice of appeal was filed on time and whether the appeal is of right or discretionary.

---

27. 345 P.3d 416 (Or. 2015).
28. State v. Nix, 345 P.3d 416, 416 (Or. 2015).

D. Relief sought

As a lawyer considers the issues on appeal, the relief the party is seeking is paramount and yet too often overlooked when preparing the appellate brief. Appellate courts generally have a limited set of actions they can take when resolving an appeal. They are:

- Dismiss the appeal if appellant did not file the notice on time, if the order is not in an appealable form, or if the appellant made a procedural error (like not timely filing a brief or paying a fee).
- Affirm the trial court's judgment or order.
- Modify the trial court's judgment or order.
- Reverse all or part of the trial court's judgment or order.
- Remand the case to the trial court for further action, including further analysis, a new trial, or new hearing.

The brief must include a succinct, plain statement of the relief the party seeks; otherwise, the party abandons the court to wonder exactly what the appellant wants. Not asking for the vote is a classic rookie politician mistake. Not asking the appellate court for specific relief is a classic litigant mistake. Be direct and to the point. Tell the court what your client wants it to do.

IV. Types of appeals: Of right, discretionary, and interlocutory

This section explores the three primary types of appeals: appeals of right, discretionary appeals, and interlocutory appeals. Each type serves a distinct purpose.

A. Of right appeals

Appeals of right are relatively straightforward and do not require a great deal of discussion. The right to appeal generally is established by statute. And as long as the appellant complies with the court's jurisdictional requirements, the appellate court must hear the appeal. Most intermediate appellate courts oversee appeals of right and may have discretionary review in certain types of appeals. Most courts of last resort, often though not always called supreme courts, generally have some form of discretionary review.

B. Discretionary appeals

Appellate courts have articulated factors they use to consider whether to accept review of a discretionary appeal. Even if a court has not articulated a specific factor, each factor provides a valuable opportunity to persuade the court either to accept or to reject a discretionary appeal. Remember, an appellee's lawyer has to persuade a court not to accept a discretionary appeal.[29]

Whether interlocutory or not, discretionary appeals require more work. With an of-right appeal, a lawyer must establish jurisdiction to get in through the courthouse door. Not so with discretionary appeals. For a discretionary appeal, the lawyer also must convince the court that it should hear the appeal. At bottom, the appellate lawyer needs to convince the appellate court that this appeal is the right case (means) to address an important legal issue (end). And the brief should answer two questions for the court: Why this appeal? Why now? In that regard, the brief should create a sense of urgency around the issue. The opposite generally is true for the appellee, who likely will want to portray the case as a lackluster, ordinary appeal on which the court should not waste any further resources.

Discretionary review authority is when a court with jurisdiction to hear an appeal has the power to decide whether to grant review. Generally, courts of last resort have discretionary review authority. The U.S. Supreme Court is such a court. It has the power to grant or deny certiorari. Exceptions prove that rule. For example, the Arizona Supreme Court has discretionary review in all but one type of case: if a jury imposes a capital sentence, the criminal defendant has the right of appeal directly to the Arizona Supreme Court.

A court with discretionary review authority generally does not explain why a case garnered the court's attention. At most, lawyers can glean insight from a dissenter's reasoning for why the court should or should not accept review, and then only if the dissenter chooses to issue a dissent to the review decision. Courts sometimes will give a little more insight beyond a single sentence, but not often.

---

29. You may be wondering about times when an appellee's lawyer also wants the court to take a discretionary appeal, perhaps because the lawyer sees the opportunity to establish precedent favorable to the client. Appellate practice is like ballroom dancing. As the lawyer becomes more advanced, the moves become more nuanced. At this stage, the goal is to build a solid foundation by learning the basic steps. This book will cover the basic steps. As a lawyer, you will refine your moves with practice.

Still, general rules apply. A common basis for granting review is that the lower courts are divided on an issue. In federal courts, this is called a circuit split.

Courts exercise this discretion cautiously. Discretionary review does not function as a mere second appeal. Rather, the goal is to address substantial errors or important legal questions. For that reason, the scope of review generally narrows when an appeal enters the discretionary process.[30] The appellate lawyer needs to plan accordingly, choosing only the most critical issues to pursue. Associate Justice Elena Kagan gave an apt description while talking about retired Associate Justice Thurgood Marshall, saying, "He just had an ability to get to the heart of a problem, to see sort of straight through to what was most important in any legal issue."[31] And like Justice Marshall, appellate lawyers always must keep their eyes on the ball.

In deciding whether to grant discretionary review, courts focus on the following factors:

- Lower courts' desire for guidance
- Issues of first impression
- Nature of the issues and legal principles
- Public importance
- Merits of the appeal
- Judicial economy
- Likelihood of recurrence

These seven points should figure prominently in any brief seeking discretionary review.[32] Each factor highlights the careful balance courts strike when

---

30. *See, e.g.*, Custer Med. Ctr. v. United Auto. Ins. Co., 62 So. 3d 1086, 1092 (Fla. 2010) ("We have consistently observed that as a case travels up the judicial ladder, review should consistently become narrower, not broader.") (internal quotations and citations omitted).

31. *See* Elena Kagan, *See A Conversation with Associate Justice Elena Kagan*, 91 U. Colo. L. Rev. 749, 776 (2020).

32. Arizona is in the process of amending its rules of procedure for special actions, which is Arizona's name for interlocutory appeals. The amended rules will list the following grounds for accepting discretionary review:

A lower court's being certified for review

Issues of privileges or immunities

Issues of first impression

Issues of statewide importance

Issues tending to evade review, including questions that may become moot before an appeal

Issues involving the welfare of children where the harm complained of can only be prevented by resolution before an appeal

deciding whether to exercise discretionary review, ensuring they use their discretionary review to correct significant errors and clarify important legal principles without overburdening the judicial system.

1. *Lower courts want guidance*

Lower courts often know what they need. And they are not afraid to ask a court with discretionary review authority to address an issue. For example, one appellate judge, who also happens to be one of the authors, dissented in a case and said, "If the Arizona Supreme Court intended such a result, it should say so."[33] The Arizona Supreme Court took discretionary review. Not every request for guidance will be quite so direct, but a resourceful appellate lawyer can find nuggets asking for it. This type of request often is found in dissenting opinions and in conflicting opinions, which are discussed in greater detail below. And courts will listen when the lower court says it does not want guidance.[34]

2. *Issues of first impression*

First impression issues often garner discretionary review. Indeed, some states have statutes allowing the state supreme court to take discretionary jurisdiction over such issues before the appellate courts even touch them.[35] Courts generally do not grant discretionary review just because a case raises a new issue, no matter how interesting it is. Generally, when an appeal presents an issue of first impression, the court is going to use that to buttress the reason for granting review.[36] But to use a relay race analogy, an issue of first impression is a great anchor to have when seeking discretionary review. It may not carry the day all by itself, but it will get the team across the finish line. Always look for at least one other factor to partner with it, but preferably several others, so you have enough to put together a full relay race team.

Issues whose resolution will materially advance the efficient management of the case, other than issues presented by ordinary dispositive motion practice

Issues concerning a decision that cannot be justified under any rule of law

Each of these grounds has some basis in case law, and a litigant seeking discretionary review, interlocutory or otherwise, may want to consider them.

33. Arizona v. Traverso, 537 P.3d 345 (Ariz. Ct. App. 2023).

34. *See* Quirion v. Veilleux, 65 A.3d 1287 (Me. 2013) (exercising its discretion to decline interlocutory appeal when the trial court did not seek interlocutory guidance by reporting the question to the higher court as provided by statute).

35. *See, e.g.*, Neb. Rev. Stat. § 24-1106.

36. *See, e.g.*, Oregon v. Turay, 532 P.3d 57 (Or. 2023).

3. *Nature of the issues and legal principles*

Courts often look for significant or fundamental errors that affected the lower court's decision. This analysis includes errors that result in a miscarriage of justice or depart significantly from the essential legal requirements.[37] The nature of the issue together with a rapid evolution in the area of law often supports the court's granting discretionary review.[38]

4. *Public importance*

The significance of the legal issues involved, especially in terms of their public importance or the need to resolve conflicts in legal principles, is another key factor. This includes cases where there is a conflict between appellate decisions or where the case involves matters of great public importance.

A common reason for granting discretionary review, even at the U.S. Supreme Court, is conflict between decisions of the lower courts. At the federal level, it is commonly called a circuit split.[39] But not all circuit splits are created equal. For example, in *Miroyan v. United States*,[40] the Supreme Court declined to grant certiorari because it had previously declined to grant review for similar claims and did not perceive a clear and significant conflict among the circuits warranting intervention. This case highlights two key issues for the appellate lawyer regarding lower court conflicts: Is there a conflict? Is the conflict sufficient to merit intervention? Many state courts face the same issue when the state's intermediate appellate courts reach different results.[41]

What else constitutes a matter of great public importance can be difficult to assess.[42] In *Thompson v. Heineman*,[43] the issue revolved around whether to require a taxpayer to show standing. The functioning of the courts can also present issues for discretionary review. In *Jones v. Georgia*,[44] the Georgia Supreme Court addressed the removal of jurors after deliberations had begun. Appeals that can have far reaching consequences on constitutional

---

37. Nader v. Florida Dept. of Highway Safety & Motor Vehicles, 87 So. 3d 712 (Fla. 2012).

38. *See, e.g.*, Carpenter v. Florida, 228 So. 3d 535 (Fla. 2017); Rhode Island v. Sinapi, 295 A.3d 787 (R.I. 2023).

39. *See, e.g.*, Murthy v. Missouri, 603 U.S. 43 (2024).

40. 439 U.S. 1338 (1978).

41. *See, e.g.*, Arizona v. Stummer, 194 P.3d 1043 (Ariz. 2008) (granting review in civil cases to resolve conflict between two opinions from the Arizona Court of Appeals).

42. Thompson v. Heineman, 857 N.W.2d 731 (Neb. 2015) (explaining the need to address issues of statewide importance).

43. 857 N.W.2d 731 (Neb. 2015).

44. 875 S.E.2d 737 (Ga. 2022).

rights also are common fodder for discretionary review.[45] Appeals involving children often present this issue, especially issues related to their time with parents in family law cases, or their placement in dependencies and parental termination matters.

Another way of looking at public importance in private causes of action is through the lens of the amount of money involved and the number of people affected. For example, in one Arizona case, the amount at issue was a relatively small dollar amount — a $35 cleaning fee — but many people were affected by that fee, making the public importance of the case much greater than the individual litigant's exposure.[46] Conversely, in the same case, the punitive damages award was a significant amount for the other side. And the effect of the opinion affected insureds and insurers statewide. The appellant's lawyer generally will emphasize the significance of the issue, while the appellee's lawyer generally will seek to minimize it.

Ultimately, matters of great public importance are as varied as the courts that hear the appeals. An appellate lawyer should focus on the precedent from the jurisdiction to frame the matter and, when appropriate, look beyond that jurisdiction's boundaries for helpful authority.

5. *Merits of the appeal*

The merits of the appeal are critical. The merits go to the likelihood an error occurred in the lower court. Courts typically require a party to show that the lower court's decision was probably erroneous and that the party is entitled to the sought-after relief.

6. *Judicial economy*

Judicial economy, or the efficient use of judicial resources, will get an appellate court's attention. For example, the New Mexico Supreme Court granted expedited review and issued an order taking control of many cases involving the legality of same sex marriage because of the high volume of cases pending around the state.[47] Courts have reached issues in the interest of judicial economy even when not raised on the appellate briefs.[48] The appellant's lawyer should look for ways that resolving the issue now will reap rewards later on, thus answering the questions why this appeal and why now.

---

45. *See, e.g.*, Oregon v. Turay, 532 P.3d 57 (Or. 2023).
46. *See* Hawkins v. Allstate Ins. Co., 733 P.2d 1073 (Ariz. 1987).
47. *See* Griego v. Oliver, 316 P.3d 385 (N.M. 2013).
48. *See, e.g.*, Nicollet Restoration, Inc. v. City of St. Paul, 533 N.W.2d 845 (Minn. 1995).

7. Likelihood of recurrence

In assessing the efficient use of judicial resources, courts consider whether the issue is likely to recur. If so, resolving it might promote judicial economy. A common example is when the issue involves a new or evolving area of law with limited jurisprudence, which potentially could waste judicial resources if not addressed.[49] Think of it as a pay-me-now or pay-me-later argument. The focus, however, is on making the point that taking this appeal (pay me less now) is more efficient than waiting for another appeal (pay me more later).

C. Interlocutory appeals

An interlocutory appeal is one in which the case between the parties is ongoing. No final judgment has been issued. Most appeals are ripe for review only once the parties' claims are all resolved and their rights set in the form of a final judgment, with some limited exceptions for post-judgment issues.[50] This concept of not allowing an appeal until that point is called the rule of finality, and it promotes judicial economy by avoiding multiple appeals in a single action.

Discretionary appeals and interlocutory appeals are not synonymous. Indeed, depending on the jurisdiction, some interlocutory appeals are of right, not discretionary. The mechanics for bringing an interlocutory appeal vary by jurisdiction and the nature of the case. Each jurisdiction will have rules regarding the eligibility and process for interlocutory appeals, reflecting that jurisdiction's legal principles and procedural frameworks.

For example, Arizona has adopted specific grounds for the appellate courts to consider when granting discretionary review of an interlocutory appeal. Many other states, such as Georgia, have adopted similar criteria.[51] Those criteria, not surprisingly, mirror the criteria for granting any discretionary appeal discussed above. But discretionary interlocutory appeals involve further analysis.

When considering whether to grant review of an interlocutory appeal, the courts must balance judicial efficiency and the need to address potentially decisive legal questions before a final judgment is entered. Courts generally will entertain interlocutory appeals if resolving the issue earlier will resolve

---

49. *See* Cryan v. Nat'l Council of Young Men's Christian Ass'ns of the United States, 887 S.E.2d 848 (N.C. 2023).

50. *See* Simmons Self-Storage Partners, LLC v. Rib Roof, Inc., 247 P.3d 1107 (Nev. 2011).

51. *See, e.g.*, Jones v. Peach Trader Inc., 807 S.E.2d 840 (Ga. 2017).

the case, saving time and resources.[52] Courts are not inclined to resolve interlocutory issues unless the resolution will move the case closer to final disposition.[53] A common concern about interlocutory appeals is they will result in piecemeal litigation.[54]

Courts also are concerned about the unintended and harmful consequences of issuing rulings on interlocutory appeals. But they often will entertain such appeals if the issue would become moot by the time the case becomes final, for example, a trial court's ruling that a party has waived a privilege.[55] When arguing for or against a court's accepting discretionary review over an interlocutory appeal, the brief should address these issues.

V. Appellate motion practice

It should come as no surprise that appellate courts are the source of active motion practices. Just like at the trial court, when a party wants the court to take a specific action, the party must file a motion.

Motions at the appellate level fall into two categories: substantive and procedural. Examples of a substantive motion include a motion to dismiss the appeal for lack of jurisdiction or a motion for reconsideration. Procedural motions address issues such as extending the deadline to file a brief or to request oral argument. And many fall somewhere in between, such as a motion to strike a brief for not complying with the court's rules, which may include a request for sanctions such as dismissing the appeal.

Appellate courts have rules for motions, such as unique formatting and requirements for filing responses and replies. A lawyer should not assume the appellate court will follow the trial court's procedural rules for motions.

The more common motions on appeal include:

- Motion to extend the time to file a brief
- Motion for oral argument
- Motion to expedite the appeal

---

52. *See* Maybury v. City of Seattle, 336 P.2d 878 (Wash. 1959).

53. *See* Bond v. Bond, 30 A.3d 816 (Me. 2011); Sabre Travel Int'l, Ltd. v. Deutsche Lufthansa AG, 567 S.W.3d 725 (Tex. 2019); Ford v. ChartOne, Inc., 834 A.2d 875 (D.C. 2003); Indus. Specialists v. Blanchard Ref. Co., 652 S.W.3d 11 (Tex. 2022).

54. *See* Maybury v. City of Seattle, 336 P.2d 878 (Wash. 1959).

55. *See* Duke v. State, 29 S.E.2d 348 (Ga. 2019) (noting the defendant would have the ability to address the issue on direct appeal after a final judgment and would not lose any rights by having to do so).

- Motion to stay the action in the trial court or the appeal
- Motion to dismiss appeal
- Motion for summary affirmance or summary reversal
- Motion for leave to file amicus brief

As with initiating an appeal, most courts set strict deadlines on when parties may file certain motions and formatting rules. Those rules also address when a party should file a response. Be sure to comply with those rules.

With that in mind, four types of motions merit attention at this point. This section addresses three of those motion types because of the dispositive effect they can have on the appeal or because of the collateral effect they can have on the parties. They are motions for stay of the trial court proceedings, motions to dismiss an appeal, and motions for summary disposition (whether affirmance or reversal). This section also briefly touches upon a fourth type of motion, motions for leave to file an amicus brief, because of its unique nature.

A. Motion to stay the action in the trial court

Often, when a party files a notice of appeal or petition for appeal, it divests the lower court of jurisdiction and transfers jurisdiction to the appellate court.[56] The primary goal of this divestiture rule is to prevent confusion and to avoid having two courts deliberating the same issues at the same time.[57]

But the exceptions and limitations of the divestiture rule vary by jurisdiction. Generally, the lower court retains the ability to enforce its judgments unless the court — either the trial or the appellate — issues a stay.[58] The last thing a lawyer wants is to have a client's assets seized unexpectedly because the other party is moving forward with enforcing the very judgment the client is appealing.[59] The lower court's ongoing jurisdiction also may extend to issuing protective orders or continuing with proceedings unrelated to the issues

56. *See, e.g.*, In re Padilla, 222 F.3d 1184 (9th Cir. 2000); Williamson v. Recovery Ltd. P'ship, 731 F.3d 608 (6th Cir. 2013); Mann-Stack v. Homeside Lending, Inc., 982 So. 2d 72 (Fla. Ct. App. 2008); Commonwealth Fin. and Admin. Cabinet v. Wingate, 460 S.W.3d 843 (Ky. 2015).

57. *See, e.g.*, Rodriguez v. Cnty. of Los Angeles, 891 F.3d 776 (9th Cir. 2018); In re Padilla, 222 F.3d 1184 (9th Cir. 2000).

58. Horvath v. Packo, 985 N.E.2d 966 (Ohio Ct. App. 2013); Cheves v. Williams, 993 P.2d 191 (Utah 1999); In re Sheshtawy, 161 S.W.3d 1 (Tex. Ct. App. 2003); Mann-Stack v. Homeside Lending, Inc., 982 So. 2d 72 (Fla. Ct. App. 2008).

59. *See, e.g.*, In re Padilla, 222 F.3d 1184 (9th Cir. 2000); United States v. PetroSaudi Oil Services (Venezuela) Ltd., 70 F.4th 1199 (9th Cir. 2023).

being appealed.[60] The exceptions generally address the lower court's practical needs and the effective administration of justice while not undermining the appellate process.[61]

When a stay is not automatic, appellate courts may issue stay orders instructing the lower court to suspend all or part of the judicial proceedings below.[62] Appellate courts also may stay an appeal and revest jurisdiction in the trial court to allow it to take some action in various situations, such as certifying finality under the relevant rules.[63]

Generally, "[t]he goal of a stay is to preserve the status quo while a court determines the merits of the appeal; issuance of the stay cannot depend on the assumption that the appeal will fail."[64] But how each jurisdiction decides when to impose a stay varies widely.

Some appellate courts require the appellant to seek a stay from the trial court before seeking relief from the appellate court. At times, appellate courts issue a stay when extraordinary circumstances make it impractical to obtain a stay from the trial court.[65] Generally, the appellate court will consider a motion for stay if the trial court has not granted one. In doing so, the appellate court will consider the reasons for the trial court's decision and the party's arguments in the motion to the appellate court.

Nevada's rules of appellate procedure identify four common factors that appellate courts consider in deciding whether to grant a stay.[66] They are "(1) whether the object of the appeal will be defeated if the stay is denied, (2) whether the appellant will suffer irreparable or serious injury if the stay is denied, (3) whether the respondent will suffer irreparable injury if the stay is granted, and (4) whether the appellant is likely to prevail on the merits in the appeal."[67] Wisconsin, for example, uses a sliding scale, called the *Gudenschwager* test, in which the court balances the likelihood of success on the

---

60. *See, e.g.*, Williamson v. Recovery Ltd. P'ship, 731 F.3d 608 (6th Cir. 2013); Rodriguez v. Cnty. of Los Angeles, 891 F.3d 776 (9th Cir. 2018); Mann-Stack v. Homeside Lending, Inc., 982 So. 2d 72 (Fla. Ct. App. 2008).

61. Nicaise v. Bernick, 542 P.3d 258 (Ariz. Ct. App. 2024); Horzely v. Horzely, 390 N.E.2d 28 (Ill. App. Ct. 1979); Jallali v. Knightsbridge Village Homeowners' Ass'n, Inc., 152 So. 3d 808 (Fla. Ct. App. 2014); Bert Allen Toyota, Inc. v. Grasz, 947 So. 2d 358 (Miss. Ct. App. 2007); Sheet Metal Workers' Int'l Ass'n Local 19 v. Herre Bros., Inc., 198 F.3d 391 (3d Cir. 1999); Reaves v. Tucker, 800 S.E.2d 188 (Va. Ct. App. 2017).

62. In re Conservatorship of Malone, 691 S.W.3d 365 (Tenn. 2024).

63. Andreiu v. Ashcroft, 253 F.3d 477 (9th Cir. 2001).

64. Daly v. San Bernardino Cnty. Bd. of Supervisors, 492 P.3d 921, 927 (Cal. 2021).

65. Bova v. City of Medford, 236 P.3d 760 (Or. Ct. App. 2010).

66. *See* Nev. R. App. P. 8(c).

67. State v. Robles-Nieves, 306 P.3d 399, 401 (Nev. 2013).

merits against the potential harm to the parties or the public.[68] Illinois, in contrast, does not use a strict formula; instead, Illinois courts engage in a balancing process that considers all elements relevant to the equitable nature of the relief sought, which can include the likelihood of success on the merits among other factors.[69] In seeking a stay, the lawyer must understand the rules in the specific jurisdiction, but these four factors are common.

Interlocutory appeals also may result in an automatic stay of the lower court proceedings.[70] For example, the Texas Citizens Participation Act provides for an automatic stay from the denial of a motion to dismiss, and it includes all other trial court proceedings pending resolution of that appeal.[71] In contrast, in Arizona, interlocutory appeals are known as special actions, a stay is not automatic, and generally the party must seek and be denied a stay at the trial-court level before seeking a stay from the appellate court.[72]

B. Motion to dismiss

If the attorney is representing an appellee, the attorney must consider whether grounds exist to dismiss the appeal. And before an appellant's attorney files a notice of appeal, the appellant's attorney must consider and frame the appeal to avoid such a motion.

To begin, a motion to dismiss is not an appropriate vehicle for alleged irregularities in proceedings relating to the appeal, such as errors in the trial court or appellate process. Those errors should be addressed on the merits in the appeal if the issue goes to the merits of the case.[73] And some jurisdictions limit by statute the use of motions to dismiss appeals.[74]

In jurisdictions that allow motions to dismiss, the motions commonly arise out of procedural errors, often related to timeliness. The impact of such errors varies by jurisdiction, but these motions generally are in order when the procedural errors affect the appellate court's subject matter jurisdiction. Many such motions focus on whether a party filed specific documents timely, in the appropriate court, and completely. Noncompliance with procedural rules can support a motion to dismiss. Examples include failure to file the notice of

---

68. Waity v. LeMahieu, 900 N.W.2d 264 (Wis. 2022) (citing State v. Gudenschwager, 529 N.W.2d 225 (Wis. 1995)).

69. Stacke v. Bates, 562 N.E.2d 192 (Ill. 1990).

70. *See* Colo. R. App. P. 4.2.

71. In re Geomet Recycling LLC, 578 S.W.3d 82 (Tex. Ct. App. 2019).

72. Grady v. Barth ex rel. Cnty. of Maricopa, 312 P.3d 117 (Ariz. Ct. App. 2013) (staying execution pending resolution of special action).

73. Caldwell v. Planning Comm'n of Calcasieu Parish, 419 So. 2d 56 (La. Ct. App. 1982).

74. *See, e.g.*, Ga. Code § 5-6-48(b).

appeal or appeal petition within the required time or in accord with specific procedural rules.[75] Failure to file an appeal bond timely also can deprive an appellate court of jurisdiction.[76]

Many courts will dismiss appeals because an appeal calls for an advisory opinion.[77] In federal court, when an appeal calls for an advisory opinion, the parties generally will move to dismiss for lack of jurisdiction because the case is not justiciable.[78] In the case of justiciability in federal court and some state courts, the issue is jurisdictional.

A variation of an appeal calling for an advisory opinion is a moot appeal. Generally, courts will not consider a moot appeal.[79] That said, even federal courts will not dismiss moot appeals if the issue is capable of repetition without review under the aptly named "capable-of-repetition-yet-evading-review" exception to the mootness doctrine. This doctrine is an appellant's friend. For the exception to apply, the appellant generally will need to show that "(1) the challenged action was in its duration too short to be fully litigated prior to its cessation or expiration, and (2) there was a reasonable expectation that the same complaining party would be subjected to the same action again."[80] A variation on the capable-of-repetition-yet-evading-review exception is the voluntary cessation doctrine, where the appellee voluntary discontinues the challenged action to moot the appeal.[81] State courts also use these same exceptions.[82]

75. *See* Peters v. Life Gen. Sec. Ins. Co., 393 So. 2d 1286 (La. Ct. App. 1980); Carson v. Eberth, 592 P.2d 112 (Kan. Ct. App. 1979); Auto Acceptance Corp. v. Veneziano, 197 A.2d 346 (Conn. Ct. App. 1963).

76. *See* Peters v. Life Gen. Sec. Ins. Co., 393 So. 2d 1286 (La. Ct. App. 1980); Carson v. Eberth, 592 P.2d 112 (Kan. Ct. App. 1979); Auto Acceptance Corp. v. Veneziano, 197 A.2d 346 (Conn. Ct. App. 1963).

77. *See* State v. Hansen, 717 N.W.2d 541, 542 (N.D. 2006) (dismissing appeal because issue was moot as to the defendant and was capable of repetition in another appeal so that it would not evade review); Plan Helena, Inc. v. Helena Regional Airport Auth. Bd., 226 P.3d 567 (Mont. 2010) (dismissing appeal because it called for an advisory opinion).

78. *See, e.g.*, Raley v. Hyundai Motor Co., 642 F.3d 1271 (10th Cir. 2011).

79. *See, e.g.*, Atlantic Coast Line R. Co. v. Wells, 54 F.2d 633 (5th Cir. 1932) (dismissing appeal because it became moot because of a Supreme Court decision); Governor Claiborne Apts. v. Attaldo, 81 So. 2d 566 (La. Ct. App. 1955) (granting motion to dismiss appeal on the ground that the case had become moot).

80. Corrigan v. Boston Univ., 98 F.4th 346 (1st Cir. 2024) (internal quotations and citations omitted).

81. *Id.*

82. *See, e.g.*, In re Earl B., 994 A.2d 269 (Conn. Ct. App. 2010); In re Joseph M., 939 N.E.2d 959 (Ill. App. Ct. 2010).

Other non-jurisdictional reasons can support dismissal, including substantial noncompliance with procedural rules.[83] Even so, courts tend not to dismiss appeals for purely technical procedural errors, especially when an error does not affect the appellate court's jurisdiction, unless the error causes the appellee prejudice or confusion.[84] For example, omitting an appellant from a notice of appeal may result in that appellant's successfully moving to dismiss.[85] Though the federal government amended the statute on which the *Torres* decision relied, the underlying requirement that an appellant adequately be identified in a notice of appeal continues.[86] Ultimately, courts have found that omitting an appellant from a notice of appeal deprives the appellate court of jurisdiction over that appellant.[87] In another instance, the appellate court dismissed an appeal because the notice of appeal erroneously said the defendant was appealing, when, in fact, it was the plaintiff.[88] Even when an appellant voluntarily moves to dismiss, courts have been unwilling to dismiss if the appellee can show prejudice.[89]

At bottom, whether representing the appellant or appellee, lawyers must focus on the procedural aspects of the appeal. The primary concern of appellant's attorney is costing clients their rights to appeal. The primary concern of appellee's attorney is whether a defect would support a dismissal without going through the cost and risk associated with a full appeal. Even for procedural errors, if the appellee can show prejudice, it may be worth pursuing a motion to dismiss.

---

83. Giovagnoli v. State Civ. Serv. Comm'n, 868 A.2d 393 (Pa. 2005) (citing Sahutsky v. H.H. Knoebel Sons, 782 A.2d 996, 1001 n.3 (Pa. 2001) (holding that failure to file a petition to open waived all claims on appeal and required dismissal)).

84. *See, e.g.*, State ex rel. Dedmon v. Carroll, 151 So. 2d 5 (Fla. 1963); Watson v. Dedmon, 145 So. 2d 564 (Fla. Ct. App. 1962).

85. Due v. Tallahassee Theatres, Inc., 160 So. 2d 169 (Fla. Ct. App. 1964) (ruling that a notice of appeal was insufficient and warranted dismissal because it did not name the appealing defendants); Torres v. Oakland Scavenger Co., 487 U.S. 312 (1988) (failing to name one of the appellants, not appellee, in the notice of appeal deprived the appellate court of jurisdiction over that appellant).

86. *See, e.g.*, Patterson v. Dist. of Columbia, 995 A.2d 167 (D.C. Ct. App. 2010) (discussing federal cases on that point).

87. *See id.* (citing, for example, Billino v. Citibank, N.A., 123 F.3d 723 (1997); Maerki v. Wilson, 128 F.3d 1005 (6th Cir. 1997)).

88. Watson v. Dedmon, 145 So. 2d 564 (Fla. Ct. App. 1962).

89. *See, e.g.*, Blount v. State Bank & Trust Co., 425 F.2d 266 (4th Cir. 1970) (denying appellant's voluntary dismissal and instead granting appellee's motion to dismiss and award appellee costs because appellant's failure to comply with briefing schedule caused trouble and expense to appellee).

C. Motion for summary disposition

Either appellant or appellee may move for summary disposition, either in the form of a motion for summary affirmance or a motion for summary reversal. Unlike a motion to dismiss, a motion for summary disposition results in a substantive, dispositive ruling from the appellate court. Appellate courts limit summary dispositions to clear-cut cases in which the outcome is plain and without the need for further briefing or review. As one federal court explained, courts should grant summary reversal only when the right to relief is "so clear, plenary briefing, oral argument, and the traditional collegiality of the decisional process would not affect [the appellate court's] decision. In sum, the merits of this action have been given the fullest consideration necessary to a just determination."[90]

Though a court may have the discretion to grant a motion for summary reversal, it generally will consider several factors in deciding whether to grant such a motion. When considering a motion for summary disposition, points for the parties to consider generally include:

- Precedent: Consider whether a higher court already ruled on the same legal issues, as it provides a clear precedent for the lower court.
- Public interest and irreparable harm: Consider whether the case involves public interest or potential irreparable harm that requires the courts to address urgent concerns.
- Fundamental, manifest, or prejudicial error: Consider whether the case involves clear error that is prejudicial or affects the rights of a party significantly.
- Nature of the legal issue: Consider whether the appeal presents issues of first impression, particularly on significant questions of public interest or serious errors in the application of the law.
- Absence of opposition: Consider whether the opposing party did not file a brief or formally oppose the motion.
- Judicial efficiency and economy: Consider whether summary disposition would promote judicial efficiency and economy by avoiding unnecessary burdens on the courts and parties.

Summary disposition is common when the outcome is mandated by a higher court's ruling. Summary reversal may be merited when the lower court

---

90. Sills v. Bureau of Prisons, 761 F.2d 792, 793–94 (D.C. Cir. 1985).

disregarded controlling precedent.[91] It may also be appropriate when the lower court decided a case without the benefit of more recent precedent.[92] With that backdrop, it is not surprising that courts often will not grant summary reversal when presented with an issue of first impression.[93]

Summary disposition also is more likely when the other party does not oppose the requested relief. For appellants, summary reversal generally will be appropriate if the appellee fails to respond to the opening brief.[94] But that general rule does not always control; it depends on the jurisdiction. For example, in Arizona, an appellate court generally may, but need not, consider an appellee's failure to file a responsive brief a confession of error when the case presents a debatable issue.[95] But the court may grant summary reversal if it finds per se prejudicial error.[96]

D. Motion for leave to file amicus brief

Amicus briefs are unique. They require leave of the appellate court to file. Additionally, appellate courts have broad discretion in deciding whether to accept an amicus brief, and they often do not.

The courts have articulated criteria aimed at ensuring amicus briefs meaningfully contribute to their understanding and resolution of the issues. If the parties can fully and adequately present the relevant issues and the amicus brief does not add significant value, a court likely will reject it. Amicus briefs

---

91. *See, e.g.*, Vietnam Veterans Against the War/Winter Soldier Org. v. Morton, 506 F.2d 53 (D.C. Cir. 1974).

92. *See* McNair v. City of Drew, Miss., 351 F.2d 498 (5th Cir. 1965) (granting motion for summary reversal and remanding to the federal district court due to appellee's failure to oppose the motion and the federal district court's having decided the issue without the benefit of more recent precedent).

93. *See, e.g.*, In re Israel O., 182 Cal. Rptr. 3d 548, 552 (Ct. App. 2015) (noting that granting "summary reversal would have abdicated our responsibility to provide de novo analysis of what appears to be a potentially significant and recurring issue of first impression").

94. *See, e.g.*, McNair v. City of Drew, Miss., 351 F.2d 498 (5th Cir. 1965); Metro Invs. Co., Inc. v. Enge, 297 N.E.2d 756 (Ill. App. Ct. 1973).

95. *Compare* United Bonding Ins. Co. v. Thomas J. Grosso Inv., Inc., 419 P.2d 546 (Ariz. Ct. App. 1966) (treating failure to file a responsive brief as a confession of error on the merits rather than by summary disposition, and reversing the trial court's ruling), *with* Flynn v. Flynn, 543 P.3d 269 (Ariz. Ct. App. 2024) (deciding not to treat failure to file a responsive brief as a confession of error, and affirming the trial court's ruling).

96. *See, e.g.*, People v. Geitner, 188 Cal. Rptr. 486 (Ct. App. 1982) (ruling summary reversal appropriate because defendant was induced to enter a plea agreement with an invalid term).

should not merely repeat the parties' arguments but should provide additional value.[97] Courts routinely reject amicus "echo" briefs.

In deciding whether to accept an amicus brief, a court's primary consideration is whether the amicus brief will assist it by presenting ideas, arguments, theories, insights, facts, or data not found in the parties' briefs.[98] Courts also assess the movant's interest in the appeal and whether the amicus brief serves an extraneous purpose.[99] As part of that assessment, a court generally evaluates whether the movant has a unique perspective or information that will assist the court beyond what the parties can provide.[100] As a last point about amicus briefs, if an appeal will have broad consequences, a court is more likely to accept the amicus brief to ensure it considers the public's interest and public policy, including the effects of the decision on non-parties.[101] For that reason, a court also is more likely to allow an amicus brief if it will help in avoiding judicial errors or unintended consequences.[102]

VI. Conclusion

Navigating the appellate process requires a commitment to detail, jurisdiction-specific knowledge, and an understanding of the differences between courts. While this chapter has provided a generalized framework for navigating appeals, as an appellate practitioner it is imperative you continue to refine your expertise through hands-on experience and ongoing study of the rules, procedures, and preferences governing your jurisdiction. By doing so, you can ensure that your clients receive effective representation and that the details that matter most are never overlooked.

97. *See, e.g.*, Prairie Rivers Network v. Dynegy Midwest Generation, LLC, 976 F.3d 761 (9th Cir. 2020).

98. *See, e.g., id.*; Voices for Choices v. Illinois Bell Tel. Co., 339 F.3d 542 (7th Cir. 2003).

99. *See, e.g.*, Columbus Monument Corp. v. City of Syracuse, 156 N.Y.S.2d 820 (2021).

100. Voices for Choices v. Illinois Bell Tel. Co., 339 F.3d 542 (7th Cir. 2003); Nat'l Org. for Women, Inc. v. Scheidler, 223 F.3d 615 (7th Cir. 2000); Ryan v. Commodity Futures Trading Comm'n, 125 F.3d 1062 (7th Cir. 1997).

101. *See, e.g.*, Lefebure v. D'Aquilla, 15 F.4th 670 (5th Cir. 2021) (granting leave for three retired federal judges to file amicus brief).

102. *See id.*

Discussion Questions

1. What are some common mistakes attorneys make when navigating the appellate process, and how can they be avoided?
2. In what ways do you think lawyers can manage client expectations and anxiety during the appellate process? What strategies can be used to set realistic goals?
3. What resources are available in your jurisdiction to help practitioners stay current with changes in appellate rules and procedures?
4. What factors do appellate courts consider when deciding whether to grant discretionary review, and how do these factors influence the strategies employed by appellants seeking review versus appellees seeking to deny review?
5. What are the key considerations when deciding whether to file a motion to stay the lower court's decision pending appeal, and how can appellants effectively demonstrate a likelihood of success on the merits?
6. As a lawyer, what responsibilities do you have to your clients, the court, and the legal system when navigating the appellate process?

Chapter 3

Ethics and Professionalism in Appellate Advocacy

In this chapter, you will learn to:

- Identify ethical issues that arise at various stages of appellate litigation
- Consider how diversity and cross-cultural competence relate to ethics and professionalism
- Develop and maintain a professional identity

I. Introduction

An effective advocate is an ethical advocate. Put differently, an advocate can be a brilliant writer and a persuasive speaker, but if they fail to meet minimal ethical standards when representing a client on appeal, then they have failed to represent that client effectively.

At this point in your legal career, you have likely taken a mandatory professional responsibility class, passed the Multistate Professional Responsibility Exam, and perhaps attended some continuing legal education courses on various topics relating to ethics. These courses and exams are focused on the Rules of Professional Conduct, which provide minimum standards for lawyers to follow. A thorough understanding of these rules is critical to recognizing the minimum standards of acceptable conduct when facing an ethical dilemma.

However, understanding these lower limits usually isn't enough to resolve the issues encountered in appellate practice. Advocates must exercise their professional discretion in choosing from several possible courses of action in any given scenario. Although each course of action may be ethically acceptable, they will lie along a spectrum when it comes to demonstrating professionalism and civility. Here, the twin goals of ethics and persuasion intersect. As discussed in Chapter 9, people tend to be most influenced by those they perceive as credible and likeable. By steering toward professional and civil options when representing a client on appeal, an advocate increases credibility and likeability, thereby increasing persuasiveness and efficacy as well.

This chapter discusses several areas of ethical concern in appellate advocacy, referring to the American Bar Association (ABA) Model Rules of Professional Conduct.[1] After completing this chapter, take some time to work on the hypothetical scenarios at the end. First determine the minimum standard of ethical conduct, and then identify two or more options that an advocate may have for addressing these issues as professionally as possible.

II. Frequently encountered ethical issues in appellate practice

The nature of appellate practice gives rise to certain ethical issues not commonly encountered in other practice areas. The issues discussed below are organized in a roughly chronological manner, as they may be encountered in representing a client on appeal. The first set of issues involves the nature of the lawyer-client relationship when representing appellate clients, focusing on the lawyer's authority to make strategic decisions on the client's behalf. The second set of issues relates to the process of identifying and raising claims on appeal. The third and fourth sets of issues are those arising in brief writing and oral argument.

1. The ABA Model Rules of Professional Conduct are models that jurisdictions are free to adopt in whole or in part and are not themselves binding in any jurisdiction. This text refers to the Model Rules for the sake of uniformity and convenience. However, when resolving any ethical issue, you should consult the Rules of Professional Conduct as adopted in your jurisdiction.

A. Issues that arise when dealing with clients

In appellate practice, lawyers exercise a good deal of discretion when it comes to identifying claims, selecting arguments, and organizing briefs. To ensure lawyers exercise this discretion in accordance with their clients' objectives, they should maintain proper communications with clients and set expectations early in the relationship.

Model Rule 1.5 requires lawyers to communicate the scope of representation to the client at the start of the lawyer-client relationship. Lawyers should explain to clients what they will and will not do in the course of the representation. If the scope of representation is limited in any way — for example, if the lawyer is ghostwriting the brief for a self-represented litigant — then the lawyer also must obtain the client's informed consent, confirmed in writing.[2]

Lawyers should also have a thorough conversation with clients regarding the allocation of decision-making authority. This allocation is often described as a means versus objectives dichotomy; the lawyer has complete authority to choose the means by which to achieve the client's objectives.[3] In practice, the distinction is not always clear. For example, the client may have a firm opinion on which claims should or should not be raised on appeal. The lawyer, however, may have a different opinion based on their professional judgment of which claims are most likely to prevail. In general, the final decision will rest with the lawyer. Even in criminal cases, a lawyer has the discretion to decide which nonfrivolous arguments to raise on appeal.[4]

Nonetheless, a lawyer who makes strategic decisions over a client's objections risks souring the lawyer-client relationship, perhaps to the point of termination. In these cases, lawyers are wise to explain their decisions thoroughly and understandably to their clients, as often as necessary. Although Model Rule 1.4 requires only that a lawyer keep a client "reasonably" informed,[5] rising above this minimum standard is often critical to maintaining a positive lawyer-client relationship and forestalling potential complaints.

Depending on your area of practice, you may encounter situations that make communication with clients difficult. Representing clients with dimin-

---

2. Model Rules of Pro. Conduct r. 1.2(c) (Am. Bar Ass'n 1983) [hereinafter Model Rule(s)].

3. Model Rule 1.2(a). Note that the Rules of Professional Conduct specify certain areas where clients have ultimate decision-making authority, such as whether to settle a civil claim and whether to testify in a criminal matter. *Id.*

4. *See* Jones v. Barnes, 463 U.S. 745 (1983) (holding that a criminal appellant does not have a constitutional right to dictate which nonfrivolous arguments court-appointed counsel must raise on appeal).

5. Model Rule 1.4.

ished capacity presents special challenges. A client's capacity may be diminished due to age, physical infirmity, or mental illness; the diminishment may be temporary or permanent. Model Rule 1.14 provides guidance for this specific circumstance. Lawyers are first reminded that even when a client has diminished capacity, the lawyer is to maintain a "normal" lawyer-client relationship to the extent reasonably possible. Thus, a lawyer should endeavor to communicate directly with the client in a manner that the client is most likely to comprehend. Model Rule 1.14 outlines situations where the lawyer may deviate from the norms of the lawyer-client relationship and seek the input of third parties when dealing with a client. If you find yourself representing a client with diminished capacity, you should consult your jurisdiction's version of Model Rule 1.14 and seek the advice of an ethics attorney, as necessary.

B. Issues that arise in identifying appellate claims

After setting expectations with the client, your next task is to review the appellate record and identify potential claims to raise on appeal. Chapter 4 covers the technical aspects of this process, but lawyers must also be mindful of ethical obligations. As a baseline, lawyers must meet the interrelated obligations of competence (Model Rule 1.1) and diligence (Model Rule 1.3). Even a lawyer handling their first appeal can be competent; the ethical duty of competence includes not only experience and skill but also thoroughness and preparation. When it comes to legal skills, the Rules of Professional Conduct recognize that a lawyer can achieve competence through self-study and consulting with more experienced lawyers.

But the reality is that a lack of diligence is sometimes a greater threat to a successful appeal than a lack of competence. Appellate practice is governed by strict timelines. Many writers, including legal writers, find it difficult to avoid procrastination. Comment 3 to Model Rule 1.3 describes procrastination in harsh terms, stating that "no professional shortcoming is more widely resented." This comment also rightly points out that procrastination "can cause a client needless anxiety and undermine confidence in the lawyer's trustworthiness."

Perhaps you have felt the stress of being plagued by procrastination while working under a tight deadline to complete a writing project. Sometimes, procrastination takes the form of writer's block, where the writer cannot get "unstuck" and break through a writing plateau. Procrastination can also be disguised by keeping busy with other tasks unrelated to the writing project. That form of procrastination takes the guise of productivity; perhaps you have heard the term "procrastibaking"? Chapter 8 provides some advice for dealing with writer's block and task anxiety.

Let's say you're now at the point where you have the requisite competence and diligence to take on the appellate record before you. As you begin identifying potential claims to raise on appeal, you must keep in mind the baseline ethical requirement that all claims be meritorious. In lay parlance, one would define a meritorious claim as a claim that has merit—what you might consider to be a "good argument." When applying the Rules of Professional Conduct, however, the definition of a meritorious claim per Model Rule 3.1 is slightly different; it is a claim that has "a basis in law and fact...that is not frivolous, which includes a good faith argument for an extension, modification or reversal of existing law." Thus, a meritorious claim, from an ethical perspective, has three elements: a legal basis, a factual basis, and good faith.[6] Indeed, the Rules of Professional Conduct do not require a meritorious argument to be a good one; the comments state that an argument with a good faith legal and factual basis is nonfrivolous, even if the lawyer believes the client will not win.

So, from an ethical perspective, in identifying claims on appeal, a lawyer can draw a few lines. The lowest line would be "meritorious claims"—those that meet the bare minimum of law, facts, and good faith (any claims that fall below the line would be considered frivolous). Next, one can draw a line labeled "good claims"—arguments that have some chance of prevailing on appeal. The top line would be "winning claims"—those that the lawyer feels reasonably certain will prevail on appeal. For any given case, these boundaries could shift as the lawyer develops the facts and law.

Diagram: Identifying Claims from an Ethical Perspective

You can see how a lawyer's ethical obligations intersect during this process of identifying claims. To comply with Model Rule 3.1, the lawyer must raise only those that cross the "meritorious" threshold. However, to comply with Model Rule 1.1, Competence, the lawyer may be required to winnow the claims further, raising in the brief only those that fall above the "good" line, or

6. *See* Model Rule 3.1 cmt. 2 ("What is required of lawyers...is that they inform themselves about the facts of their clients' cases and the applicable law and determine that they can make good faith arguments in support of their clients' positions.").

perhaps only those above the "winning" line. As stated in the section above, this process relies on the lawyer's professional judgment, thereby making the selection of claims the lawyer's call, not the client's.

At times, a lawyer's duty of competence and diligence may require the lawyer to raise claims on appeal that fall between "meritorious" and "good." We can label those claims "nonfrivolous"—arguments that a lawyer can make on appeal without violating the Rules of Professional Conduct but which have a low chance of prevailing (or perhaps no chance at all). Although lawyers should usually not dilute strong arguments with weak ones, at times the lawyer's professional obligations require breaking this rule of thumb. This is most likely to arise in criminal practice, where a lawyer's obligations are dictated by the Sixth Amendment to the U.S. Constitution in addition to the Rules of Professional Conduct. To ensure they are fulfilling a criminal defendant's right to effective assistance of counsel, a lawyer may strategically decide to include weaker arguments among the stronger ones. In fact, a lawyer may even have to file an appeal that includes only arguments that the lawyer reasonably believes will *not* prevail.[7]

You may have already made the next logical step in this analysis, wondering what a lawyer must do if a criminal defendant-appellant does not have *any* meritorious arguments to raise on appeal. The U.S. Supreme Court addressed this issue in *Anders v. California*.[8] In that opinion, the Court provided that a lawyer appointed to represent a client who has no nonfrivolous bases for appeal should request to withdraw from representation but must also file "a brief referring to anything in the record that might arguably support the appeal."[9] The client is then permitted to raise their own arguments to the court, and the court must then examine the brief and the record to determine "whether the case is wholly frivolous."[10] This practice is known as filing an *Anders* brief. If you must file an *Anders* brief at some point, be certain to check your court's local rules for additional requirements.

One final ethical consideration in identifying appellate claims is recognizing positional conflicts of interest. If you have made it this far in your representation of a client, you would have already run a conflicts check to look for actual conflicts with current or former clients of your office. But a sneaky type of conflict can creep up even when a client is cleared through the con-

---

7. For example, in capital cases, a defendant may be entitled to a mandatory direct appeal. Counsel for the defendant would have a duty to raise nonfrivolous arguments, even if they are unlikely to prevail.

8. 386 U.S. 738 (1967).

9. *Anders*, 386 U.S. at 744.

10. *Id.*

flicts-check process. Imagine you are representing an employee on appeal, seeking an advantageous ruling from a state appellate court regarding payment of workers' compensation benefits. Concurrently, in an unrelated case, you are representing an employer before the state's workers' compensation board. You realize that an advantageous ruling on appeal, although it would benefit the employee-client, would create binding precedent that would be disadvantageous to the employer-client. At this point, you have identified a positional conflict of interest. Although these two clients may have initially been unrelated and non-adverse, your position in the appellate case is now adverse to the employer-client. At this point, you would have to address the conflict, whether through informed consent or withdrawal.[11]

C. Issues that arise when writing briefs

In writing an appellate brief, you will make many decisions that have ethical implications. Will you start from scratch or recycle something you drafted for a previous client? What about using briefs written by other lawyers? How much can you rely on the assistance of nonlawyers, or perhaps the assistance of artificial intelligence (AI) drafting tools? To what extent can you criticize the lower court or opposing counsel? And to what extent must you cite unfavorable legal precedents? The sections below answer these questions from an ethical perspective.

1. *Using your prior work or another lawyer's work*

Lawyers with experience in particular practice areas (e.g., criminal appeals) will encounter similar appellate issues over time. Drafting every brief from the bottom up not only is inefficient but could prejudice the client's interests by creating unnecessary expense and delay. Thus, a lawyer is squarely in the right if they choose to reuse their previous written work. However, they must do so carefully to sidestep ethical concerns. First, both competence and diligence require careful examination of the facts and law to determine that the prior work is indeed adequate to address the current client's legal issues. Next, the lawyer must be careful to tailor the work to the current client's case. Using a former client's name in a current client's brief not only is an embarrassing mistake but could also violate the duty of confidentiality to the former client.[12]

---

11. MODEL RULE 1.7.

12. MODEL RULE 1.6(a). Confidential information is any information relating to the representation of the client, which includes the client's identity. Model Rule 1.9(c) extends the duty of confidentiality to former clients.

Finally, the lawyer must bill the current client only for the actual time spent on the brief. The lawyer may not bill for the time that it took in the past to prepare the original brief for the former client.[13]

Let's change the above scenario slightly. In conducting online legal research for a client, you find a court opinion favorable to your client's position. You download the appellate brief filed by the prevailing party and discover that the arguments are both relevant to your client's case and well written. "I couldn't say it better myself," you think, and you copy/paste portions of the other brief into your own without attribution. Now, to be certain, doing this in a brief written for a law school class would constitute academic dishonesty. In the context of legal practice, however, the analysis is less clear. Model Rule 8.4(c) prohibits lawyers from engaging in dishonest conduct. However, some ethics committees have refrained from holding that copying another lawyer's written work without attribution is per se unethical.[14] For example, the New York City Bar Association's ethics committee noted that the value of a legal brief lies in its persuasiveness and application of precedent, rather than its originality.[15] The North Carolina Bar Association's ethics committee further condoned recycling, stating that "[i]t... facilitates the preparation of competent briefs by encouraging lawyers to use the most articulate, carefully researched, and comprehensive legal arguments."[16] Nonetheless, courts have routinely disfavored the practice of copying work without attribution, particularly when combined with other misconduct, such as:

- Lying to the court when asked if the work was copied.[17]
- Filing a recycled brief referring to facts from a different case.[18]
- Submitting an application for attorney's fees including time spent "preparing" copied work.[19]

---

13. Model Rule 1.5(a); ABA Comm'n on Ethics & Pro. Resp., Formal Op. 93-379 at 6 (1993) ("A lawyer who is able to reuse old work product has not re-earned the hours previously billed and compensated when the work product was first generated.").

14. N.C. State Bar, Formal Op. 2008-14, Attribution When Using the Written Work of Another (2009), https://www.ncbar.gov/for-lawyers/ethics/adopted-opinions/2008-formal-ethics-opinion-14/; N.Y. City Bar Ass'n, Formal Op. 2018-3, Ethical Implications of Plagiarism in Court Filings (2018), https://www.nycbar.org/reports/formal-opinion-2018-3-ethical-implications-of-plagiarism-in-court-filings/.

15. N.Y. City Bar Ass'n, Formal Op. 2018-3, *supra* note 14.

16. N.C. State Bar, Formal Op. 2008-14, *supra* note 14.

17. N.Y. City Bar Ass'n, Formal Op. 2018-3, *supra* note 14 (citing In re Ayeni, 822 A.2d 420, 421 (D.C. 2003)).

18. *Id.* (citing In re Mundie, 453 Fed. Appx. 9 (2d Cir. 2011)).

19. *Id.* (citing In re Ayeni, 822 A.2d 420, 421 (D.C. 2003)).

In light of the potential negative consequences, lawyers are advised not to copy/paste entire sections of other lawyers' briefs into their work. Indeed, the better practice would be to cite favorable legal authorities and case law precedent.[20]

2. Delegating work to assistants

Another method for increasing efficiency is to rely on the assistance of others—nonlawyers, other lawyers, and technology. In the context of legal ethics, the inelegant term "nonlawyers" can refer to anything from a person (e.g., a paralegal) to legal technology, including artificial intelligence (AI). Regardless of the nature of the nonlawyer, the lawyer's ethical obligation remains the same. Model Rule 5.3(a) provides that lawyers must ensure that a nonlawyer's assistance is "compatible with the professional obligations of the lawyer." Lawyers are also generally responsible for a nonlawyer's work; per Model Rule 5.3(c), this includes ethical responsibility under certain circumstances. In the context of appellate brief writing, this means that you must review any delegated work to ensure that it conforms to your ethical and professional standards.

If you supervise another lawyer, you also take on a degree of responsibility for their conduct, including their ethical lapses. Model Rule 5.1(c) states that a supervisory lawyer is responsible for a subordinate lawyer's ethical violation if the supervisor orders the unethical conduct, ratifies it, or fails to take remedial measures after learning about it. Rule 5.1(a) also imposes upon managing lawyers a general obligation to reasonably ensure "that all lawyers in the firm conform to the Rules of Professional Conduct."

On the other hand, if you're early in your legal career, you may be more concerned with the ethical obligations of subordinate lawyers. At some point, you may disagree with a supervisor about how to resolve an ethical issue. Model Rule 5.2(b) provides a safe harbor for subordinate lawyers: if the disagreement involves an "arguable question of professional duty," the subordinate is shielded from responsibility if they act at the direction of a supervisory lawyer whose judgment call turns out to be incorrect. In circumstances where the ethical resolution of an issue is clearer cut, however, Model Rule 5.2(a) provides that a subordinate cannot use a "just following orders" defense to avoid discipline.

As stated above, lawyers also have ethical duties when it comes to using legal technology as a form of nonlawyer assistance. Chapter 12 provides some

---

20. *See id.* ("If the argument was successful in the prior case, the more typical practice would be to draw the new court's attention to the prior court's ruling, which is precedential, and presumably would add some persuasive force to the new brief.").

additional guidance and practical advice for using legal technology effectively and ethically in appellate practice.

3. *Criticizing judges, counsel, and opposing parties*

As you dive further into the brief-writing process, you will make strategic decisions regarding how to frame your arguments. Often, an argument on appeal is all about disagreeing with something that happened at the court below. You may be seeking to dismantle an opposing party's argument, refute a lower court's decision, or perhaps both. Lawyers must be careful, though, to distinguish criticizing an argument from criticizing a party, another lawyer, or a judge. Intemperate criticism can detract from the professional tone of your appellate brief. Certain types of criticism can cross an ethical line as well.

Although lawyers are free to attack the soundness or reasoning of their opponents' arguments, they should refrain from attacking the opponents. Tactics to avoid include accusations of lying, unethical conduct, and criminal conduct. For one, judges generally disapprove of these tactics; engaging in this behavior will likely diminish your credibility with the court. In one case, the Indiana Court of Appeals admonished a lawyer for including statements in an appellate brief accusing the opposing counsel of unethical conduct.[21] The court voiced its disapproval: "For the use of impertinent, intemperate, scandalous, or vituperative language in briefs on appeal impugning or disparaging this court, the trial court, or opposing counsel, we have the plenary power to order a brief stricken from our files and to affirm the trial court without further ado."[22]

Moreover, these types of uncivil tactics can also provide a basis for lawyer discipline. In a South Dakota case, a lawyer filed a reply accusing the opposing party of "despicable greed" and claiming that "her fangs [were] fully bared for all to see."[23] Based on this and a wealth of other misconduct, the South Dakota Supreme Court suspended the lawyer for 100 days. "[The disciplined lawyer's] acts of disparaging others, threatening sanctions and disciplinary complaints against opposing counsel, ... and filing retaliatory disciplinary complaints are prejudicial to the administration of justice and violative of the Rules of Professional Conduct."[24]

---

21. Lasater v. Lasater, 809 N.E.2d 380, 403 (Ind. Ct. App. 2004).
22. *Id.* at 404.
23. In re Discipline of Eicher, 661 N.W.2d 354, 358 (S.D. 2003).
24. *Id.* at 369.

Criticizing the trial judge is another ethical landmine to sidestep in appellate arguments. Again, a lawyer may ethically criticize the reasoning of a lower court's decision when crafting an effective argument. Direct attacks on judges, however, are unprofessional and under some circumstances may be unethical. Model Rule 8.2, Judicial and Legal Officials, prohibits lawyers from "mak[ing] a statement that the lawyer knows to be false or with reckless disregard as to its truth or falsity concerning the qualifications or integrity of a judge, adjudicatory officer or public legal office...." In a decision applying Rule 8.2, an Indiana lawyer was disciplined under the "reckless disregard" standard for describing a judge as "ignorant, insecure, and a racist" and "motivated by political ambition."[25] In other cases, courts have struggled to find a Rule 8.2 violation when the lawyer's criticism consisted of opinions rather than facts.[26]

Even when Rule 8.2 does not apply, other ethical rules may prohibit intemperate remarks about judges. Model Rule 8.4(d) states that it is professional misconduct to "engage in conduct that is prejudicial to the administration of justice."[27] This broad rule covers several types of misconduct. For example, a Minnesota lawyer violated Rule 8.4(d) for telling a judge, "[Y]ou are telling me that you can be impartial in this trial, which you haven't done since day one."[28] Rule 8.4(d) also covers written statements in court documents. In a Nevada case, a lawyer violated Rule 8.4(d) when his pleadings contained statements criticizing the judges who denied his client's petition for writ of habeas corpus.[29] The statements included, "[T]he Court's own Order proves that the Court is drunk with power, acting like a lawless bully, just lying and cheating to accomplish its evil objective to see [my client] dead."[30] In holding that the lawyer had violated Rule 8.4(d), the court noted that he "made serious charges of ethical and criminal violations by the justices without any supporting factual allegations or cogent argument supported by legal authority."[31]

---

25. In re Atanga, 636 N.E.2d 1253, 1256 (Ind. 1994).

26. *E.g.*, In re Yagman, 55 F.3d 1430 (9th Cir. 1995) (holding that statements of opinions are protected by the First Amendment unless based on stated or implied facts that are false).

27. Model Rule 8.4(d).

28. In re Disciplinary Action against MacDonald, 906 N.W.2d 238, 241 (Minn.), *reinstatement granted*, 909 N.W.2d 342 (Minn. 2018).

29. In re Discipline of Colin, 448 P.3d 556, 562 (Nev. 2019).

30. *Id.* at 558.

31. *Id.* at 562.

4. *Citing adverse authority and obeying court rules*

Lawyers must also strategically decide which legal authorities to cite in a brief. Largely, this is a discretionary decision reserved to lawyers in their exercise of professional judgment. But the Rules of Professional Conduct do provide a few bright lines. First, Model Rule 3.3, Candor Toward the Tribunal, requires a lawyer to disclose "legal authority in the controlling jurisdiction known to the lawyer to be directly adverse to the position of the client and not disclosed by opposing counsel."[32] The comments to Rule 3.3 further illuminate a lawyer's obligations: "Legal argument based on a knowingly false representation of law constitutes dishonesty toward the tribunal. A lawyer is not required to make a disinterested exposition of the law but must recognize the existence of pertinent legal authorities." Thus, a lawyer is required to cite unfavorable law under the circumstances outlined in Rule 3.3(a)(2), but a lawyer is permitted (indeed, required by the duty of competence) to make meritorious arguments that the law is inapplicable, distinguishable, or should be reversed, modified, extended, or narrowed, as appropriate.

The duty of candor to the tribunal includes within it a duty to update a previously filed appellate brief if the law changes prior to the court's decision. To ensure the court is properly informed of "pertinent legal authorities," a lawyer may have to file a supplemental brief or other form of supplement. For example, Federal Rule of Appellate Procedure 28(j) allows counsel to submit a supplemental letter to the circuit clerk, not to exceed 350 words, "stat[ing] the reasons for the supplemental citations."[33]

A second restriction on a lawyer's citation of legal authority relates to unpublished opinions. When a court designates an opinion as unpublished, this typically means that it does not become binding legal precedent. In addition, the ability of lawyers to cite the case in a legal filing will be limited by the court's rules. For example, the U.S. Court of Appeals for the Ninth Circuit Rule 36-3 generally restricts the citation of unpublished appellate decisions when the decision predates January 1, 2007, and is unrelated to the proceeding before the applicable court within the Ninth Circuit.[34] From an ethical perspective, lawyers are obligated to obey a court's rules.[35] Thus, failure to comply with so-called "no citation" rules may subject a lawyer to both professional discipline and court sanctions.

---

32. Model Rule 3.3(a)(2).
33. Fed. R. App. P. 28(j).
34. U.S. Ct. App. 9th Cir. R. 36-3(c).
35. Model Rule 3.4(c).

On the subject of obeying court rules, lawyers must also be mindful of other rules pertaining to the form of written briefs. Appellate courts set rules relating to word or page limits, font type, font size, margins, and line spacing. Do not assume that any uniform standard exists across state or federal courts. Again, following these rules is not just a matter of professionalism but of ethics as well.

D. Issues that arise in oral argument

Chapter 11 details the ins and outs of oral argument. For purposes of a legal ethics discussion, issues may arise as to the decision to request or waive oral argument. Once more, the question of who makes the decision — lawyer or client — relies on interpreting Model Rule 1.2(a). Unless oral argument itself is the client's objective in the representation, the lawyer ordinarily has the authority to decide whether to request it.[36] As a strategic decision, requesting or waiving oral argument is a matter of professional competence and determining which course of action best suits the client's goals.

Lawyers must also keep ethics and professionalism in mind when it comes to arguing before the court. The ethical duty of diligence requires that lawyers adequately prepare for oral argument; the extent to which the lawyer prepares may be dictated by the duty of competence. During oral argument, lawyers must demonstrate respect toward the judges, counsel, and court personnel. Model Rule 3.5(d) prohibits lawyers from "engag[ing] in conduct intended to disrupt a tribunal," and Model Rule 8.4(d) more broadly prohibits "conduct that is prejudicial to the administration of justice." Most discipline cases involving disruptive courtroom behavior relate to trial courts rather than appellate courts.[37] Nonetheless, appellate lawyers are not immune from losing their temper or otherwise conducting themselves poorly. In one case, the U.S. Court of Appeals for the Federal Circuit criticized a lawyer for pointing his finger at opposing counsel during rebuttal, referring to them as "bad lawyers," and accusing them of deception.[38] Although the court refrained from formally sanctioning this particular lawyer, the court firmly stated, "Angry, intemperate verbal attacks have no place in this court."[39]

36. Model Rule 1.2(a). Even when the lawyer has the authority to request or waive oral argument, they must still inform the client regarding the decision. *See* Model Rule 1.4.

37. *See, e.g.*, Annotated Model Rules of Professional Conduct 401–03 (Ellen J. Bennett & Helen W. Gunnarsson eds., 9th ed. 2019) (compiling several examples of Rule 3.5(d) violations in state and federal courts).

38. Nordberg, Inc. v. Telsmith, Inc., 82 F.3d 394, 398 (Fed. Cir. 1996).

39. *Id.*

E. Diversity and cross-cultural competence

An ability to work with individuals with a diverse array of backgrounds and beliefs is essential in the legal profession. Indeed, many workplaces require some type of diversity training for all employees. For lawyers, however, respecting diversity is not just an aspirational goal, nor is it solely a function of the human resources department. Rather, it is firmly embedded within the Model Rules of Professional Conduct as well as the corresponding rules in many U.S. jurisdictions. In other words, lawyers have an ethical duty to prevent and refrain from harassment, bias, and discrimination in the practice of law.

The primary source of this ethical duty comes from Model Rule 8.4, Misconduct. Model Rule 8.4(g) specifies:

> It is professional misconduct for a lawyer to... engage in conduct that the lawyer knows or reasonably should know is harassment or discrimination on the basis of race, sex, religion, national origin, ethnicity, disability, age, sexual orientation, gender identity, marital status or socioeconomic status in conduct related to the practice of law. This paragraph does not limit the ability of a lawyer to accept, decline or withdraw from a representation in accordance with Rule 1.16. This paragraph does not preclude legitimate advice or advocacy consistent with these Rules.

The comments to Model Rule 8.4 provide examples of conduct related to the practice of law: "representing clients; interacting with witnesses, coworkers, court personnel, lawyers and others while engaged in the practice of law; operating or managing a law firm or law practice; and participating in bar association, business or social activities in connection with the practice of law." As you can see, Model Rule 8.4(g) covers a wide range of activities, both within and outside the office.

Although some of the conduct prohibited by Model Rule 8.4(g) would also violate state and federal antidiscrimination laws, creating a provision within the Rules of Professional Conduct serves several important purposes. For one, it reflects the idea that the practice of law is a profession, not a trade. As part of a profession, lawyers hold themselves to a higher standard of conduct than those outside the profession. Lawyers are often viewed as leaders within their communities, and as such should model exemplary behavior.

In addition, prohibiting discrimination and harassment contributes to a more civil practice of law. Treating everyone with respect allows lawyers to better resolve conflict and achieve beneficial outcomes for clients. Moreover, civility is closely tied to lawyers' sense of job satisfaction. In a 2021 survey by the Illinois Supreme Court Commission on Professionalism, 92 percent of responding lawyers stated that incivility made their legal practice less satisfying.[40]

A deep understanding of diversity and cultural issues is also a component of lawyers' competence. As provided in Comment 5 to Model Rule 1.1, Competence, a lawyer must understand not only the client's legal problems but the factual circumstances as well. Such circumstances may include a client's background, culture, and beliefs. For example, in the United States, maintaining eye contact during conversation is generally used as a measure of a person's honesty and credibility. However, in other cultures, steady eye contact may signal rudeness or even aggression.[41] A lawyer who is unaware of this cultural difference may incorrectly assume that a client's averted gaze indicates deception, whereas the client was actually trying to show deference or respect.

At the extreme, intolerance of a client's race or religion may rise to the level of ineffective representation. In 2023, the Massachusetts Supreme Judicial Court held that a lawyer with documented hostility toward Black people and Muslims provided ineffective assistance of counsel when representing a Black, Muslim defendant.[42] Essentially, the defendant was deprived of his state and federal constitutional rights to counsel based on the "conflict of interest inherent in counsel's bigotry against persons of the defendant's faith and race."[43] The court granted a new trial, stating, "Where, as the record shows was the case here, counsel harbors a deep-seated animus for persons of the defendant's race or religion, we cannot presume zealous advocacy...."[44]

Although this case presents an acute example of bigotry, it exemplifies the danger of discriminatory behavior in the legal profession. On a smaller scale, bias and discrimination can impede the competent and effective representation of clients as well as the administration of justice in general. Even benign ignorance of cultural differences can lead to misunderstandings, which in turn may result in miscommunication, mistakes, and delay.

---

40. Ill. Sup. Ct. Comm'n on Professionalism, Survey on Professionalism: A Study of Illinois Lawyers (2021), https://civility.wpenginepowered.com/wp-content/uploads/2021/12/ILSCCP-Civility-Survey-Report-2021.pdf.

41. *See, e.g.*, Shota Uono & Jari K. Hietanen, *Eye Contact Perception in the West and East: A Cross Cultural Study*, PLoS One, Feb. 25, 2015, https://www.ncbi.nlm.nih.gov/pmc/articles/PMC4340785/.

42. Commonwealth v. Dew, 210 N.E.3d 904, 906 (Mass. 2023).

43. *Id.*

44. *Id.* at 915.

F. Creating your professional identity

If you're a law student or an early-career lawyer, you may not have had much occasion to consider your professional identity. A mandatory course on professional responsibility can help you learn the ethical rules, but those rules provide only the minimum standards for lawyers' conduct. In other words, these mandatory courses, along with the Multistate Professional Responsibility Exam, test only your understanding of the ethical "floor" — the standard below which you must not fall. Professionalism, on the other hand, deals with everything that rises above.

In any given situation, once you've determined the minimum standard of ethical conduct, deciding upon a course of action is a matter of your discretion and professional judgment, tempered by your client's objectives. It is in making these choices that lawyers forge their professional identities. For example, will you be a lawyer who puts zealous representation of the client at the forefront of every decision? Will you be a lawyer who shies away from conflict, instead seeking cooperation? No bright-line rule exists to answer these questions, but one thing is true: These decisions, in the aggregate and over time, will form your professional identity. Regardless of how you may view yourself, others will judge you more by your external actions than your internal beliefs.

With that in mind, be thoughtful when exercising your professional discretion. As an agent of your client, you are obligated to work diligently to obtain the client's objectives. The Rules of Professional Conduct recognize, however, that lawyers need not sacrifice civility when pursuing zealous representation. Comment 1 to Model Rule 1.3, Diligence, states, "The lawyer's duty to act with reasonable diligence does not require the use of offensive tactics or preclude the treating of all persons involved in the legal process with courtesy and respect." In making tactical decisions, think not only of the short-term results but also of the long-term consequences to your reputation, character, and goodwill. As a career, the practice of law is much more satisfying and sustainable when those in the profession exercise civility and courtesy in their daily interactions.

Another aspect of professionalism is the duty of lawyers to society at-large. Although no U.S. jurisdiction currently mandates pro bono publico service for lawyers, Model Rule 6.1 sets an aspirational standard of fifty hours of pro bono per year. As an appellate practitioner, you can apply your valuable skill set to support your community by participating in a pro bono appeals program. Chapter 13 discusses these types of programs in more detail. If you are a student or an early-career lawyer, engaging in pro bono representation is a way to hone your skills in a supportive environment.

III. Conclusion

Whether you are a student or lawyer, you have many resources available to learn more about ethics and professionalism. The American Bar Association requires law schools to include professional identity formation training to maintain ABA accreditation. Practicing lawyers and law students can also take advantage of continuing education programs, either through a state or local bar association or through a commercial provider. Above all, a valuable resource for developing professional identity is mentorship. Connect with lawyers, judges, and professors whom you identify as good role models. Over lunch or coffee, talk to them about their career path and the decisions made along the way. And once you have advanced in your career, pay it forward by mentoring a law student or new lawyer.

Discussion Questions

1. Can you think of a situation where an advocate's failure to meet minimal ethical standards might undermine their effectiveness, even if they are a skilled writer and speaker? How might this play out in an appellate case?
2. How do the goals of ethics and persuasion intersect in appellate advocacy, and why is it important for advocates to prioritize professionalism and civility?
3. Consider a scenario where an advocate has multiple options for addressing an ethical issue, all of which meet the minimum standards of the Rules of Professional Conduct. What factors should the advocate consider when choosing the most professional and civil course of action?
4. How might an advocate's professional identity influence their approach to ethical decision-making in appellate practice? Can you think of a situation where an advocate's personal values or biases might conflict with their professional obligations?
5. Can you think of any ethical issues that might arise in appellate practice that are not addressed in this chapter? How might you go about identifying and addressing these issues in your own practice?

Exercises

For each of the scenarios below, identify (1) the ethical issues presented; (2) the applicable Rules of Professional Conduct; and (3) your possible courses of action, taking into account minimum standards of ethical conduct as well as professional considerations.

1. You're a recent law graduate working at a firm, and you're assisting other lawyers with research and drafting while you wait for your bar exam results. You're currently helping a senior associate with an appellate brief to be filed in your state's intermediate court of appeals. You provide her a list of relevant case law in your jurisdiction, along with summaries of each case. A week or so later, the associate asks you to proofread the argument section of the brief. You notice that she did not cite a case decided last year by your state supreme court. The case deals with the same area of law and similar facts. In your assessment, this case is directly adverse to your client's position. You meet with the associate and ask her why she didn't cite the case in her brief. She tells you, "I agree that the outcome was the opposite of what our client seeks, but I think the facts are distinguishable. Also, I think the portion of the opinion discussing the law that's relevant to our case is dicta, not precedential. Anyway, I'm sure the appellant will cite the case in their reply brief." What do you do?
2. You're a junior associate in a firm. You're assigned to write a brief on a First Amendment issue, to be filed in your state's intermediate appellate court. You're also juggling several other projects and feel stretched thin. You discuss your concerns with a senior associate. He tells you that a similar First Amendment issue was the subject of an appeal in a neighboring state a couple of years ago, and that the attorneys' briefs in that case could be very helpful. After reviewing those briefs, you realize you could probably use them almost word for word, given that the facts and legal issues are nearly identical. You ask the senior associate for his advice. He tells you, "You should definitely borrow from those briefs. Plagiarism is a problem in law school, but not in litigation. In fact, it could be malpractice if you tried to make this up on your own! Copy the briefs, and just cut an hour or two off your billable time to the client." What do you do?

Part 2

Building Appellate Arguments and Drafting Appellate Briefs

Chapter 4

Appellate Foundations: Preserving the Record, Identifying Issues, and Understanding Standards of Review

In this chapter, you'll learn about:

- Preserving issues for appeal
- Reviewing records to identify appellate issues
- Understanding the different standards that apply to appellate review of lower court proceedings

I. Introduction

A successful appeal requires a solid foundation. In this chapter, we take a deeper dive into the process by which proceedings at the agency- or trial-court level can give rise to appellate claims. This chapter also provides guidance on how to review appellate records. Lastly, this chapter discusses an essential part of appellate practice: the standards of review. The outcome of an appeal may turn upon the level of deference that the appellate court must apply to the lower court's proceedings. By the end of this chapter, you'll understand these key components of building an appeal from the ground up.

II. Preserving the record

The seeds for every successful appeal are planted in the record at the trial-court level. The challenge for every trial lawyer is planning for the unthinkable: "What happens if I lose?" No baseball player bats 1.000. And no lawyer wins every case. The rules of professional conduct around the country even make it plain that a lawyer cannot promise success because at least the occasional loss is inevitable. Every trial lawyer, no matter how confident, must plan for a possible appeal by creating a record of what the parties presented and the trial court considered.

The importance of preserving the record cannot be understated. A California jurist, Justice Rebecca Wiseman of the California Appellate Division, Fifth District, is well known for her pithy summary of the importance of preserving the record.[1] She said, "When practicing appellate law, there are at least three immutable rules: first, take great care to prepare a complete record; second, if it is not in the record, it did not happen; and third, when in doubt, refer back to rules one and two."[2]

And when an appellant does not make materials a part of the record, appellate courts generally presume the omitted materials would support affirming, not reversing, the trial court.[3]

With few notable, but rarely applicable, exceptions, parties cannot present any new evidence at the appellate level. The exceptions, discussed in more detail below, are judicial notice and late-developing jurisdictional issues, such as a party's death. Subject to those limited exceptions, appellate courts limit their review to issues raised before the trial court, whether in pretrial proceedings or during the trial itself. This section considers how to ensure the contents of the trial court's record allow for appellate review.

Thus, the trial lawyer must lay the factual foundation for an appeal. The trial lawyer generally does so through the following means:

- Ensuring a complete record of every hearing
- Engaging in motion practice
- Making objections during trial
- Making offers of proof and seeking to admit evidence for appeal purposes only

---

1. *See* Protect Our Water v. Cnty. of Merced, 110 Cal. App. 4th 362, 364 (2003).
2. *Id.*
3. *See, e.g.*, Erickson v. Erickson, 521 P.3d 1089, 1099 (Idaho 2022) ("[T]he missing portions of that record are to be presumed to support the action of the trial court.") (quoting Groveland Water & Sewer Dist. v. City of Blackfoot, 505 P.3d 722, 728 (Idaho 2022)); Whaley v. Commonwealth, 567 S.W.3d 576, 591 (Ky. 2019).

- Ensuring exhibits are admitted and are made a part of the record, including checking for clerical errors
- Requesting specific factual and legal findings when appropriate

No appellate lawyer wants to tell a client that the issue might have merit but the record does not support relief, especially when it could have supported relief with a little planning.

A. Verbatim record of proceedings

Verbatim records historically have been the province of court reporters, who are human and make mistakes. Over the past twenty years, courts have begun to use audio and video recordings of proceedings, which later can be transcribed by court reporters or other individuals. And even more recently, courts have begun looking to artificial intelligence to help create a verbatim record. Each method is subject to error. And the lawyer must review those verbatim records for accuracy. Failure to do so can cost the client on appeal.

The appellate lawyer thus must ensure all the transcripts are produced, complete, and filed with the appellate court. Even when the court orders the transcripts, the appellate lawyer must ensure they are complete. To that end, the appellate lawyer must review the proceedings to ensure transcripts of all recorded proceedings are produced. Transcripts are easily overlooked, especially if they occurred in chambers or through videoconference. Appellate counsel should review all the minute entries to determine if the trial court made a verbatim record and ensure the transcript is filed with the appellate court.

Trial counsel also must make a record of events not evident in a verbatim record. For example, if the defendant is dressed in jail garb, instead of civilian clothing, for the trial, defense counsel needs to speak up and say something on the record; otherwise, the appellate court will have no way of knowing, and the trial court will have had no opportunity to address the issue. Examples of this type of issue are as varied as the facts in lawsuits. Common examples include juror behavior, such as falling asleep, or behavior by members of the public viewing the proceedings, such as wearing clothing emblazoned with slogans or logos favoring one side or the other.

Opposing counsel's behavior also can require a comment on the record. For example, let's suppose that during closing argument, counsel pulled a clear plastic baggie from his pocket. He said the baggie contained rosemary clippings. He argued the jury should compare the clippings to the photos in evidence and conclude the photo did not show rosemary. He told the jury he had clipped the rosemary from his own yard that morning. The baggie was never subject to witness testimony or admitted into evidence. Because opposing counsel did not object, the trial court did not address the issue. Ultimately, it was the video recording of the closing argument that allowed the appellate court to address the issue. Counsel had to supplement the record with the video recording because the transcript did not sufficiently show what occurred. When an appeal presents this type of issue, the appellate lawyer should consider asking the appellate court to supplement the record with the video recording itself and then direct the appellate court to the specific time when the video recording shows the events leading to the issue.

When the trial court does not make a verbatim record, trial counsel also must make a comprehensive statement on record. Many a trial court and counsel have summarized an off-the-record discussion or ruling with ten words: "Subject to the objections raised during the off-the-record discussion." That general statement preserves nothing. That said, at times, trial counsel risks the ire of the trial court when seeking to make an oral record during the proceedings. In those situations, trial counsel can simply say they will file a written record of the objections for appellate purposes.

Historically, in-chambers meetings and teleconferences were common sources of this issue. Technology has expanded the source of the issue. More and more issues are resolved in videoconferences. Email and collaborative editing programs are becoming more common. Courts have adopted such processes to speed case processing. Examples include using email exchanges to edit and finalize jury instructions and verdict forms. In those situations, the trial lawyer should ask the court to preserve all those communications and edits by placing them in the record. If it is not in the record, it did not happen. And a litigant could lose a valid issue as a result.

B. Motion practice

A key component of preserving the record is motion practice at the trial court. The court's decisions on motions often lead to grounds for appeal. Conversely, failure to file certain motions may limit the ability of a party to raise an issue on appeal.

1. *Pretrial motions and dispositive motions*

Many appeals arise because the trial court granted a motion to dismiss or motion for summary judgment, or some combination of the two. The record for a motion to dismiss generally is quite small, limited to the pleadings, documents incorporated by reference, judicial notice, and the briefing. Summary judgment rulings similarly are limited, but broader than a motion to dismiss.

The trial lawyer must ensure that the record on appeal reflects everything the trial court considered. And the trial lawyer must ensure that the documents and evidence the trial court considered were in the proper form. For some jurisdictions, the evidence must be in admissible form. Other jurisdictions apply a looser standard. Whatever the standard, appellants and appellees alike can make much of defects in the evidentiary record when the trial court ruled on a dispositive motion.

2. *Motions in limine*

The trial lawyer should use motions in limine to address significant evidentiary issues, particularly if an issue will require the trial court to conduct an evidentiary hearing. Motions in limine are used to secure an order from the trial court to exclude or limit the use of evidence. By using a motion in limine, the trial lawyer can make a better and more comprehensive record. As part of this process, the trial lawyer must raise the issue timely. Most courts impose strict deadlines on motions in limine. Many restrict oral objections to exhibits if not made in pretrial statements and the like. The trial court's goal is the efficient use of trial time. No judge wants to keep the jury waiting while dealing with an untimely raised evidentiary issue.

3. *Post-trial motions*

To preserve some issues for appellate review, many jurisdictions require specific motions at specific stages during or after the trial. If a party does not make the motion timely, the appellate court will not take up the issue. The requirements vary by jurisdiction.

Examples of common motions include directed verdict and judgment notwithstanding the verdict (in some jurisdictions, such as Arizona, these motions are known collectively as judgment as a matter of law). Other examples of post-trial motions include motions for remittitur (or to reduce the jury verdict), motions for a new trial, and motions for reconsideration.

Some courts require the trial attorney make those motions and to renew those motions at specific times. For example, trial counsel for criminal defendants often must make a motion for judgment as a matter of law (or for a directed verdict) as a prerequisite to challenging the sufficiency of the evidence on appeal. The same often is true for civil cases too.

If the trial attorney does not make those motions timely, the issue is not preserved for appeal. The appellate lawyer can help avoid these fatal errors by being involved early, before and during trial. After the fact, there is little an appellate lawyer can do. But as noted below, the failure to preserve an issue is not always fatal.

At the same time, post-trial motions can have the effect of narrowing the issues on appeal. Many jurisdictions will not allow an appellant to seek relief if the appellant filed a post-trial motion but did not ask the trial court to consider the issue. For that reason, the appellate lawyer should be involved early in the case and absolutely should be involved in drafting any post-trial motions. It is little comfort at oral argument for an appellate lawyer to have to field a judge's question by saying the lawyer did not handle that part of the case and might have handled it differently. A party's appellate lawyer may retain some dignity with such an answer, but the party still loses.

C. Trial objections

Objections during trial must be timely and specific. General objections rarely suffice. The attorney should identify the evidentiary rule, preferably by number. In the absence of specificity, appellate courts generally will affirm the trial court's ruling. The objection also must be timely. Even a short delay can result in waiving the issue. The exception for this general rule is when the issue presents concerns of plain error, also known as fundamental error.

Trial lawyers too often overlook opportunities at the end of the trial, specifically when working on jury instructions and verdict forms. In reality, the trial lawyer should be focused on both from the beginning of the trial. For the jury, the instructions and verdict forms are the four corners of what they will consider. The trial lawyer's theme should fit nicely within those four corners. And if the instructions contain errors or the verdict forms do not call out specific findings, the appellate lawyer may be without means to correct the issue.

D. Offers of proof

Offers of proof are critical to preserve an issue when the trial court overrules an objection. The trial lawyer must timely make an offer of proof as to what the evidence would have been. The offer of proof can take many forms, from asking the court to admit evidence for appeal purposes only, to offering transcripts of depositions, and to avowing what the witness would have said if the witness had been allowed to answer a question. In the hectic trial environment, lawyers often forget to make offers of proof because they must await a break in the trial proceedings, often at the end of the day. And the trial lawyer should keep in mind that the offer of proof is not designed to convince the trial court to change its ruling. Rather, it is designed to show the appellate court two things: (1) the trial court erred and (2) the error could lead the jury to reach a different verdict.

E. Admission and retention of evidence

Too often, a trial lawyer gets caught up in the moment and forgets to ask the court to admit a key piece of evidence. The trial lawyer should maintain a list of each exhibit the lawyer wants admitted by witness. Before each witness leaves the stand, the trial lawyer should review that list to ensure all the evidence was admitted.

Trials are human endeavors, so mistakes happen. Sometimes, the exhibit does not get marked as admitted. Sometimes, exhibits get mislaid. Witnesses will walk off with exhibits (one of the authors has had to have court staff chase down a witness in the elevator). And judges will do the same, noting that an exhibit is admitted but then not giving it to the clerk. The appellate lawyer needs to review the record to be sure it is complete and accurate.

F. Specific factual and legal findings

The trial lawyer should consider whether success on appeal will require the trial court to make specific factual and legal findings. Most court rules allow the lawyers to request specific findings when the court rules on motions. Importantly, the lawyer must make that request timely, usually within a specific time period before the court rules on the motion. Sometimes, statutes and case law also require specific factual and legal findings.

If a trial lawyer fails to request specific factual findings or does not object to the sufficiency of the findings, the appellate court may not be able to address the issue.

G. Facts not in the record: Judicial notice and late-occurring jurisdictional facts

The judicial notice exception rarely applies, but it may provide relief if the trial court did not address some fact. An appellate court occasionally will take judicial notice of the fact. The fact must be of consequence. The appellate lawyer will need to comply with the specific jurisdiction's requirements for judicial notice. Most commonly, courts require the fact to be generally known, easily and accurately verified, and beyond reasonable question. Even so, if a fact is subject to judicial notice and affects the case outcome, the lawyer should ask the trial court to take judicial notice, not wait until the appeal stage. Otherwise, the litigant likely will face a waiver argument.

Late occurring facts may arise at the appellate level. The most common affect justiciability of the issue. A common example is the death of a party before the judgment becomes final. The effect of this type of fact is to moot the appeal or at least some of the appellate issues. When such factual issues arise, the appellate lawyer will need to ask the appellate court to supplement the record with the necessary documentation.

III. Reviewing appellate records

As the above shows, the appellate lawyer must review the record carefully. The goal goes beyond just making sure the record is complete. While ensuring the record is complete, the appellate lawyer also is searching for appealable issues. Trial counsel often will have a list of issues, but the appellate lawyer must bring a focused eye to the task. Trials are human endeavors. None are perfect. Mistakes occur at many stages, but few mistakes merit relief on appeal.

The appellate lawyer's job is to identify any errors at the trial court, whether preserved or not, and then winnow the issues down to those errors worth pursuing on appeal. The first job is to understand the facts and the controlling law underlying the ruling being appealed. The lawyer then must consider the information in the record and whether it will support an appeal. And even if the appellate court agrees that an error occurred, the appellate lawyer must consider whether the error will support reversal and whatever other relief the appellant seeks. In that regard, if the issue was waived, ask whether one of the exceptions applies.

A key part of the appellate lawyer's analysis is the standard of review the appellate court will apply, discussed later in this chapter. If the appellate court will engage in a *de novo* review, the appellant has a better chance of prevailing. If the appellate court will engage in an abuse of discretion review, the appellate lawyer must not only ensure that the record supports the requested relief but also that it does not support the trial court's ruling. The appellant has a much tougher row to hoe under that standard of review.

When reviewing the record, an appellate lawyer must also consider trends at the relevant appellate court. In *Loper Bright Enterprises v. Raimondo*,[4] the U.S. Supreme Court recently abandoned *Chevron* deference. That change may prove to be such a trend. Not all state courts had embraced the *Chevron*

4. 603 U.S. 369 (2024).

doctrine prior to the Supreme Court's decision, and even those that did had backed away from it before *Loper*.[5] But for those courts that had embraced it, whether *Loper* suggests a trend for other deference doctrines is an issue for courts and appellate lawyers alike. A wise appellate lawyer will address the trend and whether it should or should not extend to the case before the court.[6] In that regard, the appellate lawyer must consider the temperament of the bench to which the appellate lawyer is arguing. At courts of last resort, that task is easier. Lawyers often draft briefs for intermediate appellate courts without knowing the makeup of the panel. Even so, by the time oral argument is set, the lawyer generally knows who will be taking the bench and can focus oral arguments on those judges.

IV. Standards of review

Most standards of review can be divided into four broad categories: factual findings, discretionary rulings, legal conclusions, and mixed questions of law and fact. Appellate courts apply the most deferential standard, generally called the "clear error standard," to the trial court's factual findings. After all, it is the trial court's job to make factual findings. Appellate courts also are deferential to trial courts when the trial courts make discretionary decisions, generally called the "abuse of discretion standard" or "arbitrary and capricious" standard. The *de novo* standard of review applies when the appellate court is deciding an issue of law, such as interpreting a constitutional provision or a statute. Mixed questions of law and fact are subject to a mixed standard of review.

This section does not aspire to identify and articulate every standard of review. Instead, it provides a brief overview of the more common standards and when they apply. The appellate lawyer will need to review the jurisdiction's law on the standards of review carefully. Different jurisdictions use different terminology. And the appellate lawyer must be aware of and work with any jurisdiction-specific nuances.

Which standard of review an appellate court applies can change the outcome. And which standard of review the appellate court chooses may depend on how the lawyer frames the issue. Can the appellant's lawyer frame the appeal as involving a legal issue subject to a *de novo* review? Can the appellee's lawyer frame the appeal as involving a factual issue subject to an abuse of discretion review? Too often, appellate lawyers cite the standard of review

5. *See, e.g.*, A.R.S. § 12-910 (expressly rejecting *Chevron* doctrine in Arizona in 2018).
6. *See, e.g.*, United States v. Boler, 115 F.4th 316, 322–23 (4th Cir. 2024).

early in the brief and never mention it again. But for the appellate court, the standard of review is front and center at all times. Every brief must discuss the standard of review and apply it to the case before the court.

A. Factual findings: Clear error and substantial evidence

The clear error standard of review represents one of the most deferential standards of review. Substantial evidence follows closely. Each jurisdiction may use slightly different names and may articulate the standards in slightly different ways. But at bottom, the standards apply to the factual findings at the trial court, whether done by a trial court or a jury. And they limit the appellate court to addressing the most egregious factual errors.

When looking for clear error, an appellate court will not overturn a trial court's factual finding unless the appellate court is left with the "definite and firm conviction that a mistake has been committed."[7] The standard requires appellate courts to exercise restraint and respect the fact finder's unique ability to assess witness credibility and evidence directly. Under this standard, an appellate court will not substitute its reasoning for the fact finder's reasoning even if the appellate court might have come to a different conclusion if it had been the fact finder.[8] For that reason, even if evidence in the record supports a contrary finding, the appellate court will not disturb the finding.

Under the clear error standard, an appellate court will affirm a fact finder if the findings are plausible given the entire record, even if the appellate court would have weighed the evidence differently.[9] As such, when a fact finder chooses between two permissible views of the evidence, the fact finder's choice between them cannot be clearly erroneous. For example, even if evidence in the record supports the appellant's argument, if that evidence is subject to any credibility assessment or weighing, appellate courts generally will not tread on the fact finder's decision.

For an appellant to prevail under this standard, the evidence of the fact generally needs to be incontrovertible. For example, clear error might apply if a trial court found that a person took no drug tests even though testimony from the other side and drug testing reports in the record show the person did. It might not apply if the person's own testimony is the only evidence

---

7. Easley v. Cromartie, 532 U.S. 234 (2001); *see also* Alexander v. S.C. State Conf. of the NAACP, 602 U.S. 1 (2024).

8. *See* Bose Corp. v. Consumers Union of United States, Inc., 466 U.S. 485 (1984).

9. Alexander v. S.C. State Conf. of the NAACP, 602 U.S. 1 (2024).

because the trial court could conclude the person was not credible. The U.S. Supreme Court provided insight into the standard in *Anderson v. City of Bessemer City.*[10] The Court ultimately concluded the district court's finding was not clearly erroneous.

The substantial evidence standard differs slightly from the clearly erroneous standard.[11] The substantial evidence standard generally adds a reasonableness component to the analysis, making it a slightly less rigorous standard.[12] This standard allows the appellate court to invade the decision-making if it concludes that evidence supports the trial court's or agency's findings but the findings were not reasonable in light of the evidence. As such, an appellant should focus on the differences in the standards when the substantial evidence standard applies.

An appellate lawyer will find nuanced differences in how jurisdictions apply these standards and related degrees of deference and scrutiny involved in each. As a general rule, the clearly erroneous standard requires a higher degree of certainty about a mistake compared to the substantial evidence standard, which focuses on the reasonableness of the evidence supporting the conclusion.

And even if the appellant establishes clear error or a lack of substantial evidence, the appellant still must show the error made a difference or constitutes reversible error.

B. Discretionary rulings: Abuse of discretion or arbitrary and capricious

Like the clear error and substantial evidence standards, the abuse of discretion standard and the arbitrary and capricious standards are similar but not interchangeable. They generally apply when the appeal involves a discretionary issue. Be sure to use and apply the correct standard for the jurisdiction.

Appellate courts generally apply the abuse of discretion standard when reviewing trial court or quasi-judicial discretionary decisions. Under this standard, courts look for whether there has been a clear error of judgment (not to be confused with the clear error standard of review). In applying this standard of review, the appellate court goes beyond just ensuring the trial court applied correct legal principles. It also assesses whether the trial court

10. 470 U.S. 564 (1985) (reviewing the Fourth Circuit's clearly erroneous ruling, based on a meticulous review of the record).

11. *See* Dickinson v. Zurko, 527 U.S. 150 (1999).

12. *Id.*; Biestek v. Berryhill, 587 U.S. 97 (2019).

exercised its discretion in a reasonable manner within the bounds of the law. Evidentiary rulings often are subject to this standard. By way of example, in *Old Chief v. United States*,[13] the Supreme Court concluded the trial court abused its discretion by admitting evidence that was deemed prejudicial. In that case, the district court admitted evidence of the defendant's earlier conviction. The defendant objected and offered to stipulate to the conviction. The stipulation could have satisfied the element of the offense without revealing the nature or details of the earlier crime. The Supreme Court concluded the district court abused its discretion because the decision raised the risk of a verdict tainted by improper considerations.[14] Key to establishing error under this standard is showing the prejudicial nature of the evidence admitted against the alternatives offered by the defendants, such as stipulations.[15]

Appellate courts commonly apply the similar, but narrower, arbitrary and capricious standard of review for administrative decisions. For this standard, the appellate court will focus on whether an agency reached its decision after considering all the relevant factors and whether the agency made a clear error of judgment. As with the abuse of discretion standard of review, the appellate court's review under this standard is highly deferential to the agency. At its core, this standard prevents an appellate court from substituting its judgment for that of the agency. It instead requires appellate courts to assess whether the agency's decision-making process was reasonable and based on relevant factors.

In summary, the clear error standard discussed above primarily focuses on the factual correctness of the trial court's findings. The abuse of discretion standard and the arbitrary and capricious standard apply when the appellate court is reviewing for reasonableness and adherence to the law. The abuse of discretion standard allows for a more thorough review of the decision-making process and focuses on whether the trial court or quasi-judicial body made a decision within a permissible range based on the discretion involved. In contrast, the arbitrary and capricious standard focuses more on the rationality and justification of the decision within the confines of an agency's authority and the evidence presented.

---

13. 519 U.S. 172 (1997).

14. *Id.*

15. *Id.* at 184–85 ("Thus the notes leave no question that when Rule 403 confers discretion by providing that evidence 'may' be excluded, the discretionary judgment may be informed not only by assessing an evidentiary item's twin tendencies, but by placing the result of that assessment alongside similar assessments of evidentiary alternatives.") (citing J. Strong, McCormick on Evidence 780, 782 & n.41 (4th ed. 1992); 22 C. Wright & K. Graham, Federal Practice and Procedure § 5250 (1978)).

Both standards respect the trial court's or agency's knowledge of the case and the evidence, but the standards apply to different aspects of the decision-making process. And both standards have a prejudice component.

C. Legal rulings: *De novo* — generally

Appellate courts generally give no deference to a trial court's legal conclusions, such as when the appellate court reviews a trial court's constitutional or statutory interpretation rulings. The standard requires the appellate court to undertake an independent, comprehensive review. Generally, absent waiver, appellate *de novo* review is analogous to resetting an electronic device to factory settings.

Appellate courts apply the *de novo* standard of review to constitutional and statutory interpretation issues to ensure "a unitary system of law."[16] To do otherwise would open the door to widely differing interpretations depending on the trial court. This standard reflects the appellate courts' role of ensuring legal accuracy and uniformity.[17] Countless books and articles have been written about *de novo* review as it applies to constitutional and statutory interpretation. Paradigms and corollaries abound. Because the appellate court has broad review powers under a *de novo* review, an appellate lawyer should present alternative arguments—unambiguous and ambiguous—to show the provision's meaning.

Most jurisdictions begin by deciding whether the plain language of the constitution or statute is ambiguous. Plain language analysis looks at the words in the provision and other similar provisions (*in pari materia*). The appellate court will look for statutory definitions and the plain meaning of the words used. If the appellate court decides the plain language is unambiguous, it generally will not refer to secondary interpretation paradigms and corollaries. But even after finding a provision unambiguous, appellate courts have sometimes been known to address the secondary interpretation rules to buttress the court's overall conclusion.

If the appellate court decides a provision is ambiguous, then secondary rules come into play. Each jurisdiction's secondary rules of statutory interpretation vary slightly. To begin, the appellate lawyer must consider the jurisdiction's controlling precedent. Then the appellate lawyer should consider other helpful secondary rules unless the jurisdiction has rejected it. The appellate court will be in the best position to decide whether to adopt a specific second-

---

16. Ornelas v. United States, 517 U.S. 690, 697 (1996).

17. *See, e.g.*, Bailey v. Bayles, 52 P.3d 1158, 1164 ¶ 18 (Utah 2002).

ary interpretation rule. The appellate lawyer should not leave a valuable tool on the table just because the jurisdiction has not addressed it before.

When an appeal involves *de novo* review, the policy reasons for reaching a particular result are paramount. When engaging in a *de novo* review, appellate courts often involve lengthy policy discussions to support the court's decision. In any appeal, the appellate lawyer should answer the question "why?" in the briefing. When the court is engaged in a *de novo* review, the appellate lawyer must make strong policy arguments. The briefing should back up the proposed interpretation by explaining why it makes sense and why a particular outcome will further, not undermine, other precedent or stated goals.

Some courts apply a slightly different standard to an agency's statutory interpretation. Until recently, the Supreme Court did.[18] But not all state courts embraced the federal *Chevron* deference, and some that did have backed away from it. And though the Supreme Court has abandoned the *Chevron* deference for statutory interpretations, the extension of the *Chevron* deference to an agency's interpretations of its own regulations, known as *Auer* deference, remains an open question even in the federal courts.[19]

D. Mixed questions of fact and law

When considering a mixed question of fact and law, appellate courts will apply a deferential review to the trial court's factual findings. Not so for the trial court's interpretation of the law. And not so for how the law applies to the specific facts. Those legal issues generally are subject to *de novo* review. When faced with this standard, the appellate lawyer must consider how to approach the issue. As Justice Elena Kagan noted, the answer may be elusive:

> Mixed questions are not all alike. Some require courts to expound on the law, and should typically be reviewed *de novo*. Others immerse courts in case-specific factual issues, and should usually be reviewed with deference. In short, the standard of review for a mixed question depends on whether answering it entails primarily legal or factual work.[20]

Because the standard of review may be case-dispositive, the appellate attorney should seek to frame the issue in a way that gives their client the most favorable standard.

---

18. *See Loper Bright Enters.*, 603 U.S. at 412.

19. *See, e.g.*, *Boler*, 115 F.4th at 322–23.

20. United States Bank Nat'l Ass'n ex rel. CWCapital Asset Mgmt. LLC v. Vill. at Lakeridge, LLC, 583 U.S. 387, 388 (2018).

E. Unpreserved issues: Plain or fundamental error

Under the waiver doctrine, appellate courts do not take up issues on appeal if the party did not present those issues to the trial court. Appellate courts use waiver to ensure that the trial court performs its fact-finding role and that the appellate courts limit their role to looking for legal error at the trial court.[21] State courts are in accord.[22] Courts offer several reasons for this approach, namely "judicial economy—trial courts make factual findings and appellate courts pronounce the law . . . [because] trial judges are the only ones who have the unparalleled opportunity to determine the credibility of the witnesses and the weight to be afforded the evidence."[23]

That said, depending on the jurisdiction, some notable exceptions apply to the waiver doctrine. The most common examples include:

- Subject matter jurisdiction and statutory exceptions. An appellate court may raise a waived issue *sua sponte* if the issue involves subject matter jurisdiction or if there is a statute or rule that allows or requires the court to address the issue.[24]
- Manifest injustice and prejudice.[25] An appellate court may intervene if the issue is astonishingly erroneous but undetected and addressing it would avoid great and manifest injustice, provided that raising the issue does not unfairly prejudice any party.
- Fundamental rights and plain error doctrine.[26] The "plain error" or "fundamental error" doctrine allows an appellate court to address errors implicating fundamental rights, even if these were not preserved during the trial. Criminal defendants convicted following a trial generally have a right to this review even if their appellate lawyer concludes that the case involves no appealable error.
- Errors affecting substantial rights. An appellate court has the inherent authority to address errors in civil cases even if no

---

21. *See, e.g.*, Pullman-Standard v. Swint, 456 U.S. 273, 291 (1982) (noting that even when appellate issue turns on omitted factual finding, appellate court should remand to the trial court to resolve the factual omission).

22. *See, e.g.*, *Bailey*, 52 P.3d at 1164 ¶ 18 ("The appellate court is entrusted with ensuring legal accuracy and uniformity and should defer to the trial court on factual matters.").

23. Carousel Farms Metro. Dist. v. Woodcrest Homes, Inc., 442 P.3d 402, 407 ¶ 19 (Utah 2019).

24. *See, e.g.*, State v. Johnson, 416 P.3d 443 (Mont. 2017).

25. *See, e.g.*, *id.*

26. *See, e.g.*, State v. Hatfield, 426 P.3d 569 (Mont. 2018).

> objection was raised at the trial court if those errors affect substantial rights in the most egregious circumstances. In those cases, the appellate court can apply plain or fundamental error principles. Common examples include cases involving children, such as legal custody, parenting time, and parent rights.

In summary, appellate courts have mechanisms under certain limited conditions, like the plain or fundamental error doctrine and statutory exceptions, to allow them to address issues that were not preserved at the trial level. An appellate lawyer should consider whether one of those exceptions might apply to an otherwise unpreserved issue.

For this type of issue, the appellate lawyer remains tied to the record created at the trial level, so the appellate lawyer may opt not to pursue an issue if the record is not strong enough. And the failure to preserve the issue may affect whether the appellate court will presume prejudice or require the appellant to show prejudice. For example, when an appellant preserves an issue before the trial court rules, the appellate court may apply a reversible error standard of review, which may result in the appellate court's presuming prejudice or placing the burden of proof of prejudice on the appellee. But if the appellant did not preserve the issue and the trial court did not consider it, the appellate court may apply a plain error or fundamental error review or require the appellant to show prejudice.

When seeking review of issues not preserved at the trial-court level, the appellate lawyer must contemplate an important distinction between waived and forfeited rights.[27] In *Olano*, the Supreme Court articulated a three-prong test for plain error. As *Olano* explained, the distinction between waiver and forfeiture is longstanding.[28] Forfeiture occurs when a party fails to assert a right timely, but "waiver is the intentional relinquishment or abandonment of a known right."

If an appellate court can attribute an appellant's failure to preserve an issue before the trial court to the trial lawyer's strategy or tactics, the appellate court generally will not take up the issue.[29] The error also must be plain under existing law.[30] And the error must affect an appellant's substantial rights to be considered prejudicial for purposes of plain or fundamental error review.[31]

---

27. United States v. Olano, 507 U.S. 725, 731 (1993).
28. *Id.* at 733.
29. *See id.* (discussing and contrasting waiver from forfeiture).
30. *Id.* at 734.
31. *Id.*

Even so, the appellate court's exercise of plain or fundamental error review is discretionary.[32] The Supreme Court has said that appellate courts should correct a plain forfeited error affecting substantial rights if the error would "'seriously affect the fairness, integrity, or public reputation of judicial proceedings.'"[33]

Though the above Supreme Court cases addressed appeals from defendants in criminal cases, plain or fundamental error extends to appellants in civil cases, though only in "extraordinary circumstances."[34] In cases involving constitutional issues, the appellate courts may engage in slightly different standards of review, such as plain or fundamental error versus reversible error. Plain or fundamental error generally applies when the issue is constitutional in nature and the appellant otherwise waived it by not raising the issue before the trial court. Instead, the appellant must show the constitutional defect involved substantial rights.

F. Prejudice

Establishing prejudice often is the last mountain an appellate lawyer must climb. Who bears the burden, if anyone, of showing prejudice depends on the nature of the appeal. As discussed above, the appellate court at times will presume prejudice or require the appellee to show no prejudice, such as when the appellate court applies plain or fundamental error. In other instances, the appellee may show the appellant did not experience prejudice.

In most instances, the appellant must show prejudice. And many an appellate lawyer has experienced a Pyrrhic victory: The appellate court agrees an error occurred, so the battle is won. But then the appellate court declines to grant further relief because the appellant did not show prejudice, so the war is lost.

In most appeals, the appellant will bear the burden of establishing prejudice. But for certain actions, such as claims of ineffective assistance of counsel in a state postconviction relief or federal habeas proceeding, appellate courts may shift the burden of showing prejudice to the appellee or presume prejudice.[35] For such claims, the court may presume prejudice if the defendant was

---

32. *See, e.g.*, Henderson v. United States, 568 U.S. 266, 272 (2013).

33. *Id.* at 267.

34. Boutros v. Avis Rent a Car Sys., LLC, 802 F.3d 918, 924 (7th Cir. 2015) (quoting Williams v. Dieball, 724 F.3d 957, 963 (7th Cir. 2013)).

35. *See, e.g.*, United States v. Cronic, 466 U.S. 648, 659 (1984) ("The presumption that counsel's assistance is essential requires us to conclude that a trial is unfair if the accused is denied counsel at a critical stage of his trial.").

denied counsel at a critical stage in the proceedings, if the State interfered with counsel's assistance, or if "counsel is burdened by an actual conflict of interest."[36] But even that standard is subject to further nuance because a defendant must show counsel's conflict adversely affected counsel's performance.[37]

V. Conclusion

This chapter has explored the critical building blocks of a successful appeal: preserving issues at the lower court, identifying viable issues through a thorough review of the appellate record, and understanding the standards of review. Mastering these fundamental concepts will allow you, as an appellate advocate, to ensure your appeal is built on a solid foundation. The next few chapters will explain how to take the issues you have identified, build them into well-crafted arguments, and incorporate them into a professionally written and formatted brief.

Discussion Questions

1. How have advances in technology made it easier to preserve issues at the trial court? How have advances in technology made this process more difficult?
2. How might a trial lawyer's decision to preserve certain issues for appeal impact their litigation strategy and relationships with the court, opposing counsel, and clients?
3. What are the advantages to applying standards of review that afford deference to a lower court's or agency's decision? What are the disadvantages?

---

36. *See* Strickland v. Washington, 466 U.S. 668, 692 (1974).

37. *Id.*; Smith v. Robbins, 528 U.S. 259, 287 (2000) (discussing *Strickland*).

Chapter 5

Crafting Compelling Arguments

In this chapter, you will learn to:

- Select arguments to present on appeal
- Determine how to most effectively organize your arguments
- Construct the most common types of legal arguments
- Draft effective point headings
- Identify and avoid logical fallacies

I. Introduction

The Argument section is the heart of an appellate brief. In the Argument, an appellate advocate must present the best case on behalf of the client, often distilling complex facts and legal issues in the process. Effective appellate advocacy requires more than just strong research and writing skills; it demands a deep understanding of how to identify, organize, and structure arguments in a logical and persuasive manner. In appellate practice, advocates must often combine multiple types of arguments to write a coherent and cogent brief. This chapter will guide you through the process of:

- Selecting the most promising arguments to present on appeal
- Determining the optimal organization for the arguments in your brief

- Introducing and connecting arguments using roadmaps and point headings
- Constructing the most common types of legal arguments, including rule-based, analogical, and policy-based arguments
- Identifying and sidestepping logical fallacies that can undermine an otherwise strong argument

II. Selecting arguments to present on appeal

In Chapter 4, you learned how to identify which appellate issues were properly preserved at the trial court. An argument usually cannot be raised for the first time on appeal; however, many exceptions exist to this general rule. Therefore, a key task in reviewing an appellate record is to determine whether any non-preserved issues are nonetheless viable to raise before the appellate court.

Once you've identified the viable issues, you need to develop them in the appellate brief. Simply listing arguments is not enough; you must thoroughly present and support each argument with authority and analysis. "Merely mentioning an argument in an appellate opening brief is insufficient."[1] Courts will frown upon a brief that includes a laundry list of potential issues without further development. Indeed, the court may refuse to consider an issue that's raised in a brief without any argument.

Sometimes, an advocate can identify many possible arguments to present on appeal, but some will be stronger than others. As discussed later in Part 3, one persuasion strategy is to curate arguments to present only the strongest ones. This strategy allows the court to focus on the high points of your argument while keeping weak arguments from diluting a strong case. However, you should consider the risks of not raising an argument on appeal. Failing to raise an argument can result in waiver or forfeiture, making it difficult or impossible to raise the argument later. This can happen, for example, if an advocate fails to raise an argument in a first appeal but then seeks to raise it in a second appeal, e.g., after a remand to the trial court.[2]

---

1. MacMillan v. Schwartz, 250 P.3d 1213, 1220 (Ariz. Ct. App. 2011).
2. *E.g.*, Bradley v. Village of Univ. Park, 59 F.4th 887, 898 (7th Cir. 2023) (holding that a party who conceded an issue during an appeal was bound by that waiver in subsequent proceedings in the same case, including a second appeal following a remand).

Once you have thoroughly reviewed the record, identified all possible arguments, and selected your viable winning arguments from the list, you'll be able to separate them into two broad categories. Within the first category you have your substantive arguments. These arguments relate to the substantive legal issues in the civil or criminal matter that were adjudicated in the lower court. For example, if you're appealing a tribunal's denial of your client's workers' compensation claim, then your substantive arguments will come from the body of workers' compensation law in your jurisdiction. In the second category, you have procedural arguments. These arguments relate to the judicial process itself, from the inception of your client's matter up to the appeal. Procedural arguments often relate to decisions that the lower court made, such as accepting jurisdiction, applying a certain legal standard in granting or denying motions, or excluding evidence. Sometimes, the actions of other court personnel can generate procedural arguments. Examples include a prosecutor's misconduct in bringing charges or a juror's contact with witnesses. Other procedural arguments relate to what you're asking the appellate court to do, such as accept jurisdiction or apply a certain standard of review.

As you might expect, this chapter is designed to help you craft appellate arguments in general, rather than focusing on a particular area of substantive law. For example, this chapter can't help you choose the strongest arguments relating to a topic like medical malpractice. For those decisions, you'll have to conduct your own legal research and consult secondary sources like treatises and practice guides. However, the table below can help you identify some common procedural arguments that could apply regardless of the underlying substantive area of law.

Procedural Argument	Examples
Jurisdiction	• Challenging the court's subject matter jurisdiction (e.g., lack of federal question or diversity jurisdiction in federal courts) • Arguing that the lower court lacked personal jurisdiction over a party • Claiming that the court's jurisdiction is precluded by statute (e.g., the lower court has not yet rendered a final decision as required by 28 U.S.C. § 1291)
Justiciability	• Asserting that a case is not ripe for review • Claiming that a case is moot (e.g., due to changed circumstances or settlement) • Arguing that a party lacks standing • Arguing that a political question or other non-justiciable issue precludes review
Standard of review	• Arguing that an issue presents a factual question rather than a pure question of law, thereby meriting a more deferential standard of review • Arguing over the level of deference to be afforded to an agency's interpretation of regulations
Lower court error	• Improper admission or exclusion of evidence in a jury trial • Failure to honor a defendant's constitutional rights in a criminal case, such as the right to a speedy trial, an open hearing, or effective assistance of counsel • Incorrect jury instructions • Abuse of discretion in granting or denying a motion to dismiss • Commission of prosecutorial misconduct or prosecutorial error, such as improper statements made during a closing argument • Ex parte contact between a lawyer and a juror

Lastly, criminal lawyers representing defendants have special obligations when faced with a seemingly frivolous appeal. If, after careful examination, counsel believes the case lacks merit, they should inform the court and request withdrawal. However, as the Supreme Court held in *Anders v. California*, the defendant's counsel must first submit a brief that "[refers] to anything in the record that might arguably support the appeal."[3] This brief should be shared with the client, allowing them time to raise any points they wish. Ultimately, it is the court's responsibility, "after a full examination of all of the proceedings, to decide whether the case is wholly frivolous."[4]

To sum up, when *identifying* appellate issues, you'll want to think broadly, looking for both substantive and procedural arguments. When it comes to *selecting* appellate issues for your brief, however, you'll want to critically analyze the issues you've identified. If you have identified threshold procedural issues, such as lack of standing, that can resolve an appeal without examining the underlying substantive issues, you'll probably want to raise them. When it comes to the substantive arguments, you'll want to consider the repercussions of failing to raise them on appeal as well as the potential drawbacks of raising arguments that are unlikely to succeed. After you have selected your arguments, your next step is to determine how best to organize them within your brief. The next section will guide you in that process.

III. Organizing appellate arguments

Once you've determined the arguments you'll present on appeal, the next step is to organize them in a clear and compelling way. The best approach will always depend on the specific case, but this section provides some general guidelines to help you make these decisions in a reasoned manner.

A. Large-scale organization

In this section, the term *large-scale organization* refers to how you'll organize the numerous appellate issues that you'll cover in the Argument section of your brief. In contrast, *small-scale organization* refers to the organizational scheme you'll use for each individual argument.

Often, the discretion you have in organizing arguments is dictated by the side you represent on appeal. An appellant's or petitioner's opening brief has

3. 386 U.S. 738, 744 (1967).

4. *Id.*

the most flexibility in terms of which arguments to present and how to present them. In contrast, an appellee's or respondent's brief is often organized to respond point by point to the opening brief, meaning that its organization will be dictated by the appellant's choices. However, the appellee may strategically deviate from this order if it best suits their argument. For instance, if the appellee has a strong counterargument that undermines the appellant's primary argument, they may want to present that counterargument first.

An appellant's reply brief is optional, but it is advisable if the appellee has raised different arguments or cited new or different legal authorities that merit a response. A reply brief should do what it says and reply to the respondent's or appellee's brief. It shouldn't simply repeat the appellant's arguments from the opening brief, and it definitely shouldn't introduce new arguments. Because a reply brief is crafted around the appellee's brief, and because it has stricter word/page limits, the organizational choices are similarly constrained.

When you have the flexibility to make large-scale organizational decisions, you may consider a few different strategies for choosing a logical and persuasive order of arguments.

1. *Threshold arguments first*

Some arguments, such as those based on jurisdiction or justiciability, can potentially resolve an appeal without addressing the underlying substantive legal issues. Consequently, if you have threshold arguments in your appeal, you should place those up front in your brief.

2. *Strongest arguments first*

A basic but effective strategy is to lead with your most compelling argument. Doing so allows you to place your strongest argument in a position of emphasis and to take advantage of the primacy effect. However, this approach may not always be the best choice, especially if the arguments are interrelated or need to be presented in a specific order.

3. *Topical grouping*

This approach makes sense when there are multiple arguments that relate to a specific issue or topic. For example, in a case involving employment discrimination, you may have a group of arguments relating to sex discrimination and another group relating to age discrimination. Thus, it would make sense to group the arguments together based on their related claims.

4. *Chronological order*

You may want to organize arguments chronologically, especially when relating to a sequence of events or arguments raised at the trial court. For instance, in a case involving a dispute over the timeline of events, you may want to present arguments in the order they occurred, starting with the earliest events.

5. *Arguing in the alternative*

When arguing in the alternative, you explain that even if the court agrees with the other side's argument, your client still wins. For example, in an appeal the parties may be arguing over how the court should interpret a term within a controlling statute. An argument in the alternative would state, "Even if the court agrees with my opponent's interpretation, my client still prevails because ___." Thus, a logical order would be to present your primary argument first, followed by the alternative argument.

B. Connecting multiple arguments within a brief using roadmaps and point headings

At this point in developing your Argument section, you have selected which arguments to raise and determined a logical and persuasive order for presenting them in your brief. Before diving into small-scale organization, let's take a look at two additional components of large-scale organization: roadmaps and point headings. They play a critical role in structuring the Argument and keeping the reader on track.

1. *Roadmaps*

A brief with more than one argument must start with a roadmap section. The roadmap serves multiple functions. As the name indicates, it tells the reader where the brief is going and how it will get there. After reading the roadmap, a judge should understand which arguments your brief will address and in which order. Depending on the nature of your arguments, your roadmap can also accomplish other goals:

- Introducing general legal principles that apply to the entire Argument
- Providing historical context to the factual or legal issues

- Stating the standard of review to be applied (if your court doesn't require a separate standard of review section in the brief)
- Referencing your theme
- Providing persuasive conclusions for each legal argument

For example, let's say your client, Alpha, is the plaintiff-appellant appealing a district court's grant of summary judgment in a copyright infringement matter. The defendant-appellee, Beta, is arguing that its copying of the plaintiff-appellant's work qualifies as fair use under the Copyright Act. Fair use is assessed using four statutory factors, and your brief will present a separate argument for each factor, each separated by its own point heading. Before launching into your four-factor analysis, you'd provide a roadmap section like the example below:

> **I. The Court should reverse the trial court's grant of summary judgment because Beta's copying of Alpha's work does not qualify as fair use as a matter of law.**
>
> Alpha has established a prima facie case of copyright infringement. Alpha has a valid copyright in its photograph, *Eiffel Tower II*, and Beta violated Alpha's exclusive rights to reproduce its photograph and create derivative works. R. at 75–76; 17 U.S.C. § 106; *Ellison v. Robertson*, 357 F.3d 1072, 1076 (9th Cir. 2004). Beta admits that it took advantage of Alpha's creative efforts by creating an advertisement that openly copied *Eiffel Tower II*. Beta seeks to justify its copying with the affirmative defense of fair use. R. at 17.
>
> Determining fair use requires a court to examine four statutory factors: (1) the purpose and character of the use, (2) the nature of the copyrighted work, (3) the amount and substantiality of the portion used, and (4) the effect of the use upon the market for the copyrighted work. 17 U.S.C. § 107. These factors must be analyzed "in light of the purposes of copyright," such as incentivizing creators to invest their resources in producing original works. *Campbell v. Acuff-Rose Music, Inc.*, 510 U.S. 569, 578 (1994). In the instant case, Beta's secondary work is insufficiently transformative and causes cognizable market harm to Alpha's original work. Therefore, Beta's copying does not qualify as fair use. *See id.* at 566–67, 579.

In the example above, the advocate starts broadly by defining copyright infringement before addressing the fair use defense. In the first paragraph, the advocate points out that Beta admitted to copying Alpha's copyrighted work, thereby focusing the Argument solely on the affirmative defense of fair use. In the second paragraph, the advocate lists the four statutory factors. Because the advocate doesn't indicate that any factor is undisputed, the reader will anticipate that the Argument will address all four factors. Also, because the advocate doesn't state otherwise, the reader will also expect the factors to be addressed in the order listed in the roadmap.

In addition to setting forth the general rules and mapping out the Argument, the advocate also reinforces the theme. The main point heading and roadmap indicate that "copying to take advantage of a creator" is likely the theme that runs throughout the brief. Lastly, the final two sentences of the roadmap provide persuasive conclusions. These conclusions forecast the main points of the argument—within the four-factor analysis, the two important points will be (1) lack of transformation and (2) cognizable market harm.

The excerpt above exemplifies a primary roadmap that would appear at the start of the Argument section. Keep in mind that within each argument, any sub-arguments must also be preceded by a mini roadmap. Typically, these mini roadmaps simply explain any general rules that pertain to both sub-arguments and then map out the sub-arguments.

Let's say that in the example above, the advocate wants to discuss the third factor, amount and substantiality of the portion used, by breaking down the third factor into two sub-arguments. One sub-argument will address amount, and the other will address substantiality. The mini roadmap may look like this:

> The third fair-use factor assesses both the amount taken of the copyrighted work and the substantiality of what was copied. 17 U.S.C. § 107; *see Campbell,* 510 U.S. at 586. Here, the third factor weighs in Alpha's favor because Beta took both a large amount of Alpha's work and its creative heart.

Although this mini roadmap is brief, it effectively maps out the two sub-arguments and provides a persuasive conclusion. The reader can quickly grasp that the advocate intends to address both amount and substantiality, in that order.

Roadmaps are an essential part of creating a well-structured and organized Argument. As discussed in the next section, carefully crafted point headings can complement the roadmaps and serve as effective signposts for the reader.

2. *Point Headings*

Clear and effective point headings are a crucial part of a well-crafted appellate brief. Serving to reinforce your roadmap and provide visual landmarks, point headings provide a concise overview of the argument's structure and guide the reader through the logical progression of your case. This section explains the importance of point headings in appellate briefs and provides guidelines for crafting headings that effectively convey your argument's structure and message.

a. Characteristics of effective point headings

A point heading is like the headline of a news story. Written well, the headline quickly tells the reader what the story is about. Written poorly, the headline creates confusion and perhaps even inadvertent humor, as in the classic "Man Helps Dog Bite Victim."

Just as an effective headline summarizes the story below, an effective point heading summarizes an entire argument (for a main point heading) or its individual components (for subheadings). Thus, a primary characteristic of an effective heading is that it summarizes the text in a manner that is both accurate and easily comprehended.

In a persuasive legal document like an appellate brief, an effective point heading also states a persuasive conclusion. Or put another way, the point heading tells the court (1) what you want the court to do and (2) why the court should do it. When you craft a persuasive heading, you should write a sentence that the court could copy/paste into its own order or opinion.

Generally speaking, an effective point heading is also written as a concise sentence with easy-to-understand language and simple sentence structure. If necessary, your heading could refer to a case or statute by name, as in "*Auer* deference" or "The Copyright Act." But you should avoid putting citations in point headings. A point heading should not exceed one sentence.

b. Types of point headings

As noted above, a main point heading precedes an argument, and subheadings introduce components of that argument, such as those based on individual factors or elements. Depending on the complexity of the legal claim, the sub-arguments may be further subdivided and introduced by their own point headings. Here's an example of effective point headings from a criminal appeal.

I. The Court should vacate Ms. Byron's conviction because her trial defense counsel was ineffective, thus depriving her of her Sixth Amendment right to counsel.

A. The trial defense counsel had an actual conflict of interest because he concurrently represented Ms. Byron's co-defendant.

1. Ms. Byron and her co-defendant had directly adverse interests because Ms. Byron's alibi defense implicated her co-defendant.

2. The trial defense counsel's defense of Ms. Byron was materially limited by his duty to zealously represent her co-defendant.

B. The trial defense counsel's conflict adversely affected his performance because he failed to raise Ms. Byron's alibi defense during the trial.

In the example above, the main point heading is introduced by a Roman numeral. This heading introduces the argument (ineffective assistance of counsel) and tells the court what the party wants the court to do (vacate the conviction). The subheadings, introduced by capital letters, introduce two primary components of an ineffective assistance of counsel claim based on a conflict of interest: the defense counsel represented clients with adverse interests, and the conflict adversely affected the defense counsel's performance.[5] As you can see, the first component of this argument is further subdivided into two parts. Here, the advocate presents two arguments to support the claim of an actual conflict of interest: (1) representing directly adverse clients and (2) material limitation of the representation.[6]

Note that the subheadings do not repeat the procedural component of the main heading—the part that describes what the party wants the court to do. Instead, the subheadings present a persuasive conclusion for the subcomponents of the argument. As the argument is further divided, the structure of the subheadings remains the same; each should provide, in a complete sentence, a persuasive conclusion.

---

5. Strickland v. Washington, 466 U.S. 668, 692 (1984) (quoting Cuyler v. Sullivan, 446 U.S. 335, 350, 348 (1980)).

6. *See* Model Rules of Pro. Conduct r. 1.7 (Am. Bar Ass'n 1983).

c. Best practices for crafting effective headings

As discussed in Chapter 7, Formatting Briefs for the Modern Reader, point headings should be written as complete sentences and formatted using sentence case, meaning the words are capitalized as they would be in an ordinary sentence. This format is the easiest to read and comprehend. To set the point heading apart visually from the text, it should be in bold typeface. Consult Chapter 7 for further details regarding formatting point headings.

Another best practice is to ensure that the wording of each point heading is consistent with the rest of your Argument. For instance, the point headings should be consistent with your roadmap. If your roadmap maps out an argument based on three factors, then you should have, at a minimum, a subheading for each factor. The language used in the headings should reflect the language used in your roadmap. For example, if your roadmap describes the first factor as "the purpose and character of the secondary use," then the heading for that roadmap shouldn't read, "the character and purpose of the secondary use."

The language used in point headings should also be consistent with your argument's theme. For example, let's say the theme of your argument is that the opposing party "stole" your client's work. If so, then you wouldn't want to state in a point heading that the opposing party "borrowed from" your client's work. "Borrowing" implies taking something only temporarily, which differs from "stealing," where there's no intent to return the item.

Lastly, a good way to check your point headings is to examine just your headings without the associated text, as in the example above. Reading just the headings should provide a complete outline of your argument. You should be able to readily discern the action your client wants the court to take, the primary argument to support that position, and the subcomponents of that primary argument. The point headings should refer not only to legal standards but also to some facts that are specific to your client's case. In a way, each point heading is a mini-argument—the law as applied to specific facts.

As this section has explained, effective point headings are the backbone of a well-organized and persuasive appellate brief. Remember that point headings can be a powerful tool to showcase your argument's strengths and guide the court toward a favorable decision. Following the guidelines above will allow you to write headings that complement your arguments and make a lasting impression.

C. Small-scale organization of individual arguments

So far, this chapter has examined the choices you can make in terms of large-scale organization—taking multiple arguments, determining the most effective sequence, and introducing and connecting them with roadmaps and headings. Once you are comfortable with the large-scale organization of your Argument section, you can consider how to best organize each individual argument, i.e., small-scale organization. This section provides guidelines for how to organize individual legal arguments for maximum persuasive power.

1. Follow an analytical paradigm

At a basic level, an effective way to organize an individual legal argument is by providing the reader with the relevant law and then applying that law to your client's facts. This classic paradigm is reflected in the many acronyms law students learn in their first year of study—IRAC, CRAC, CREAC, CRUPAC, TREAT, and so on. At least one or two of these should be familiar to you. For our purposes, let's use CREAC as a model. This acronym represents a clear and logical structure:

> C—Conclusion (clearly state the conclusion you want the court to reach)
>
> R—Rule (set forth the relevant legal rules)
>
> E—Explanation (explain the rules using illustrations from precedent case law)
>
> A—Application (apply the legal rules to your client's facts)
>
> C—Conclusion (summarize once more the conclusion you want the court to draw from this analysis)

This basic framework can be adapted to suit almost any type of legal argument. Later in this chapter, we'll explore specific types of arguments commonly presented on appeal and provide further guidance on how to tailor your approach to each.

2. Start with your primary argument, not the opposing side's argument

Sometimes you may be inclined to start by explaining your opponent's primary arguments, then telling the court why your opponent is wrong. For example, if your client is appealing an adverse ruling by the lower court, your first thought might be to summarize the adverse ruling from the opposing party's perspective. You can then explain why the opposing party is incorrect and argue that the law actually favors your client's position. But it's almost always a better approach to start with your primary argument—why your client should prevail—before addressing and rebutting the other side.[7] For one, starting with your opponent's position sacrifices an important position of emphasis. Also, starting with a positive position is often easier to comprehend than a negative position. In other words, explaining "Here's why we win" is usually a better sell than "Here's why we don't lose."

For example, suppose you represent XYZ Corporation which was sued by ABC Corporation for a breach of contract. XYZ was supposed to deliver goods to ABC by a certain date and failed to do so. Below you'll find two simplified argument constructions:

1. ABC argues that XYZ's actions constituted a breach of contract because XYZ failed to meet the delivery deadline. However, XYZ argues that the delay was excusable due to unforeseen circumstances.
2. XYZ's delivery delay was excusable based on unforeseen circumstances. Therefore, XYZ did not breach its contract with ABC.

The second construction is cleaner, easier to comprehend, and, for those reasons, more persuasive.

3. *Always balance the facts and the law*

When crafting the argument section of an appellate brief, it is essential to remember that all arguments are a delicate balance of facts and law. The facts of the case are just as crucial as the legal principles that govern them. Simply citing statutes and case law is not enough; the argument must be grounded in the specific details of the record and supported by adequate factual evidence.

Conversely, an argument that relies solely on the facts, no matter how compelling or sympathetic, will ultimately fall short without sufficient legal support. The law provides the framework for understanding and interpreting the facts, and a successful argument must demonstrate a clear understanding of this interplay.

4. *Pay attention to hierarchies of authority*

Not all legal authorities are created equal, and it is vital to consider the hierarchies of laws and courts when constructing an argument. Statutes take precedence over case law, and the authority of case law depends on the court that issued it. Understanding these hierarchies is essential to effectively applying the law and building a persuasive argument.

---

7. *See, e.g.*, Thomas L. Hudson, *Structuring Appellate Briefs*, 21 J. App. Practice & Proc. 85, 91–92 (2021).

5. Apply the law, not cases

It is also important to remember that the goal is to apply the law, not simply to cite cases. Cases are useful for illustrating legal principles and providing support for an argument, but they should not be the sole focus. Instead, use cases to demonstrate how the law applies to the specific facts of the case. This concept is discussed further below in the section on constructing arguments using analogical reasoning.

6. Connect arguments and sub-arguments to create a cohesive and logical flow

Dovetail your arguments using transitional language to connect ideas and show how they relate to each other. This will help to build a strong and persuasive argument that is greater than the sum of its parts.

To sum up, the large-scale and small-scale organizational strategies discussed in this section work in tandem to create clear, compelling, and cohesive arguments. By carefully sequencing arguments, using roadmaps and point headings to connect the dots, and employing analytical paradigms to build individual arguments, you can craft a brief that guides a reader through your logic. The next section looks at specific types of arguments that appear in appellate briefs and provides best practices for drafting them for maximum effect.

IV. Constructing standard forms of legal arguments

In appellate briefs, advocates use various types of legal arguments to support the client's position and persuade the court. Below you'll find explanations and drafting advice for the most common types of legal arguments. By understanding the finer points of each argumentative form, you can tailor your approach to best fit the needs of your appellate briefs.

A. Arguing from precedent: Analogical reasoning

Analogical reasoning is a powerful tool in legal analysis. Indeed, it's probably the first type of legal reasoning you learned in law school because it's so closely tied to the common law principles of precedent and stare decisis. Because courts are obligated to follow binding precedent, an advocate can make a compelling argument by demonstrating the similarities or differences between a client's case and a case that has already been decided.

Effective analogical reasoning, however, requires more than simply finding cases that resemble a client's case. A skillful advocate will consider the following guidelines when arguing from precedent.

1. *Use cases to illustrate legal rules*

Because analogical reasoning depends on highlighting factual similarities and differences, it's easy to lose sight of the purpose of incorporating precedent case law into your analysis. Case law, even from the U.S. Supreme Court, does not exist unto itself; cases are the means by which legal rules are applied to real-world factual scenarios. Thus, once your research has led you to precedent case law, your task is to determine what legal principles the cases were applying to the facts and then synthesize those principles together to articulate the overarching legal rules.

An example may be helpful here. In *United States v. Jones*,[8] the U.S. Supreme Court took up the appeal of an individual who was convicted based in part on evidence obtained when the Government tracked his vehicle's location. The Government did this by surreptitiously installing a GPS tracking device on the vehicle. The Court held that this practice constituted a Fourth Amendment search because the Government had "physically occupied private property for the purpose of obtaining information" and had done so without a valid search warrant.[9]

One way to formulate the legal principle from this case would be to state, "The Government is not allowed to install a GPS tracking device on a suspect's car without a search warrant." Although this may be a true statement, it's a facts-focused way of explaining what the case is about. A rule-focused way to articulate the legal principle would be to state, "The Government violates the Fourth Amendment's prohibition against unreasonable searches when it physically invades a suspect's personal property, without a warrant or consent, to collect incriminating information." This is a rule-focused approach that allows for the legal principle from the case to be more readily synthesized into other rules derived from Fourth Amendment jurisprudence. A rule-focused approach also makes the legal principle easier to apply to other cases with different facts.

Understanding this rule-based approach to using case law allows for more structured legal analogies. Before analogizing your client's case to precedent, you must start by explaining the case law precedent. If you're used to the CREAC paradigm described above, this would be the E section: explaining

---

8. 565 U.S. 400 (2012).

9. *Id.* at 404.

the law using case illustrations. The most effective case illustrations start with the legal principles before describing the facts and holding from the case.

Once you have illustrated the relevant legal principle using case law precedent, you can craft an analogy to your client's case. Again, an effective analogy will start with the legal principle and build from there. Start with an up-front conclusion about how the legal principle applies to your client's case, then point out the factual similarities and distinctions that support the analogy to precedent.

The example below demonstrates how to craft a rule-forward case illustration with a corresponding analogy.

> The Government violates the Fourth Amendment's prohibition against unreasonable searches when it physically invades a suspect's personal property, without a warrant or consent, to collect incriminating information. In *United States v. Jones*, 565 U.S. 400 (2012), the Government placed a GPS tracking device on a suspect's car. Although the Government had obtained a warrant for the tracking device, it installed the device after the warrant had expired. *Id.* at 403. The suspect was eventually convicted of drug trafficking based in part on evidence of his vehicle's whereabouts obtained through the tracking device. *Id.* at 403–04. The Court affirmed the D.C. Circuit's reversal of the conviction, holding that the Government had violated the Fourth Amendment. *Id.* at 412–13. The Court reasoned that the physical intrusion of the tracker in the suspect's personal property constituted a search. *Id.* at 404–05. The Court focused on the notion of trespass rather than looking solely at whether the suspect had a reasonable expectation of privacy in his vehicle's whereabouts. *Id.* at 407–09.
>
> Likewise, in the instant case, the Government's placement of an Apple AirTag in the Appellant's backpack constitutes a search. In *Jones*, the Court focused on the nature of the Government's physical intrusion into the suspect's personal property—his car. Similarly, the Government physically intruded into the Appellant's backpack when police instructed the school security officer to place the AirTag in the backpack's lining. As in *Jones*, the AirTag was installed without a valid warrant and without the Appellant's consent. To be sure, the Appellant had knowingly left her backpack unattended in a public-school classroom when the AirTag

> was installed. However, *Jones* focused on the nature of the Government's trespass rather than the suspect's expectation of privacy. Applying the reasoning from *Jones*, this Court should hold that the Government violated the Appellant's right to be free of unreasonable searches or seizures.

2. *Focus on the relevant facts*

Crafting effective analogies also requires that factual comparisons draw upon relevant facts and avoid factual distractions. Although case illustrations may require some degree of factual background or context, these details should be kept to a minimum. The illustrations should focus instead on the legally relevant facts, i.e., the facts upon which the court relied in reaching its decision. For this reason, legally relevant facts are also referred to as outcome-dispositive facts. Likewise, when crafting analogies, you should compare only legally relevant facts from case law precedent to legally relevant facts from your client's case.

3. *Choose influential cases*

The persuasive value of analogical reasoning is tied to the weight of the legal authorities that support the analogies. Not all cases are equal. In your research, you may find a case that has very similar facts to your client's situation and also reaches an outcome that's favorable to your client. Although this case could allow you to create a favorable analogy, you'll also have to examine the jurisdiction, level of court, date of decision, type of decision (e.g., reported or unreported), type of opinion (e.g., majority, dissent, concurrence), and any subsequent history. Also, always use a citator like Shepard's or KeyCite to check that the cases you're citing are still good law.

4. *Anticipate counterarguments*

In analogical reasoning, an opponent has many opportunities for counterargument, such as:

- Pointing out factual distinctions that weaken your analogy
- Arguing that you have failed to focus on the legally relevant facts in creating your analogy
- Creating analogies to other cases that lead to a different outcome
- Undermining the precedent case's value by citing subsequent cases that have criticized or otherwise undermined its reasoning

An effective advocate must anticipate these counterarguments. In an opening brief, for instance, an appellant can address the counterarguments proactively, thereby weakening the appellee's arguments. Look at the Apple AirTag example above—can you see how the author addressed the anticipated counterargument?

B. Rule-based arguments

As powerful as analogical reasoning may be, not every argument requires it. When a legal principle, or rule, has a straightforward application to your client's facts, you can apply the rule without any need to analogize to case law precedent.

In its structure, a rule-based argument mirrors the construction of a logical syllogism. As described later in this chapter's discussion of fallacies, a syllogism has three parts: a major premise, a minor premise, and a conclusion that follows logically from the premises. In a legal argument, the major premise consists of a clear articulation of the relevant legal rule. The minor premise presents the relevant facts from the client's case. The third component is the conclusion derived from applying the rule to the facts.

Here's a simple example of rule-based reasoning, structured as a syllogism:

> Major premise: Arizona Rule of Professional Conduct 1.8(l) prohibits a lawyer from representing a client when the opposing party is represented by the lawyer's close relative or cohabitant unless the client provides informed consent.
>
> Minor premise: Doug Smith represented a criminal defendant in a trial that was prosecuted by Laurie Smith, his daughter, without obtaining the client's informed consent.
>
> Conclusion: Therefore, Doug Smith violated Rule 1.8(l).

In the above example, the rule and the facts are plainly stated without ambiguity. As with all legal reasoning, effective rule-based reasoning requires accuracy in both the rule and facts. Any flaw could lead to an error in reasoning.

For many advocates, applying a rule without any reference to case law can seem unusual, even uncomfortable. A syllogism can seem naked if it isn't clothed in case law precedent and analogical reasoning. That's why you'll often see rule-based reasoning paired with analogical reasoning. At times, the pairing isn't strictly necessary but rather is used as reinforcement. In such cases, a parenthetical citation may suffice.

> Rule 1.8(l) prohibits a lawyer from representing a client when the opposing party is represented by a close relative or cohabitant, unless the client provides informed consent. In the instant case, Doug Smith represented a criminal defendant in a case prosecuted by Laurie Smith, his daughter. Doug Smith did not inform his client of the relationship, nor did he obtain his client's consent. Therefore, Doug Smith violated Rule 1.8(l). *See Johnson v. State*, 501 P.2d 220 (Ariz. 2019) (holding that a prosecutor violated Rule 1.8(l) in a matter where the public defender was the prosecutor's son).[10]

At other times, a rule's application isn't 100% clear. What if Rule 1.8(l) doesn't explicitly state whether the prohibition applies to lawyers who are the stepchildren of opposing counsel? What if Laurie Smith is Doug Smith's stepdaughter? In such a case, the rule may have to be paired with a fuller illustration of case law precedent:

> Rule 1.8(l) prohibits a lawyer from representing a client in litigation when the opposing party is represented by a close relative or cohabitant. A stepchild qualifies as a close relative under this rule. *Johnson v. State*, 501 P.2d 220 (Ariz. 2019). In *Johnson*, a lawyer prosecuted a defendant charged with felony theft. *Id.* at 222. The public defender representing the defendant was the prosecutor's stepson. *Id.* Although Rule 1.8(l) doesn't explicitly include stepchildren in its list of close relatives, the court held that the prosecutor violated Rule 1.8(l) nonetheless. *Id.* at 225. The court reasoned that Rule 1.8(l)'s list of close relatives was intended to be illustrative rather than exhaustive, as indicated by the word "including." *Id.* at 224. Moreover, the policy supporting the principle of conflict-free representation applied equally in cases of both adoptive and biological children. *Id.*
>
> Here, Doug Smith also violated Rule 1.8(l). He prosecuted James Wendell, who was represented by Laurie Smith, Doug's stepdaughter. This case is wholly analogous to *Johnson*, where the defense attorney was the prosecutor's stepson. Therefore, Doug Smith violated Rule 1.8(l).

10. For simplicity's sake, this and the following example use fictionalized case law.

Whether used on its own or in conjunction with analogical reasoning, rule-based reasoning is most effective when advocates keep the following considerations in mind:

- Rely on authoritative rules. When conducting your research, ensure that your rule is derived from legal authorities that are current. If relying on a regulation, ensure that you also look at the authorizing legislation. Use a citator to see if subsequent case law, legislation, or constitutional amendments have limited the rule's application.
- Address exceptions, exemptions, and other limitations. Many rules, regardless of their source, are implemented with exceptions or exemptions. In other cases, the limitations develop over time as courts interpret and apply the rules. Failure to consider the rule's limitations may create a flaw in your logical reasoning, thereby opening the door to an opponent's counterargument.
- Ensure your structure and reasoning are sound. Organizing rule-based reasoning in the manner of a three-part syllogism is effective because the structure is easy to follow. However, you'll have to be mindful of both formal and informal logical fallacies. This chapter discusses fallacies and provides tips for avoiding them in your writing.

C. Statutory interpretation

Resolving the meaning of a statute's language is a legal question that arises frequently in appeals. When an appeal deals with an issue of statutory interpretation, the parties argue over the definition of one or more terms in a statute. Moreover, the parties may also argue over the legal doctrines the court should apply in interpreting the statutory language.

Historically, both state and federal courts have applied many doctrines to interpret a statute's text. Over time, certain doctrines have receded while others have become more prevalent. For example, over 100 years ago, the U.S. Supreme Court's approach was to focus on the intent of the lawmakers who enacted the statute.[11] This approach allowed a focus on extrinsic evidence of intent, such as legislative history. Nowadays, the related doctrine of

11. *E.g.*, Eliot T. Tracz, *Words and Their Meanings: The Role of Textualism in the Progressive Toolbox*, 45 Seton Hall Leg. J. 353, 355–56 (2021).

purposivism seeks to discern a statute's purpose and interpret it in a way that furthers its purpose.[12]

Generally speaking, the modern trend is toward textualism, a doctrine that focuses on the words alone rather than relying on extrinsic evidence of legislative intent.[13] If a text is unambiguous, then a court is to apply the plain meaning of the words.[14] To be certain, numerous arguments may arise over how to determine a word's plain meaning.[15] Should courts consult a particular dictionary? Should judges consider a word's meaning in contemporary society, or what the word would have meant when the law was enacted?

On the other hand, if a statute's text is ambiguous, then judges must apply additional doctrines to resolve the ambiguity.[16] One method is to examine the disputed statutory provision in light of the meaning and purpose of the entire statute.[17] By looking at statutory context, judges strive to define the disputed term in a manner that's consistent with how the same or similar language is used in other parts of the statute. Judges also seek to apply a meaning that isn't contrary to the statute's purpose.

Judges also use interpretative guidelines called canons of statutory construction. There are numerous canons that judges can draw upon. Some are related to the text itself, such as interpreting "and" as conjunctive and "or" as disjunctive.[18] Others relate to substantive concepts, such as the canon of constitutional avoidance. This canon states that if a statutory text is open to more than one plausible interpretation, then the court should use the interpretation that avoids creating a constitutional issue.[19] Other frequently used canons of construction include the following:

- Expressio unius: This canon states that "the expression of one thing implies the exclusion of others."[20] For example, if a statute criminalizing driving under the influence applies to operating "motor vehicles," then

---

12. Cong. Research Serv., R45153, Statutory Interpretation: Theories, Tools, and Trends 11–13 (updated Apr. 5, 2018), https://crsreports.congress.gov/product/pdf/R/R45153/2 [hereinafter CRS Report R45153].

13. *Id.* at 13–15.

14. *Id.* at 19–20.

15. *See, e.g.*, William N. Eskridge, Jr., Brian G. Slocum, & Kevin Tobia, *Textualism's Defining Moment*, 123 Columbia L. Rev. 1611, 1616–17 (2023).

16. *E.g.*, Tracz, *supra* note 11, at 361.

17. *See* CRS Report R45153, *supra* note 12, at 23–24.

18. *See id.* at 26, 54.

19. *Id.* at 29.

20. *Id.* at 54 (quoting Antonin Scalia & Bryan A. Garner, Reading Law: The Interpretation of Legal Texts 107 (2012)).

the presumption is that non-motorized vehicles, like standard bicycles, are excluded from the statute.

- Ejusdem generis: This canon is applied when a statute lists a series of specific things and then one general category of things. The canon states that the general category should be interpreted in a way that restricts its meaning to the specifically listed items.[21] For example, if a statutory provision applies to "shirts, blouses, vests, jackets, and other clothing," the term "other clothing" would be interpreted to exclude shoes, which are categorically different in nature than the items specifically listed.
- Ordinary meaning: This canon instructs that words in a statute should be given their everyday meaning unless the statute itself states that a different meaning should be applied. For example, if a statutory provision uses the word "hammer," then the court should apply the ordinary meaning (i.e., the thing in a toolbox that pounds nails into the wall) unless the statute provides a specialized definition of "hammer."
- Whole-text canon: When a court interprets part of a statute, this canon provides that the court should consider the entire statute as a whole.[22] A related canon states that if a word or phrase is used one way in a statute, it's presumed to mean the same things in other parts of the statute unless otherwise specified.[23]

As you can see from this brief overview, statutory interpretation arguments can be intricate and multilayered. Advocates often argue not only over a word's meaning but also how the court should arrive at that meaning. With that in mind, here's some general advice for writing a statutory interpretation argument:

- Look for definitions within the statute itself. Sometimes, statutes contain a definitions section that explains the meaning of words and phrases as they are used within the statute. At other times, a term is defined within a subsection of a statute. Keep in mind that the definition may appear in a different subsection than the one that's being disputed in the appeal.

---

21. Jay Wexler, *Fun with Reverse Ejusdem Generis*, 105 Minn. L. Rev. 1, 1 (2020).
22. CRS Report R45153, *supra* note 12, at 60.
23. *Id.* at 58 (referring to this as the presumption of consistent usage canon).

- Understand how judges interpret statutes in your jurisdiction. If you know that your court adheres strictly to textualism, then you don't want to frontload your brief with arguments about legislative history.
- Don't overlook the value of case law precedent. A common mistake is for advocates to rely too heavily on canons of construction when crafting a statutory interpretation argument while disregarding other legal authorities. A canon of construction is an interpretative tool, not a source of primary law or mandatory authority. Don't fail to consider case law precedent. Your legal research may reveal cases that have interpreted other provisions within the same statute or that have interpreted the same or similar terms as used in other statutes. Citing binding precedent will carry more weight than referring to canons of construction or judicial philosophies.

D. Policy arguments

In appellate brief writing, policy arguments can arise when dealing with novel issues and cases of first impression. The parties may be arguing for the court to interpret or apply the law in an unprecedented way. In such cases, both parties will likely argue that their proffered interpretation or application best furthers an important public policy. These types of arguments can be persuasive when the court has no binding precedent upon which to rely. Without mandatory authority, the court will turn to other justifications, including policy.

When including policy arguments in an appellate brief, you must remember that you're still making a legal argument. Sometimes policy arguments are looked down upon as being too vague or "mushy."[24] To avoid this criticism, ensure that your policy arguments are (1) connected to other forms of legal argument, (2) specific regarding the relevant policies, and (3) supported by legal authorities from which the relevant policies are derived.

Turning to the first requirement, an effective policy argument should be tied to another form of legal argument like analogical reasoning, rule-based rea-

---

24. Ellie Margolis, *Closing the Floodgates: Making Persuasive Policy Arguments in Appellate Briefs*, 62 MONT. L. REV. 59, 61 (2001) ("Many of us probably see policy as unimportant, or so 'mushy' as not to serve an important role in appellate argument.").

soning, or statutory interpretation. In the U.S. legal system, courts are meant to interpret and apply the law, not create or maintain public policies. That task belongs to the legislature. Therefore, a "pure" policy argument won't typically go far with an appellate court. However, policy can dovetail nicely with other forms of legal argument when the court is grappling with a novel issue.

For example, let's say you're drafting a brief that contains a novel argument to apply common law tort principles to social media platform providers. To supplement your analogies to cases involving product liability, you can point to the policy behind product liability law (prevention and mitigation of consumer harm) and argue that this policy should also justify application of these principles to social media providers.

Or, in a case of statutory interpretation, you may use policy arguments to bolster other forms of argument such as textualism, application of canons of construction, and case law precedent. Your brief could argue that your proffered interpretation of ambiguous statutory language would better support the legislature's policies, express or implied, than your opponent's interpretation.

The second requirement is that your argument be specific regarding the relevant policies. In other words, a broad reference to "public policy" will not be effective in an appellate brief. To integrate a policy argument into your brief in a persuasive manner, you'll have to articulate specific policies that your argument supports. Relatedly, you must also cite legal authorities for those policies. You can derive policy arguments from various authorities, such as statutory language, legislative history, case law precedent, and administrative regulations. Many policy arguments derive from concepts related to shared societal values, economic incentives, or judicial efficiency.[25] Regardless of how universal or true a policy may seem, you should still ground it by citing one or more supporting authorities.

Finally, keep in mind that policy arguments are especially prone to logical fallacies. The next section discusses logical fallacies and how to avoid them in your legal writing. If you're drafting a policy argument for an appellate brief, you should review these fallacies carefully to ensure you're not incorporating them into your argument.

25. *See id.* at 72–79.

To draft an effective policy argument, keep in mind these additional guidelines:

- Identify not only the specific policy at stake but its implications as well. Depending on the nature of your argument, you may be emphasizing either positive or negative consequences of a particular policy. You may consider using empirical arguments, discussed below, to support your arguments relating to policy implications.
- Use an analytical paradigm to structure your policy argument. Like any other legal argument, a policy argument can be logically expressed by stating the policy, then applying the policy. When you state the policy, be sure to identify it clearly and support it with legal authority. When you apply the policy, demonstrate to the court how the policy, as applied to the specific facts of the case at bar, will lead to a desirable outcome.
- Address potential counterarguments. As with any other argument, you'll want to anticipate and refute the opposing side's arguments against your position. In the context of a policy argument, you must anticipate that your opponent may argue that your proposed policy isn't valid or applicable, or that your proposed argument doesn't actually support the policy that you've identified.
- Acknowledge the court's limitations and role in policy making. Arguing that the court should make policy through its decision will likely fall flat. Instead, your argument should acknowledge that courts don't make policy, but that their decisions can support the proper implementation of public policy.

E. Empirical arguments (Brandeis briefs)

A Brandeis brief is a type of legal brief that combines legal arguments with social science research and data to support a client's position. It's named after Louis D. Brandeis, a U.S. Supreme Court Justice who pioneered this approach in the early twentieth century. In 1907, Justice Brandeis, then a practicing lawyer, represented Florence Kelley and Josephine Goldmark in a case involving the work hours for women who were laundry workers.[26] At the time, the brief

---

26. Muller v. Oregon, 208 U.S. 412 (1908).

was notable because it relied primarily on empirical evidence rather than legal authorities to support its argument.[27]

Since 1907, appellate courts have become more accustomed to reviewing briefs that incorporate social science research and empirical data alongside traditional legal authorities. Brandeis briefs are commonly used in cases involving complex social issues, such as civil rights, environmental policy, and public health, where social science research can provide valuable insights and support for the legal argument. Nowadays, an appellate advocate may consider including social science research in any matter that lends itself to empirical data.

Emphasizing empirical data over legal authorities carries a risk, however. More likely than not, the judges who make up your appellate court have no background in social science research and little experience in sorting through and interpreting empirical studies. At the appellate level, judges don't have the benefit of hearing directly from expert witnesses who can explain the research, its methodology, and its results.

Notwithstanding these risks, social science research can play an influential role in appellate practice. Advocates can take steps to mitigate the risks. When writing a Brandeis brief, consider incorporating the following best practices:

- Use social science research to enhance your legal argument rather than displace it. No matter how convincing the research may be, the court is still obligated to follow the law in reaching its decision. Think about how the empirical data can provide context, illustrate impacts, or otherwise support your legal argument.
- Ensure your research is credible and accurate. The validity of social science research depends upon accuracy in the collection and analysis of data. Any failures along the way can render results unreliable. For example, in 2023, the research of a well-known Harvard professor was called into question over allegedly falsified data.[28] The research, which had been widely cited, dealt with whether including an attestation at the beginning rather than the end of a document increased the respondents' honesty.[29] This example illustrates how even

27. *The Brandeis Brief—In Its Entirety*, Louis D. Brandeis Sch. of Law Library (last updated Dec. 1, 2018), https://louisville.edu/law/library/special-collections/the-louis-d.-brandeis-collection/the-brandeis-brief-in-its-entirety.

28. Noam Scheiber, *Researcher Is Accused of Fakery*, N.Y. Times, June 24, 2023, at B1, https://www.nytimes.com/2023/06/24/business/economy/francesca-gino-harvard-dishonesty.html.

29. *Id.*

reputable sources are prone to inaccuracy. If you're uncertain about how to analyze empirical studies to validate their findings, reach out to social scientists or other academics at your local university for their assistance.

- Clearly explain the research's methodology and limitations. To be a credible advocate, you must be transparent. Rather than presenting your social science research in a conclusory fashion, explain how the study was performed and be up-front about any constraints that affect its findings.
- Explain the research in plain English; avoid technical terms and scientific jargon. Your goal isn't to show off your knowledge of social science. Instead, your goal is to make the science understandable so the court agrees with your client's position.
- Present data in a clear and compelling manner, using visual aids like charts, graphs, or tables. Nowadays, it's perfectly acceptable to use visual aids in a brief. Judges will appreciate your efforts to make scientific research accessible and understandable. Keeping in mind that visual aids can be easily manipulated, strive for accuracy and transparency. Use expert assistance, as needed, to ensure that your visual aids provide a valid and credible summary of the research's findings.

V. Identifying and avoiding logical fallacies in appellate advocacy

Regardless of how well you organize the Argument section of your brief, if your arguments contain logical fallacies, they will falter under scrutiny. The flawed reasoning associated with logical fallacies can undermine your argument's foundation, erode credibility, and dilute your persuasive power. The challenge is that logical fallacies are all around us—in everyday conversations, social media posts, news stories, and political stump speeches. It's no wonder they can readily creep into your legal writing.

Fortunately, once you learn about logical fallacies, you'll be able to spot them in your own writing and in your opponents' arguments. This section will examine logical fallacies, covering their definitions, examples, and significance in appellate advocacy. Through this examination, you'll gain a comprehensive understanding of logical fallacies that will enable you to recognize and avoid them, which will strengthen your arguments.

A. Logical fallacies defined

A logical fallacy is an error in reasoning. The term itself comes from two Latin words: "fallacia," meaning deceit, and "logica," relating to logic or reason. In the context of classical logic and rhetoric, a fallacy refers to a flaw in the reasoning process that can render an argument invalid, misleading, or unsound. The study of logical fallacies dates back to ancient Greece. The philosopher Aristotle, in his study of deductive reasoning, identified circumstances where flawed premises, inaccurate language, and other errors could undermine an argument.[30]

Philosophers further divide logical fallacies into two categories, formal and informal. A formal fallacy arises from a flaw in the logic. As discussed above under rule-based reasoning, deductive reasoning takes the form of a syllogism:

- Premise 1
- Premise 2
- Conclusion

Here's an example of how a syllogism works:

- All dogs are mammals.
- Lassie is a dog.
- Therefore, Lassie is a mammal.

In deductive reasoning, if the two premises are true, then the conclusion must be true as well. The syllogism above is valid because both premises are true (you search "Lassie the dog" online to verify the second premise) and the conclusion logically follows them.

But sometimes, a syllogism has a structural flaw, as seen in the next example.

- If the sky is clear, then it is not raining.
- It is not raining.
- Therefore, the sky is clear.

Did you catch the error? The reasoning here is backwards. Although the premises may be true, the reasoning relies on the consequence (not raining) rather than the condition precedent (sky is clear). Even if it's not raining, something else could be happening, like a blizzard, that would make the sky

30. *See, e.g.*, Hans Hansen, *Fallacies*, Stanford Encyclopedia of Philosophy (updated Aug. 30, 2024), https://plato.stanford.edu/entries/fallacies/.

unclear. This is a formal fallacy called affirming the consequent. The flaw lies in the form of the argument.

On the other hand, informal fallacies may be structurally sound but contain flaws in the premises. The rules or facts set forth may be incorrect, oversimplified, or otherwise unsound. An example of an informal fallacy would be the slippery slope argument. Here's an example:

> If we raise the minimum wage, then businesses will be forced to lay off employees, causing unemployment to skyrocket and the economy to collapse.

This argument demonstrates the slippery slope fallacy because it presumes that raising minimum wage will create a disastrous chain reaction that will lead to economic collapse. The argument fails to provide evidence to support this claim, and it fails to consider any intervening factors that would prevent or mitigate these consequences.

For purposes of our discussion, it's not all that important to know the distinction between formal and informal fallacies. Instead, the section below will focus on highlighting fallacies that frequently arise in legal arguments, followed by advice on how to avoid fallacies in your own writing.

B. Frequently encountered fallacies in legal writing

Although many types of fallacies exist, certain ones tend to crop up more frequently in legal writing than in other contexts. The structure of legal reasoning, including its reliance on precedent, lends itself to particular logical fallacies. In the previous section, you learned about the slippery slope fallacy. The following list provides several other fallacies commonly found in persuasive legal writing.

1. Ad hominem: Attacking people (e.g., parties, counsel, judges) instead of addressing the opposing arguments.
2. Cherry-picking: Choosing to present only favorable facts or authorities and ignoring unfavorable ones.
3. Hasty generalization: Drawing conclusions about legal principles or case outcomes based on insufficient legal authorities, such as one or two cases.
4. Straw man: Manufacturing or mischaracterizing an opponent's argument, and then refuting that argument rather than the opponent's actual argument.

5. False dichotomy: Presenting only two options when other options exist.
6. Appeal to authority: Accepting or presenting an argument as valid based only on its authoritative source.
7. Red herring: Focusing on something irrelevant to distract from the important issues.
8. Bandwagon: Assuming something is true or valid just because many people believe or accept it.
9. Quoting out of context: Providing a helpful quote from an authority while leaving out facts or context that are essential to understanding the quote's true meaning.
10. Circular reasoning: Making an argument where the premise and the conclusion are actually saying the same thing.
11. False analogy: Drawing an analogy between two things that aren't actually similar.
12. Non sequitur: Stating a conclusion that doesn't follow from the preceding argument.

As you can see from this list, logical fallacies take many forms. This list provides just a sample of fallacies that pertain to legal reasoning. Many other fallacies exist, especially informal fallacies. If you'd like to learn more, you can easily find books and articles that explain more about philosophy, logic, and fallacies.

If this list of fallacies made you feel a bit nervous about your own writing, take heart. The first step in avoiding fallacies is to understand them. The following section provides a few more practical tips.

C. Best practices to avoid fallacies in appellate arguments

This section provides concrete guidance to help you avoid the logical pitfalls created by fallacies. Spotting fallacies and eliminating them from your legal reasoning will make your written and oral arguments more precise and persuasive. As you work on your appellate briefs, consider the following advice:

- Know the common fallacies. Continue to learn about the frequently encountered fallacies, both the ones listed in this chapter and others you find through your own research. See if you can identify logical fallacies in other contexts, like commercials and testimonials.

- When arguing from precedent, be careful not to oversimplify implicit legal rules. Also beware of overstating case law precedent when explaining or applying it. Do not stretch your analogies too far.
- In rule-based reasoning, such as applying a statute or court rule, be sure the logical structure of your reasoning is sound. Interrogate your reasoning to ensure that your conclusions flow logically from your premises.
- When making statutory interpretation arguments, clarify (when possible) ambiguous terms and phrases. Be transparent about any canons of construction you're applying. Consider arguments in context, such as the larger statutory scheme or purpose.
- When making policy arguments, look out for arguments that rely heavily on dramatic or disastrous consequences, such as slippery slope arguments and emotional appeals. Avoid the false dichotomy by considering all the potential policy choices and their consequences rather than presenting only your best option and the worst alternative.
- When making empirical arguments, be careful not to overstate the results of empirical research. Don't overstate the application of data-driven conclusions to real-world situations. Ensure that the studies you cite use sound methodologies and come from reliable sources.
- Always ensure that your argument adequately addresses the counterarguments rather than presenting only your client's best argument. Consider the opposing party's perspective and look for their own fallacies in reasoning.
- Be scrupulous when quoting language from legal authorities. Ensure that you're not cherry-picking only the best quotes while ignoring their context.
- Seek feedback from others: Ask peers or mentors to review your writing to look for logical fallacies or gaps in your reasoning.

Following this advice will help you write with clean logic and argue with precision. Doing so will not only make you a more persuasive advocate but will enhance your reputation as well. The advice above will also help you find and address the logical fallacies in an opponent's brief or oral argument.

Exercise

For each statement below, see if you can identify one or more of the fallacies that have been discussed in this chapter.

1. Either we adopt this new policy or we'll be stuck with the same ineffective approach we've had for years.
2. Justice John Roberts said, "If children do not understand the Constitution, they cannot understand how our government functions." Therefore, a copy of the Constitution should be displayed in all elementary school classrooms.
3. Five federal circuits have adopted the "reasonable person" test; therefore, this circuit should follow suit.
4. In two recent cases, courts ruled in favor of plaintiffs, so it's clear that the trend is toward plaintiff-friendly decisions.
5. The opposing party is an undocumented immigrant, so he obviously has no regard for the law.
6. The government's restriction on this type of firearm is legal because it is a restriction that the government may lawfully impose.
7. Just as the government regulates the pharmaceutical industry to protect the public from harm, the government should regulate social media platforms to protect our children.
8. If we allow the government to regulate social media platforms, soon we will live in a regime where free speech is a distant memory.

VI. Conclusion

Constructing effective appellate arguments requires both deliberate planning and thoughtful execution. By carefully selecting and organizing your arguments, crafting persuasive point headings, and avoiding logical fallacies, you can create a compelling argument that guides the court toward your client's desired outcome. Your goal is to make the court's decision seem inevitable by deftly weaving together the facts and law. By following this chapter's guidelines, you'll be well-equipped to meet that goal.

Discussion Questions

1. What are the key considerations in determining the order of arguments in an appellate brief?
2. What is the difference between an empirical argument and a policy-based argument? Provide an example of each.
3. How do you construct an argument based on analogical reasoning, and what are the key elements to include?
4. What are the key components of an effective point heading?
5. Choose three different logical fallacies and come up with a real-life example of each one. Try looking at advertisements, YouTube wellness influencers, or political speeches for inspiration.

Chapter 6

Drafting Effective Briefs: Beyond the Argument

In this chapter, you will learn strategies for drafting the other sections of an appellate brief, including how to:

- Open an appellate brief with a precisely formatted Cover and Tables
- Set the stage for the Argument by writing a persuasive Introduction, Statement of the Case, Issues Presented, and Summary of the Argument
- Close out the brief with the Conclusion and Certificates

I. Introduction

In Chapter 5, you learned how to organize and structure the heart of the appellate brief—the Argument. But a heart needs a body, and a brief needs a cover, certificates, and everything in between. Each part of the appellate brief requires a different strategy. Some components, like the tables, are all about good formatting. Other sections, like the Introduction, require some finesse to be effective.

In this chapter, you'll learn how to draft and format all the components of an appellate brief, aside from the Argument. This chapter will use the Federal Rules of Appellate Procedure for reference, but the advice applies equally to briefs filed in state courts.

The basic parts of an appellate brief,[1] in order, are:

- Cover Page
- Table of Contents
- Table of Authorities
- Introduction
- Jurisdictional Statement
- Issues Presented
- Statement of the Case
- Summary of the Argument
- Standard of Review
- Argument
- Conclusion
- Certificates

This chapter will discuss all the above components except for the Argument, which is discussed in Chapter 5. Keep in mind that this basic format can vary from court to court or lawyer to lawyer. Some advocates omit an Introduction; others combine the Standard of Review with the Argument. Regardless, by the end of this chapter you'll be equipped with strategies to write an effective and complete appellate brief.

II. First impressions: Cover Page, Table of Contents, and Table of Authorities

These sections of the appellate brief require careful formatting rather than insightful writing. Nonetheless, attention to detail is critical. The cover page and tables will make a first impression on the judges reading your brief. Their assessment of the quality of your argument and the time you took to craft it will be influenced by their perception of these initial components. Sloppy formatting and spelling errors may indicate that graver errors exist within the brief's pages.

---

1. Depending on the jurisdiction, some of the items above may be optional. For example, the Introduction is often an optional component according to procedural rules. The Standard of Review may be a separate section, or it may be incorporated into the Argument. In addition to the sections discussed in this chapter, Federal Rule of Appellate Procedure 28(a)(1) requires a corporate disclosure statement, if applicable under Federal Rule of Appellate Procedure 26.1.

A. Cover Page or Case Caption Page

Jurisdictions that still require paper filing may refer to the very first page of the brief as the Cover Page. Other jurisdictions use the term "Case Caption Page," especially those that use only electronic filing. This page provides the basic information about the case, including the parties, the case number information from the lower court and the appellate court, and the attorneys. Each jurisdiction will have its own format. Some courts will even provide a template to encourage uniformity. Completing this part of the brief is ministerial, but mistakes can create glitches. Details always matter. Moreover, if you omit this page or fail to format the caption correctly, your filing could be rejected.

B. Table of Contents[2]

Just as a book has a table of contents at the beginning, so does an appellate brief. The table must identify the key parts of the brief and their corresponding page numbers. It also will include the point headings and subheadings that appear in the Argument section. In addition to serving as a means to navigate the brief, the table of contents provides a roadmap for the appellate judges (and their staff). Because the point headings create an outline of the argument, the table of contents represents the lawyer's first real opportunity at persuasion. (Chapter 5 discusses best practices for crafting substantive, persuasive point headings.)

C. Table of Authorities

This section identifies each legal authority the litigant cited in the brief and the corresponding page numbers. Oftentimes, it is a shortcut for judges and their staff to find a particular issue in the brief. A quick scan of the Table of Authorities can also tell the reader what types of legal authorities the author relied on, and how frequently the author used these authorities. A Table of Authorities is organized by the type of legal authority cited: Cases, Statutes, Other Authorities, Rules, Treatises, Regulations, and Constitutional provisions.[3]

---

2. Increasingly, courts are abandoning the Table of Contents and the Table of Authorities because technology has made them somewhat obsolete. Counsel can include hyperlinks and bookmarks in electronically filed documents. These types of documents are also word-searchable, further diminishing the utility of tables in a brief. See Chapter 7 for a further discussion of formatting electronically filed briefs.

3. These are the categories that appear in Microsoft Word's Table of Authorities formatting tool.

Here's a simplified example (with fictionalized case law):

Table of Authorities

Cases

Smith v. Jones, 123 F.3d 456 (1998) 5, 7

Johnson v. Williams, 456 F.2d 789 (2001) 7, 9, 13

Statutes

28 U.S.C. § 1331 4

42 U.S.C. § 1983 6

Regulations

42 C.F.R. § 405.900 .... 9, 11

A note on page numbers: In older briefs, you may see the word "passim" in the Table of Authorities. Passim is a Latin word that roughly translates to "spread throughout." In a Table of Authorities, it would be used when an authority was cited frequently throughout the brief, in lieu of listing the actual page numbers. Nowadays, using passim instead of page numbers is disfavored. Indeed, some courts (like the U.S. Supreme Court) have banned its use altogether.

You can use macros in word processing software to automatically generate the Table of Contents and Table of Authorities. You can consult free online resources on how to format tables, or you may be fortunate enough to have someone to help you with this. You can always create tables by hand, the old-fashioned way, but errors may occur. Even if you use software to assist you, always double-check the tables for accuracy before filing your brief.

III. Setting the stage: Introduction and Jurisdictional Statement

Once you get past the cover and tables, the Introduction and Jurisdictional Statement present your first substantive opportunities to argue and persuade. The Introduction, although usually optional in an appellate brief, allows you to prime the reader and frame your argument. The Jurisdictional Statement is an essential component of the brief. Without jurisdiction, the appellate court cannot consider the litigant's case. The guidelines below will help you draft these sections with persuasion and precision.

A. Introduction

The Introduction provides a unique opportunity for advocacy. Because it's typically not a required section in an appellate brief, you have a lot of flexibility in how you draft this section. In addition, its up-front location lets you take advantage of priming, a persuasive writing technique discussed in Chapter 9. In the Introduction, you can grab the reader's attention, articulate your persuasive theme, and frame the forthcoming arguments. The excerpt below, taken from the Introduction to an appellees' brief in a marriage equality case, accomplishes these purposes.

> This case is about marriage, "the most important relation in life," *Zablocki v. Redhail*, 434 U.S. 374, 384 (1978), and equality, the most essential principle of the American dream, from the Declaration of Independence, to the Gettysburg Address, to the Fourteenth Amendment.
>
> Fourteen times the Supreme Court has stated that marriage is a fundamental right of all individuals. This case tests the proposition whether the gay and lesbian Americans among us should be counted as "persons" under the Fourteenth Amendment, or whether they constitute a permanent underclass ineligible for protection under that cornerstone of our Constitution.
>
> The unmistakable, undeniable purpose and effect of Proposition 8 is to select gay men and lesbians — and them alone — and enshrine in California's Constitution that they are different, that their loving and committed relationships are ineligible for the designation "marriage," and that they are unworthy of that "most important relation in life."[4]

Upon reading this Introduction, the court will know immediately what this case is about. Indeed, the first sentence begins with, "This case is about...." The Introduction uses engaging and compelling language, stating that denying the "fundamental right" of marriage to gay and lesbian individuals will create "a permanent underclass." The core of the appellees' argument — that Proposition 8 violates the Fourteenth Amendment to the U.S. Constitution — is apparent. Like the trailer to a movie, this Introduction conveys the

4. Brief for Appellees at 1, Perry v. Schwarzenegger, 591 F.3d 1147 (9th Cir. 2010) (quoted in Thomas L. Hudson, *Structuring Appellate Briefs*, 21 J. App. Practice & Proc. 85, 87 (2021)).

essential points of the story and whets the appetite for the forthcoming substantive discussion.

Certainly, some appeals are more mundane in nature and may not lend themselves to a dramatic theme as exemplified above. Still, you shouldn't forgo the Introduction. As discussed further in Chapter 9, a key component of persuasion is reducing cognitive load for the decision-maker who reads your brief. The Introduction can assist in doing so by providing a framework through which the reader can view the rest of the brief. Think of it this way: The Introduction provides a tiny on-ramp to the other parts of the brief, such as the Issues Presented, Statement of the Case, and Summary of the Argument. Each section builds upon the previous one, paving the path to the Argument itself.

When writing the Introduction, keep in mind these best practices:

- Keep it short. The Introduction shouldn't take up multiple pages within your brief. Often, a couple of paragraphs should suffice. You don't want the Introduction to duplicate other sections, like the Summary of the Argument.
- Keep it simple. One method is to think of it as the thirty-second pitch of your main Argument.[5] What are the essential details? Avoid lengthy quotations or citations, and don't get mired in unnecessary factual details.
- Introduce your theme. Chapter 10 explains how storytelling techniques, including themes, can enhance the persuasive value of your legal writing. Every case lends itself to a theme.
- Incorporate persuasive writing techniques. Few rules, if any, govern the content of the Introduction. This is your chance to incorporate the advice provided in Part 3 of this book. Storytelling devices and engaging word choice work particularly well in the Introduction.
- Consider writing this section last. Drafting the other parts of the brief, especially the Statement of the Case and Argument, should give you a good idea of the points to include in the Introduction.

---

5. *See* Hudson, *supra* note 4, at 87.

B. Jurisdictional Statement

The Jurisdictional Statement establishes the court's jurisdiction over the appeal. This section is critical. A mistake here could result in losing the appeal for lack of jurisdiction. Before drafting, the lawyer must do the legwork and confirm the court's jurisdictional basis. Writing the Jurisdictional Statement should be a perfunctory step by the time the lawyer is drafting the brief.

Federal Rule of Appellate Procedure 28(a)(4) requires the jurisdictional statement to contain the following:

- The basis for the district court's or federal agency's subject-matter jurisdiction over the matter
- The basis for the appellate court's jurisdiction over the appeal
- Applicable filing dates
- A statement that the appeal is from a final order or judgment, or another basis for jurisdiction

Each of these components of the jurisdictional statement should be supported by references to the applicable statutory provisions and relevant facts.

An effective jurisdictional statement should be brief and straightforward. The language tends to be standard. Here's an example:

> The United States District Court for the District of Wyoming had jurisdiction over this matter pursuant to 28 U.S.C. § 1331, which grants jurisdiction over civil actions arising under federal law. This cause involves a claim under Title VII of the Rights Act of 1964, 42 U.S.C. § 2000e. This Court of Appeals has jurisdiction of this appeal pursuant to 28 U.S.C. § 1291. On April 14, 2024, the district court entered a final judgment that disposed of all issues. The notice of appeal was filed on April 24, 2024.

IV. Crafting the questions: Issues Presented[6]

This section is where the litigant lays out the exact issue or issues on appeal. It is the lawyer's next opportunity to persuade the judges and their staff. It should be precise, succinct, and crisp. Legal writing experts recommend no

6. In certain jurisdictions, the Issue Presented is called the Question Presented, e.g., in briefs filed in the U.S. Supreme Court.

more than seventy-five words per issue statement.[7] The issues should also be presented from the client's perspective, meaning that the issues should usually be written in such a way that the answer to the legal question is a "yes" rather than a "no." (If you choose to frame the issue in a way that a "no" answer favors your client, then be sure to present the legally relevant facts persuasively. The court should be able to easily discern which conclusion you want the court to reach.)

In general, the Issue Presented comprises three parts: (1) the controlling law, (2) the legally relevant facts, and (3) the legal question (or conclusion, depending on the format you use). As long as it contains these three components, the Issue Presented can be formatted in several ways. Below you'll find guidelines for three common ways of structuring the issues.

A. Format 1: "Whether" statements

In appellate briefs, the Issue Presented is frequently written as a statement that starts with the word "whether." Here's an example from the Petitioner's Brief in *Bostock v. Clayton County*:

> Whether discrimination against an employee because of sexual orientation constitutes prohibited employment discrimination "because of... sex" within the meaning of Title VII of the Civil Rights Act of 1964, 42 U.S.C. § 2000e-2.[8]

Taking a close look, you can see that this concise statement contains the three components of an Issue Presented:

1. Controlling law: "Title VII of the Civil Rights Act of 1964, 42 U.S.C. § 2000e-2"
2. Legally relevant facts: "discrimination against an employee because of sexual orientation"
3. Legal conclusion: "constitutes prohibited employment discrimination 'because of... sex.' "

Additionally, the Issue Presented is written from the client's perspective because the conclusion the client wants the court to reach is a "yes" answer to the question "whether this type of discrimination constitutes prohibited employment discrimination."

---

7. *See* Mireille Butler, *Frame It: How to Use a Deep Issue Statement to Make a Lasting First Impression*, Wash. State Bar News (Apr. 1, 2021), https://wabarnews.org/2021/04/01/frame-it-how-to-use-a-deep-issue-statement-to-make-a-lasting-first-impression/.

8. Brief for Petitioner at i, Bostock v. Clayton Cnty., 590 U.S. 644 (2020) (No. 17-1618).

Although the "whether" format is traditional, as far as writing style goes, it's fairly bland. Depending on the nature of the appellate case, an advocate could make this style of Issue Presented more engaging by providing descriptive facts or colorful word choice. If, however, you'd prefer to write your Issue Presented in the form of a question, you could use the Under/Does/When format described next.

B. Format 2: Under/does/when construction

There's a good chance you learned the "under/does/when" format during your first year of law school. It's a classic method to include all three components of the Issue Presented, formatted as a one-sentence question. In this construction, "under" describes the controlling law, "does" asks the legal question, and "when" provides the legally relevant facts.

Depending on the author's stylistic choices and the nature of the issue, the organization and language used in the under/does/when format can vary. Look at the example below, taken from the Petitioner's brief in *Texas v. Johnson*:

> Does the public burning of an American flag during the course of a political demonstration constitute free speech subject to the protection of the First Amendment?[9]

Although the statement begins with the word "does," it actually starts with the legally relevant facts, i.e., "public burning of an American flag during the course of a political demonstration." It then provides the legal question, i.e., whether those facts "constitute free speech." Last, the statement provides the controlling law, "the First Amendment," but omits the word "under."

Here, the Petitioner wants the Court to answer the question in the affirmative and therefore constructs the Issue Presented accordingly: "Yes, the public burning of the American flag constitutes free speech."

This format works well when the three components of the Issue Presented can be clearly and logically expressed in a single sentence. In this example, the determinative facts are fairly simple, and the issue turns more upon the legal question — whether public flag burning is a form of free speech. In other circumstances, the issue may be more fact-intensive, and you may have difficulty placing all legally relevant facts into one declarative statement or question. The next format, the deep issue, works better in those circumstances.

9. Brief for Petitioner at i, Texas v. Johnson, 491 U.S. 397 (1989) (No. 88-155).

C. Format 3: The deep issue

The deep issue format deviates from the two formats above by phrasing the Issue Presented in a series of sentences. Legal writing expert Bryan Garner popularized the name "deep issue," but others have described it as "statements plus question" or "multiple sentence" format.[10] Here's an example of an Issue Presented phrased as a deep issue:

> New York, like all states, allows merchants to charge higher prices to consumers who pay with a credit card instead of cash. But New York's no-surcharge law, N.Y. Gen. Bus. Law § 518, requires merchants to label that price difference as a cash "discount" and makes it a crime—punishable by up to one year in jail—to label it as a credit card "surcharge." The question presented is whether New York's no-surcharge law unconstitutionally restricts speech.[11]

Once again, this Issue Presented contains the three required components:

1. Controlling law: "New York's no-surcharge law, N.Y. Gen. Bus. Law § 518" and the First Amendment (by implication).
2. Legally relevant facts: "New York, like all states, allows merchants to charge higher prices to consumers who pay with a credit card instead of cash.... [the law] requires merchants to label that price difference as a cash 'discount'...."
3. Legal question: "whether New York's no-surcharge law unconstitutionally restricts speech."

In the deep issue, however, these three components appear in a series of sentences rather than one statement or question. Broadly speaking, the deep issue is structured with the first two or three sentences providing the controlling law and the legally relevant facts, and the final sentences providing the legal question or conclusion.[12] The deep issue format works well when the Issue Presented is fact intensive. It also works well when the controlling law must be explained in detail. Using more than one sentence allows the writer to provide these additional details without sacrificing clarity. However, using multiple sentences can lead to wordiness. The deep issue format is also less

---

10. See Clay Greenberg & Matthew Weingast, *Persuasive Issue Statements*, Writing Ctr. at Georgetown Univ. L. Ctr. 8–10 (2015), https://www.law.georgetown.edu/wp-content/uploads/2018/07/Geenberg-Weingast-Issue-Statement.pdf.

11. Butler, *supra* note 7 (quoting Brief for Petitioner at 1, Expressions Hair Design v. Schneiderman, 137 S. Ct. 1144 (2017) (No. 15-1391)).

12. *Id.*

traditional than the formats discussed above, so it may deviate from the reader's expectations.

Regardless of which format you use, keep these best practices in mind when drafting the Issue Presented:

- Keep the issue statement concise. Even the deep issue example above uses only seventy-five words.
- Include only legally relevant (i.e., outcome-determinative) facts. Save background facts for later in the brief.
- Describe the law with the utmost precision. Quote sparingly if needed for accuracy.
- Consider how the standard of review affects how you write the Issue Presented. For example, instead of writing, "did the lower court err," you could write "did the lower court abuse its discretion" if that's the standard in your case.
- Ensure the way that you phrase your Issue Presented is consistent with how you argue the issues in the Argument and how you wrap up your brief in the Conclusion.

V. Telling a story: Statement of the Case

Figuratively speaking, the entire appellate brief is an opportunity to tell your client's story. In a literal sense, the Statement of the Case *is* your client's story. Some courts will break this into two sections, the procedural history and factual history (i.e., Statement of Facts). Either way, this section of the brief tells the reader two things: (1) procedurally, how did the parties get to the appellate court, and, (2) substantively, what are the facts of the case. The goal here is to be persuasive but not argumentative.

Accuracy here is critical. If the lawyer misstates the procedural or factual record, the appellate court will find it. Law clerks have been known to take certain joy in finding such errors, particularly when they are dispositive.

And remember, the lawyer's reputation is on the line at that point. The lawyer does not want to lose credibility, and even minor mistakes can create doubt. This is especially true when it comes to accurately citing the record on appeal. Though lawyers generally do not lose cases because of mistaken record cites, it starts them at a disadvantage. And if a lawyer identifies a mistake, the best avenue is to correct it promptly and professionally. Nothing helps restore a judge's confidence in a lawyer like having the lawyer admit to and own a mistake.

A. Procedural History

As the name implies, this section of the brief describes the path the case took to reach the appellate court. Although procedural history may appear dry at first blush, it's an essential part of the story. The history provides context to the Argument. Indeed, the procedural history may even be an essential component of the Argument, e.g., if the case turns upon issues related to removal, abstention, or law of the case.

Writing an effective procedural history means striking a balance when it comes to details. You don't want to omit the relevant steps in the procedure, but you also want to avoid getting mired in irrelevant points. The reader expects that if you chose to include something in the brief, it must be important. Including unimportant details thereby detracts from the emphasis provided to the important details. At a minimum, Federal Rule of Appellate Procedure 28(a)(6) requires the Statement of the Case to "describ[e] the relevant procedural history, and identify[] the rulings presented for review."

B. Statement of Facts

Of all the sections of the appellate brief, the Statement of Facts provides the best opportunity to employ persuasive storytelling techniques. At first glance, you may think that the Statement of Facts should be relatively easy to write because you don't have to cite or analyze the law—you just have to tell the court what happened. However, telling a persuasive story has its own challenges. For one, you have to decide which facts to include. The standard advice is to include all legally relevant facts, i.e., the facts that are outcome-determinative to your client's appeal. Federal Rule of Appellate Procedure 28(a)(6) uses the description "facts relevant to the issues submitted for review."

Beyond that, you'll want to include facts that accomplish one or more of these purposes:

- Provide context or background to the client's situation
- Allow the court to relate to the client on a human level
- Explain the motives behind the client's or other party or nonparty's conduct
- Support the narrative theme of your brief

Some words of caution: You must include both favorable and unfavorable facts. You want your presentation of facts to appear unbiased, even when you're using persuasive writing techniques to subtly support your client's position. Including unfavorable facts also allows you to draw the sting if you're filing the opening brief.

You'll also want to avoid including unnecessary details for the reasons discussed above in Section A, Procedural History. To determine whether a fact is necessary or unnecessary, ask yourself whether it is (a) legally relevant or (b) accomplishes one of the other purposes listed above. If not, then you should probably omit it. Names, dates, and locations can often fall into the unnecessary category if they aren't essential to establishing a legal position or understanding the client's story.

Although the Statement of Facts should be persuasive, it shouldn't be argumentative. Do not include any legal conclusions, and do not characterize the facts in a manner that implies a legal conclusion. For example, let's say you're writing a Statement of Facts in an employment discrimination case. The underlying legal dispute is whether the employer's treatment of the employee amounted to discrimination as a matter of law. In the Statement of Facts, you'll want to avoid writing this:

The employer discriminated against the employee.

Using the adage "show, don't tell," you should include the facts that support this conclusion. But still, don't write this:

> The employer discriminated against the employee by terminating her employment two days after she returned to work from military leave.

Instead, you'll want to write this:

> The employer terminated the employee two days after she returned to work from military leave.

In the Argument, you'll use these facts to argue that the employer's conduct amounted to discrimination as a matter of law.

A good Statement of Facts will be organized clearly and logically. Depending on the nature of the appeal, the facts could be organized chronologically, topically, or with a combination of these approaches. It's often helpful to start the Statement of Facts by introducing the key parties and their relationship to each other. Depending on the court in which you're filing the brief, you may decide to use formal titles (e.g., Petitioner, Respondent), or you may choose to use names to make the narrative easier to follow. If your Statement of Facts is long or convoluted, consider including point headings to keep the reader on track. Chapter 5's discussion of effective point headings will be helpful here. Just keep in mind that in the Statement of Facts, the point headings cannot be argumentative.

For a discussion of persuasive writing techniques that you can use when drafting the Statement of Facts, review Chapter 9, The Science of Persuasion: Modern Theories and Strategies, and Chapter 10, Advanced Persuasive Writing Techniques.

VI. Previewing your case: Summary of the Argument and Standard of Review

Although every section of a brief plays a supporting role, the Summary of the Argument and Standard of Review are the gateway to the Argument. The Summary of the Argument provides the court a concise synopsis of the key points of the Argument and its legal framework. The Standard of Review, even when brief, can be outcome-determinative for the litigant. As discussed below, thoughtful drafting choices can help you maximize the persuasive value of these two sections.

A. Summary of the Argument

The Summary of the Argument puts a little meat on the bones of the issue statement. As the name implies, this section provides a synopsis of the entire Argument section, which immediately follows. A deft advocate, however, will use this section to do more than simply condense the forthcoming arguments.

A well-crafted summary advances the litigant's objectives in two ways.[13] One, it previews the Argument. Indeed, some judges look first at the Summary to get an idea of the brief's main points. Even if the court does not require this summary as a separate part of the brief, as a best practice tip, include it at the beginning of the Argument section. It should provide a roadmap for what's to come.

Two, it provides yet another opportunity for persuasion. It should be short, to the point, and leave the judge and the judge's staff saying, "Well of course!" Indeed, because it's concise and light on citations, the summary is an excellent place to showcase the persuasive writing techniques discussed in Chapters 9 and 10.

To write an effective summary, follow these guidelines:

---

13. *See* Judith Fischer, *Summing It Up with Panache: Framing a Brief's Summary of the Argument*, 48 John Marshall L. Rev. 991, 993 (2015).

- Ensure that the summary contains "a succinct, clear, and accurate statement of the arguments made in the body of the brief" that does "not merely repeat the argument headings," as required by Federal Rule of Appellate Procedure 28(a)(7).
- Keep the summary simple; do not include quotations, and "cite only key cases."[14]
- Strive to keep the summary concise — a few pages, or no more than 5 to 10 percent of the total word count.[15]

B. Standard of Review

This section briefly states the standard of review that the appellate court should apply to the issues. Per Federal Rule of Appellate Procedure 28(a)(8), the standard of review can be incorporated into the body of the Argument, or it can be a standalone section with its own heading.

Chapter 4 discusses the various standards of review that appellate courts apply to lower court or agency decisions. The standard of review section tends to be fairly brief, but it must still cite applicable legal authorities and relevant facts. In some instances, the parties' briefs may include arguments about the applicable standard of review. In such cases, these arguments would be incorporated into the main Argument.

Here's an example of a straightforward standard of review section:

> This is an appeal from the district court's abstention pursuant to the *Younger* doctrine. Therefore, the standard of review is *de novo. See Bean v. Matteucci*, 986 F.3d 1128, 1132 (9th Cir. 2021).

The Argument follows these sections. Although this chapter doesn't focus on drafting the Argument, it helps to think of the Argument in the context of the greater brief. The Argument is the main course, with the appetizer courses above and dessert courses below. To be effective, the lawyer must carefully draft all parts of the brief, including the Argument, so they flow naturally and lead the court to the desired conclusion.

---

14. Antonin Scalia & Brian A. Garner, Making Your Case: The Art of Persuading Judges 97–98 (2008).

15. Fischer, *supra* note 13, at 995.

VII. Closing it out: Conclusion and Certificates

The Conclusion and Certificates immediately follow the Argument and bring the brief to a close. The Conclusion provides an opportunity to reinforce your arguments. Drafting the Certificates with precision lets you demonstrate your respect for court rules and attention to detail.

A. Conclusion

This section should mirror the Summary of the Argument section, but it should not repeat it verbatim. No lawyer wants to sound redundant, but they need to track what has been said so far. The old adage of "say it three times" comes into play with this section. It should be brief, a paragraph, maybe two. And the party should unambiguously ask for the relief requested. It should provide a concise dessert course that goes down easy based on the groundwork the lawyer laid above. Do not leave the judge thinking "Great brief. Great issue. What do you want me to do about it?"

Sometimes, advocates do not take advantage of this opportunity to have the last word. Instead, they write Conclusions that look like this:

For the foregoing reasons, the lower court's decision should be affirmed.

This lone sentence conveys to the reader "I only wrote this Conclusion because I had to." An advocate who's looking for opportunities to persuade will write a substantive Conclusion, as seen in the excerpt below:

> For all the reasons set forth above, Petitioner prays that this Honorable Court reverse the erroneous judgment of the Eleventh Circuit Court of Appeals that he cannot state a claim for relief under Title VII on the theory that he was subjected to discrimination "because of sex" when he was fired for being gay. That Title VII so protects him and every other employee, whether gay or straight, is the best reading of the statute and the one that comports with the congressional intent to "strike at the entire spectrum of disparate treatment of men and women in employment." *Oncale*, 523 U.S. at 78 (citing *Meritor*, 477 U.S. at 64).[16]

16. Brief for Petitioner at 57–58, Bostock v. Clayton Cnty., 590 U.S. 644 (2020) (No. 17-1618).

Here, this advocate used the Conclusion section to their advantage in the following ways:

- Reminding the Court of the Petitioner's requested relief
- Summarizing the key points of the Argument
- Reinforcing the theme ("protects him and every other employee, whether gay or straight")

Typically, the Conclusion doesn't have to contain citations. The example above has a citation because the advocate strategically chose to quote key language from a case.

B. Certificate of Compliance

Every court has some requirements for appellate briefs. Some examples include margin widths, font types, page lengths, and word counts. Most courts require the lawyer to certify that the brief complies with those requirements. And courts these days use technology to confirm the certificate is accurate.

Some courts, like the U.S. Court of Appeals for the Ninth Circuit, use a standardized form for the certificate of compliance.[17] In other federal courts, the Certificate of Compliance would be drafted similarly to the example below.

CERTIFICATE OF COMPLIANCE

> This brief complies with the word limits of Federal Rule of Appellate Procedure 32(a)(7) because this brief contains__words, excluding the parts of the brief exempted by Federal Rule of Appellate Procedure 32(f).
>
> This brief complies with the typeface requirements of Federal Rule of Appellate Procedure 32(a)(5) and the type style requirements of Federal Rule of Appellate Procedure 32(a)(6) because this brief has been prepared in a [describe typeface and font].

---

17. *Instructions for Form 8. Certificate of Compliance for Briefs*, U.S. Court of Appeals for the Ninth Circuit, https://cdn.ca9.uscourts.gov/datastore/uploads/forms/form-08instructions.pdf (last visited Sept. 2, 2024).

C. Certificate of Service

Notice is as important at the appellate court stage as it is at the trial court stage. Every court will have a specific mechanism for the lawyer to confirm the party served the filing on the other parties. Depending on the jurisdiction, an electronically filed brief may not need a separate certificate of service in the body of the brief.

If the court does require a certificate of service, it will likely look like the example below.

> CERTIFICATE OF SERVICE
>
> I hereby certify that on [date], I electronically filed this Appellant's Brief with the Court using the CM/ECF system. I certify that the following parties or counsel are registered CM/ECF users and will receive service through the CM/ECF system.
>
> [Name and address of parties served.]
>
> I further certify that on [date] I served a copy of this Appellant's Brief by [U.S. Mail/Overnight delivery/Facsimile/Email/Hand delivery] on the following parties or counsel:
>
> [Name and address of parties served.]

D. Request for attorney fees and costs

Courts generally have broad discretion to award attorney fees to the prevailing party. But the process varies greatly depending on the jurisdiction. If a client hopes to recover attorney fees and costs on appeal, the attorney needs to follow the process. Often, the party must make the request early in the appeal process, sometimes in the first brief the party files. In some jurisdictions, the party may need to make a separate filing. And if the client is seeking an award, the lawyer should renew the request in the conclusion section of the brief, even if not procedurally required.

VIII. Conclusion

An effective appellate brief is more than just a compelling Argument section. Careful attention to every part of an appellate brief, even those that seem fairly routine, helps you to present your case in a cohesive manner. Each part of the brief serves a unique purpose. Filing a professional document with consistent formatting, style, and tone allows you to reinforce your credibility and showcase your advocacy skills.

Discussion Questions

1. What are some common mistakes or oversights that lawyers make when drafting the non-argument sections of an appellate brief? How can you avoid these mistakes in your own practice?
2. In what situations might you choose to deviate from the basic format of an appellate brief, such as omitting the Introduction or combining sections? What are the potential risks and benefits of such deviations?
3. How can you balance the need for brevity and concision in certain sections of the brief (e.g., the Summary of the Argument) with the need to provide sufficient context and support for your arguments? What strategies can you use to ensure that your brief is both clear and comprehensive?

Chapter 7

Formatting Briefs for the Modern Reader

In this chapter, you will learn to:

- Consult court rules and guidelines for formatting briefs
- Make formatting decisions for both electronic and hard-copy briefs
- Increase your brief's listenability for text-to-speech

I. Introduction

Once you have determined the content and structure of your appellate brief, you'll have to make some decisions about formatting. Forty-plus years ago, these decisions were limited by technology. For instance, when lawyers used typewriters to format briefs, they had no choice about typeface. Almost all typewriters used the Courier typeface. Nowadays, word processing software allows a writer to choose from a seemingly endless array of typefaces and fonts (Comic Sans, anyone?). In addition, although many jurisdictions still require both paper and electronic filing, chances are a judge will be reading your brief on a screen, or perhaps even listening to it using a text-to-speech program.

As you can infer, many of an advocate's decisions when it comes to formatting are dictated by existing and evolving technology. As discussed below, local court rules, whether state or federal, will provide some guidelines. When making other decisions about formatting, your primary concern should be enhancing the readability of your brief. Making a brief easy to read reduces cognitive load and allows the reader to focus on content rather than format. In turn, this makes your brief more persuasive, as discussed in Chapter 9, The Science of Persuasion: Modern Theories and Strategies.

II. Local court rules and guidelines

When formatting a brief, the starting point should always be the appellate court's rules. In the federal system, Federal Rule of Appellate Procedure 32 provides guidelines regarding paper size, line spacing, typeface, and type styles. For example, Rule 32(a)(5) states that a brief can use either a proportionally spaced font (like Times New Roman) that is 14 point or larger, or a monospaced font (like Courier) that is no more than 10 ½ characters per inch. Federal appellate courts may also issue local rules to supplement the Federal Rules. For example, the U.S. Court of Appeals for the Tenth Circuit supplements Rule 32 with 10th Circuit Rule 32. This rule states, "The court prefers 14-point type as required by [the Federal Rules], but 13-point type is acceptable. Footnote font size should be the same as that used in the body of the brief."[1]

Now, it appears that this rule permits briefs in either 14-point or 13-point type. However, the court's website states, "Notwithstanding the local rule that permits 13-point font, use 14 point. The larger type is much easier to read and does not affect your available argument space."[2] Although one could argue that the rule takes precedence over the website, a wise advocate would use 14-point typeface in the Tenth Circuit.

Some federal courts provide more specific guidance on typefaces. The D.C. Circuit provides a Handbook of Practice and Internal Procedures to further supplement its local rules.[3] This Handbook states, "Certain typefaces can be easier to read, such as Century and Times New Roman. The Court encourages the use of these typefaces." Once again, it's not enough to look at the court's local rules, which in this case are silent on preferred fonts.

---

1. *Fed. Rules of Appellate Procedure (Effective Dec. 1, 2023) and Tenth Circuit Rules (Effective Jan. 1, 2024)*, U.S. Court of Appeals for the Tenth Circuit, https://www.ca10.uscourts.gov/sites/ca10/files/clerk/2024FRAPandLocalRules_FINAL.pdf.

2. *Filing Your Appeal-Briefing*, U.S. Court of Appeals for the 10th Circuit, https://www.ca10.uscourts.gov/briefing (last visited Sept. 8, 2024).

3. *Court Rules & Operating Procedures*, U.S. Court of Appeals D.C. Circuit, https://www.cadc.uscourts.gov/internet/home.nsf/Content/Court+Rules+and+Operating+Procedures (last visited Sept. 8, 2024).

In state courts, formatting guidelines can vary widely by jurisdiction. In California, a brief can use "[a]ny conventional font" that is 13 point or larger. Contrast that with Maryland, where briefs filed in the Supreme Court must use one of eight specified typefaces, including Times New Roman, Georgia, and Lexend.[4] Courts often have distinct preferences regarding typefaces, as discussed further below.

Although this discussion of local rules has focused on typeface requirements, keep in mind that court rules cover all aspects of brief formatting — margins, paper size and type, and word limits, to name a few. Moreover, courts provide rules specifically for electronic briefs, as explored further in the following section.

III. Formatting briefs for screen readers

Regardless of your jurisdiction's filing requirements (paper, electronic, or both), chances are a judge will read your brief on a screen. And not all screens are equal; the reading experience on a high-quality desktop monitor versus a six-inch phone screen will be quite different. The advice below focuses on tailoring your brief for maximum screen readability.

A. Typefaces

Before diving into the finer points of typefaces, it's important to understand the terminology. Most of us would refer to Arial and Helvetica as different fonts, but technically they are different typefaces. Within each typeface is a family of fonts. Thus, within the typeface Arial you would find fonts like Arial Bold and Arial Narrow. To be true to the terminology, this chapter primarily refers to typefaces rather than fonts. In ordinary conversation, you'd probably use the terms interchangeably.

Typefaces have many distinguishing characteristics. The primary ones that come up in legal writing are proportional spacing versus monospacing and serif versus sans serif. In a proportionally spaced typeface, each letter takes up an amount of space proportional to its relative size. Thus, a slender "i" takes up less space than a broader "w." In a monospaced typeface, each letter takes up the same amount of space on the page. Common examples of proportionally spaced typefaces are Times New Roman, Georgia, and Century

4. *Filing Briefs with the Supreme Court*, Supreme Court of Md., https://www.courts.state.md.us/scm/filingbriefs (last visited Sept. 8, 2024).

Schoolbook. The most common example of a monospaced typeface is Courier, which approximates the typeface of a classic typewriter.

A typeface with serifs is one where the letters have strokes at the end of the lines. For example, an "r" in a serif font will appear to have little feet at the bottom; these are the serifs. A sans-serif typeface omits these strokes. Thus, typefaces like Garamond and Baskerville are serif fonts, while Arial and Helvetica are sans serif. ("Sans" is the French word for "without.")

These distinctions may relate to readability. A brief search will yield volumes of research on which typefaces are the most readable under different circumstances—screen versus print, bright versus low light, books versus websites. When it comes to serifs, much of the research is conflicting. A general consensus appears to be that serif typefaces, with their feet and hats, tend to keep the reader more "in-line," thus increasing readability. However, researchers also have found that sans-serif fonts, lacking ornamentation, are more readable, especially on road signs and websites. More consensus exists for proportional versus monospaced typefaces. The proportionally spaced typefaces are generally preferred for readability.

Even a layperson examining the various typefaces and fonts available in programs like Word can discern that some are more pleasant to read than others. You probably wouldn't want to read a brief written in Brush Script, or Comic Sans, or the one that looks like drippy Halloween letters. After eliminating these obvious non-starters, choosing among different proportionally spaced serif typefaces is usually a matter of either court rules or personal preference. Examining court rules among the federal circuits yields these generally preferred choices in no particular order:

- Georgia
- Times New Roman
- Century Schoolbook
- Bookman Old Style

Ultimately, the safest choice would be one of these conventional, proportionally spaced serif typefaces. Of course, you may be able to choose a different typeface/font and still comply with your court's local rules. Some lawyers may choose a typeface based on "soft" characteristics like formality, stateliness, or a general vibe. Look up "font psychology" and you'll find robust discussions about what your font choice says about you. My advice is to be better known for the quality of your writing than the creativity of your typeface.

A final note on typeface relates to another subject of debate among some writers—whether to place one or two spaces between sentences. In some ways, this is a generational debate, as lawyers who learned to type in the 1980s or earlier were likely taught to place two spaces at the end of a sentence. Some say this relates to readability when using the standard monospaced typeface on a typewriter. The modern approach is to have one space between sentences. If you use a proportionally spaced font, then using more than one space between sentences is not required to increase readability. But unless your employer or court imposes a rule, it's largely a matter of preference.

B. White space and point headings

Although the differences between typefaces vis-à-vis readability can be marginal, studies have revealed distinct advantages to including headings and white space in documents, especially those on screens.

The term "white space" refers to any negative space in a text, whether in a book, a brief, or a web page. In a context like web design, the "white" space could be any color, but for legal writers, the negative space is invariably white. In a brief, white spaces can be found:

- In the margins
- Between lines of text
- Between paragraphs
- In the indentations of paragraphs
- Beneath headings
- In charts, diagrams, or bulleted lists (like this one)

White space enhances readability by visually breaking up the text. Have you ever had a visceral "do not read" reaction to a chunky block quotation? You were probably daunted by the cognitive effort involved in plowing through a wall of text. The effort may seem minimal on a small scale, but you can imagine the cumulative effect over hours or days of brief-reading.

Creating a visually pleasing brief also requires judicious use of white space. Here, legal writers can take a cue from the worlds of art and design. In photography and other visual media, negative space serves vital purposes like bringing a design into balance and drawing a viewer's focus. Likewise, white space in a brief can balance the text on the page. Anything that breaks up the text (like the bulleted list above) tends to draw the reader's focus, as well.

Point headings serve a similar function in a brief, depending on how they are formatted. A short heading, set in bold and spaced apart from the primary text, provides a visual landmark. Studies employing eye-tracking technology demonstrate that screen readers tend to follow an F-shaped pattern of viewing text on a screen. The reader's eyes spend the most time scanning the left side of the text (assuming the text is meant to be left-to-right) and the headings. This tells us two things. For one, because visual landmarks help the reader move through the text, we should put point headings in briefs. Second, because readers tend to spend more time on headings, we should make sure the headings contain helpful information and are formatted for maximum readability.

Using bold typeface to set the headings apart from primary text is one technique to enhance their utility as landmarks. Placing white space before and after headings can also serve this purpose. Within the heading, think carefully about capitalization. Consider the three options below:

> **THE DISTRICT COURT ERRED IN GRANTING SUMMARY JUDGMENT BECAUSE THE RESPONDENT RAISED A GENUINE ISSUE OF MATERIAL FACT REGARDING THE DISPUTED PARCEL'S VALUE.**
>
> **The District Court Erred in Granting Summary Judgment Because the Respondent Raised a Genuine Issue of Material Fact Regarding the Disputed Parcel's Value.**
>
> **The District Court erred in granting summary judgment because the Respondent raised a genuine issue of material fact regarding the disputed parcel's value.**

Nowadays, most readers will find the first option to be the least readable. In part, this is because contemporary readers equate all-caps with shouting. Beyond that, an all-caps sentence isn't one we're used to reading. The second option is better, to be sure. It uses the title case, in which only major words are capitalized. For many, the title case has an air of authority as we are used to seeing it in the titles of books and articles. Nonetheless, most will find the third option to be the most readable because its capitalization matches that of an ordinary sentence.

A traditional method for formatting point headings would require a different style for each level, with main headings being in all caps and subsequent headings using combinations of capitalization conventions, underlining, and italicization. Contemporary practice prioritizes readability. Unless your jurisdiction (or your supervisor) specifies a heading format, you're advised to format all headings like the third example above—bold typeface with sentence case.

C. Hyperlinks, bookmarks, and images

An advantage of an electronic brief is the ability to supplement its content with hyperlinks to other sources, such as the electronic record on appeal and legal authorities. In both state and federal jurisdictions, some courts encourage hyperlinks and others require them. For example, the U.S. Court of Appeals for the Ninth Circuit permits hyperlinks but cautions that "[h]yperlinks do not replace citations to the record, Excerpts of Record, or legal authority.... Hyperlinks are simply mechanisms for accessing material cited in a filed document and are not considered part of the appellate record."[5] In Arizona, the Court of Appeals, Division One, allows hyperlinks, but Division Two requires them "when citing to the record on appeal or to other items."[6]

When hyperlinks are permitted, it's a good practice to include them. Creating hyperlinks takes time, however, both to insert them into the brief and then to check their validity. Therefore, you'll want to build that time into your writing process. Also, realize that hyperlinks may decrease a document's readability. The reader has to decide whether to click on the link, and clicking takes the reader away from the primary document.

Similarly, appellate courts often require or strongly encourage bookmarks in electronically filed briefs. For example, Rule 8.74(a)(3) of the California Rules of Court requires all electronic documents to have "an electronic bookmark to each heading, subheading, and the first page of any component of the document, including any table of contents, table of authorities, petition, verification, memorandum, declaration, certificate of word count, certificate of interested entities or persons, proof of service, exhibit, or attachment."

A bookmark is similar to a hyperlink, but it allows the reader to navigate within the document itself. In a document read on a screen, clicking bookmarks makes it easier for the reader move among the parts of a brief compared to swiping or scrolling. You can use software like Adobe Acrobat to create bookmarks within a PDF brief. Legal technology companies also sell software specifically designed for formatting legal briefs that allows users to create bookmarks.

A final consideration is the inclusion of images in electronic briefs, both those contained in the record (like photos) and demonstrative images (like charts and tables). Sometimes, an appellate argument benefits from including

---

5. *Filing and Service Using CM/ECF*, U.S. Courts for the Ninth Circuit, https://www.ca9.uscourts.gov/efiling/faqs/filingservice/#filing-standards-hyperlinks (last visited Sept. 8, 2024).

6. Ariz. R. Civ. App. P. 13(a).

images contained in the record. For instance, an argument involving artwork and copyright can save many words of description by including images of the artwork in question. When transferring images from the record into your brief, ensure that the image is as sharp as possible, is not digitally altered, and is followed by a citation to the record.

You can further enhance your argument by including demonstrative images, especially when the argument describes timelines, processes, or relationships. For example, rather than verbally describing a sequence of events, you can summarize the events in a chart. Look at the sequence of events summarized below.

> On May 16, 2023, the Appellant purchased a 2020 Honda Accord from the Appellee's dealership. On May 18, 2023, the Appellant brought the Accord to a mechanic after hearing a strange noise when braking. On May 19, 2023, the Appellant retrieved the Accord from the mechanic, who told Appellant that she had to replace defective brake pads with new brake pads. Later that day, Appellant called Appellee's dealership to ask about a partial refund of the purchase price. Appellant did not receive a return call until over a week later, May 28, 2023.

These events could instead be summarized in this chart:

May 16, 2023	Appellant purchased a 2020 Honda Accord from Appellee's dealership.
May 18, 2023	Appellant heard a strange noise while braking and took the Accord to a mechanic.
May 19, 2023	Mechanic informed Appellant that she had to replace defective brake pads. Appellant called Appellee to request a partial refund of the purchase price.
May 28, 2023	Appellee returned Appellant's call.

The chart has a few advantages over the paragraph of text. For one, the chart uses fewer words (62 versus 93). The chart also breaks up the text, includes white space, and creates a visual landmark. As discussed above, these features make the information easier to read and process, especially for someone reading on a screen.

D. Complying with electronic filing requirements

As you have learned, complying with a court's rules regarding electronic filing of appellate briefs can directly affect formatting choices. When it comes to formatting tools like hyperlinks, you may have to include them even if you'd prefer to leave them out. Therefore, you must be comfortable not only with what the rules require but also with how to comply using current technology.

In addition to what's highlighted above, courts may also impose electronic filing requirements like searchable text, redaction of sensitive information, and electronic pagination. Even the methods used for electronic filing can be daunting at first. Federal jurisdictions use CM/ECF (Case Management/Electronic Case Filing), while state courts use comparable platforms. Although not terribly complicated, these systems also tend not to be intuitive.

Fortunately, courts usually provide self-help resources on their websites. Video tutorials, instructional PDFs, and FAQs can guide a new user through both the rules and the technology. Perhaps your workplace provides assistance in electronic filing, either in the form of a human legal assistant or legal technology. Nevertheless, you should become familiar with the electronic filing process. Ultimately, as the lawyer, you're responsible both for your brief's content and its timely filing.

IV. Formatting hard-copy briefs

When it comes to hard-copy (i.e., paper) briefs, the formatting advice for screen readers generally holds true. Clear typefaces, distinct headings, and sufficient white space improve readability of documents whether read on a screen or on paper. But appellate courts have distinct requirements when filing a hard copy brief, again governed by the jurisdiction's rules.

Typically, a hard-copy appellate brief is bound (like a book or pamphlet). Outside the U.S. Supreme Court, federal and state courts generally accept briefs that are 8 x 11 ½ inches—the size of a standard piece of paper. The U.S. Supreme Court requires that briefs be sized at 6 ⅛ x 9 ¼ inches. Court rules also prescribe the paper's color and weight, whether the brief is to be printed on one side only, and the margin size, among other requirements. Federal Rule of Appellate Procedure 32(a)(2) specifies the color of the cover: "Except for filings by unrepresented parties, the cover of the appellant's brief must be blue; the appellee's, red; an intervenor's or amicus curiae's, green; any reply brief, gray; and any supplemental brief, tan." State courts may have different requirements.

To determine what your court requires, consult its rules and any supplemental guidelines, or handbooks. Keep in mind that courts may reject a brief that doesn't conform to the rules. Having to refile a brief creates additional delay and expense, and refiling can create real problems for your client if you end up missing a deadline. Like many things in the practice of law, following the rules is critical to success.

V. Writing for text-to-speech

As noted earlier in this chapter, some judges use text-to-speech (TTS) software to listen to a brief in lieu of, or in addition to, reading it. The reasons for doing so vary; it could be personal preference, a time saver, or a disability accommodation. We can expect this practice to become more prevalent with advances in artificial intelligence. In the past, a hallmark of TTS technology was a distinctive computer voice, with stilted cadences and odd pronunciation. Nowadays, AI-powered TTS allows for voices that are more fluid and human-like. Indeed, media companies such as *The Atlantic* are using TTS companies like Audm to convert magazine articles into highly listenable podcasts.

Although TTS technology is constantly improving, a writer can still employ best practices to ensure that what looks good on the page also sounds good to the ear. You can get a baseline by using TTS to listen to something you have already written. Many legal writers do this as a step in the editing process, to weed out misspellings, missing words, and clunky sentences. If your writing sounds good to you, then ask a few other people to listen and gather their opinions.

If you'd like to improve the listenability of your writing, you can take a cue from broadcast journalism. Long before TTS technology, journalists writing for radio and television had to break down complex news stories into sound bites easily understood over the airwaves. We can derive and adapt their time-tested methods. Broadcast listeners are often battling distractions like a morning commute; therefore, broadcast writing tends to be shorter, snappier, and more vivid. Some other advice adapted from broadcast journalism includes the following:

- Write conversationally. In conversational speech, we tend to use contractions, rely on simpler vocabulary, and avoid jargon or foreign phrases. Audiences generally expect a bit less formality and a bit more familiarity when listening versus reading. Writing in this manner will also make the TTS conversion smoother.

- Use shorter sentences. Although a standard rule of thumb is to average twenty words per sentence, broadcast journalists often set the number lower, closer to twelve words.
- Stick to one thought per sentence. A long, convoluted sentence can be difficult for a listener to comprehend. Likewise, long sentences are hard for TTS to fluently read.
- Pay attention to punctuation. TTS technology relies on punctuation to employ appropriate inflection and pauses when reading aloud. Inserting superfluous commas or dropping an occasional period will disrupt the flow.
- Reconsider block quotations and string citations. As discussed below in Chapter 9, block quotations and string citations disrupt the reader's flow and increase cognitive load, thereby decreasing the persuasive power of your writing. Now, imagine TTS reading aloud a string citation. Of course, quotations and citations are a necessary part of legal argument, and creating a solid argument is more important than creating a listenable argument. But if you have a choice, think about trimming citations and quotations to make your brief more readable and more listenable.

You could also turn to the many resources available for podcast writers and producers. A key metric for podcasters is episode consumption, which is the percentage of a podcast that a person listens to before dropping off. Increasing consumption requires sustaining listeners' attention. Therefore, skilled podcast writers will use the following tactics:

- Rely on vivid, colorful language rather than neutral or abstract terms.
- Use the active voice instead of passive.
- Avoid nominalizations by using verbs instead of nouns.
- Place attention-grabbing information up front, rather than saving it for the end.

These techniques are discussed in further detail in the following chapters dealing with persuasion and the fundamentals of good legal writing. Fortunately, it's possible to use a handful of intersecting and overlapping techniques to produce writing that is readable, listenable, and persuasive.

VI. Conclusion

This chapter has explored the crucial role that formatting plays in creating an effective appellate brief. Modern readers consume texts in various media, each with its own set of conventions and expectations. When it comes to appellate briefs, a skilled legal writer will prioritize readability and navigation. To stay current with evolving technology, you must adjust your writing and formatting practices to communicate your arguments to judges who may be reading on a screen or listening through text-to-speech software. Making informed decisions about formatting and language will allow you to craft a compelling brief, no matter the circumstances.

Exercises

1. *Your local rules.* Find the local rules in the court in which you practice or plan to practice one day. What do the rules say about typeface, font size, margins, etc.? Now, look at the court's website. Does the website contain additional information to supplement these rules, including local practice guides or handbooks?
2. *Finding your typeface.* Take a paragraph you have written and reproduce it using the typefaces mentioned in this chapter (and others, if you'd like). Which do you find most readable? Which do you prefer for your own writing?
3. *Reading aloud.* Many free apps allow you to upload a document and hear it read aloud by a variety of AI-powered voices. You can also use the "Read Aloud" feature in Microsoft Word. Using one of these apps, listen to a paragraph or two of something you're writing. (Don't upload any confidential client information, though.) Which of your writing techniques converted well to TTS? Where could you use some improvement?

Part 3

A Contemporary Advocate's Guide to Persuasive Writing

Chapter 8

Fundamentals of Good Legal Writing

In this chapter, you will learn to:

- Develop a writing process
- Write more clearly and concisely
- Maintain a professional tone in your writing
- Cite authorities appropriately and avoid plagiarism

I. Introduction

This chapter provides strategies to improve your legal writing, from the writing process itself to the editing and polishing stage, that will help you write more accurately, clearly, and concisely. Although this book is about appellate advocacy, the writing advice here could apply to many types of legal writing — memos, trial briefs, and client correspondence, to name a few examples.

Note that this chapter does not cover the basics of writing mechanics, like verb tenses, proper comma usage, or pronoun-antecedent agreement. This book's appendix lists some texts you can consult to fortify your knowledge of these concepts, as needed. In addition, many writers use artificial intelligence-driven apps to check their writing and provide suggestions relating to grammar, punctuation, and other aspects of writing mechanics. These apps can be very useful to legal writers, subject to the cautions discussed further in Chapter 12.

II. Developing your writing process

Perhaps the greatest challenge for legal writers is developing a sound writing process. People sometimes believe that writers are divided into two camps: the naturally talented writers and the rest of us. Naturally talented writers, the belief goes, can sit at a desk and effortlessly dash off a compelling legal argument. For the rest of us, writing is a struggle.

In truth, writing is not like walking or breathing; it doesn't come naturally. Certainly, the desire to communicate is a natural one, but doing so in written form is a skill that can be developed. As with any skill, a deliberate approach can ensure that the time spent on writing is productive. Just as an athlete wouldn't walk into a gym without a training plan in place, a writer should develop a process.

A. Pre-writing

The writing process actually begins before a single word is written. Pre-writing can encompass a variety of tasks: contemplation, planning, and outlining.

The contemplation phase provides space for the writer to think freely about the writing project before committing pen to paper. Using visualization is one way to make productive use of this phase. In a quiet state, with eyes closed, imagine your brief is fully written. In your mind's eye, consider the message you wish to impart.

For many, however, the contemplation phase can also be a barrier. Writers with perfectionistic tendencies have difficulty moving past contemplation. After all, when nothing is written, no mistakes have been made. This leads to procrastination, a form of anxiety that in turn produces more anxiety as time passes and deadlines loom. Too much contemplation can also lead to "analysis paralysis," where helpful thinking turns into overthinking.

One technique to overcome procrastination is to have empathy for the "you" of the future. As discussed by Hal Hershfield in his book *Your Future Self*, you can adopt better habits today by connecting with your future identity.[1] For most people, our future selves seem strange and distant. The more you

---

1. Hal Hershfield, Your Future Self (2023).

can visualize your future self as a real person, with real emotions and needs, the better you can make choices in the present. After all, you wouldn't want your future self to be anxious, exhausted, and pulling an all-nighter to finish a brief— right?

Another tool for moving from contemplation to planning is free writing. Whether on a laptop or pen and paper, commit to a certain period where you will simply write down what you're thinking. Do not worry about spelling, grammar, Bluebook formatting, or citations to the record. Free writing is writing for your eyes only. Creative writers often use free writing to get unstuck. Legal writers have more constraints; creativity cannot displace legal precedent or historical facts. But, for those who have trouble getting started, free writing can jump-start the pre-writing process.

When it comes to dealing with writer's block, artificial intelligence can also lend a hand. Generative AI programs like ChatGPT can help with planning a timeline, outlining an argument, or revising topic sentences. Sometimes, just getting words on a page is enough to get going, and generative AI can definitely help. Just be certain to check any output you receive from generative AI, as it is prone to bias and "hallucinations" (coming up with nonexistent resources, including case law). In general, AI works best for tasks like planning, organizing, and checking grammar. As of this book's writing (2025), it's not very good at legal research and is incapable of meaningful legal analysis.

In the planning phase, a legal writer takes on an investigatory role. Examining the record can reveal bases for appeal. Researching the law allows arguments to be revealed, sorted, and perhaps discarded. During this phase, good writers have a go-to method of keeping track of their findings. Lawyers use a variety of methods to take notes and compile research. The analog approach keeps everything on paper, sorted into notebooks, file folders, legal pads, or index cards. Nowadays, legal technology permits even old-fashioned advocates to approximate the analog approach, but with the benefits of searchable files, less paper waste, and backups to the cloud. The key is to have a method and to use it consistently.

Once the legal writer has adequately investigated the record to identify appellate issues and researched the law to determine the best legal arguments, they can transition to the final stage of pre-writing: outlining. At this point, your outline should be a skeleton of your final brief. For an argument outline, you'll want to create main headings for main arguments and subheadings for nested arguments. The main argument's structure is often dictated by the structure of the legal rule or principle at issue. See Chapter 5, Crafting Compelling Arguments, for further discussion.

Beyond the headings, the structure of the outline is up to you. Some writers prefer a traditional structure, using Roman numerals, letters, and so forth. Others prefer less structure, instead opting for topic sentences with bullet points underneath. One benefit of a looser structure is the ability to copy/paste and shift arguments around without having to reformat the outline. However, you'll have to exercise some discipline to keep your outline from becoming too messy to be helpful. Ultimately, though, the best structure is the one that you're most likely to use.

B. Writing

In the writing phase, you'll fill in the outline you have created, fleshing out the skeleton, so to speak. Now, can some writers launch into the writing phase without creating an outline first? Certainly, some do. Again, the writing process that works best is the one that works best for you. However, consider the risks of writing without an outline. Imagine taking a road trip without any planning—no maps, no GPS, no destinations to reach by particular dates. In some ways, this seems like a fun adventure, especially if you have time to meander and backtrack as you wind your way across the country. But when writing an appellate brief, most likely you won't have time to meander and backtrack. If you're in private practice, you probably can't bill for that time, either. Therefore, having a plan of some sort (i.e., an outline) is a good idea for most legal writers.

In this chapter and others, you'll find plenty of guidelines and advice for writing the appellate brief. Keep in mind that the advice above for overcoming writer's block applies equally in the writing phase as in the prewriting phase.

C. Editing and polishing

The U.S. Army teaches its leaders to plan in reverse. When planning a mission, a leader must start with the goal and work backwards. Doing so allows the leader to critically analyze the amount of time needed to accomplish each phase of the mission. Legal writers can also use backwards planning to ensure they have enough time to accomplish each phase of the writing process. Importantly, backwards planning helps you to carve out sufficient time to edit and polish your brief before it's due.

To engage in backwards planning, start with the due date of your brief—the date and time you plan to file it. Then, work backwards. How much time do you want to set aside for editing and polishing? Consider a minimum of two to three days so you can have a twenty-four-hour break between the first and second edit. Doing so allows you to read your brief with fresh eyes. Once you move back three days from the brief's deadline, that becomes the new point from which to continue backwards planning. Here's what a plan might look like:

> July 17, 5:00 pm: Brief must be filed with the court and served on the parties.
>
> July 14: Begin editing the final draft of the brief.
>
> July 7: Begin writing the brief.
>
> July 3: Begin outlining the brief.
>
> July 1: Begin pre-writing.
>
> June 26: Begin additional legal research.
>
> June 20: Begin reviewing the record and identifying potential arguments.

Of course, the plan must be modified as needed to account for real life. Using the example above, what if you are assigned the appellate brief project on June 30? You'll have to compress your timeline quite a bit, but you should still allot time for each phase of the research and writing process.

Even when you're up against a tight deadline, build in time for editing and polishing. *Editing* allows you to identify and fix typographical, grammatical, and structural errors in your writing. Even the best writers make mistakes in first drafts, especially when juggling a writing project with all the casual writing that's incidental to modern life, such as texts and emails. In this book's appendix, you'll find a sample editing checklist that you can use or modify. Use it to create your own checklist that includes your personal writing pitfalls. Perhaps you tend to sprinkle commas liberally throughout your sentences. If so, you'll want to check for comma splices. Or maybe you're inclined to use an apostrophe when writing "it's," even when you're writing it as a possessive ("the car and its passengers"). Put it on the checklist.

Once you have finished editing, you'll ideally have at least one day to set aside the brief before you move to the next phase. At this point, you'll have already corrected any misspellings, grammatical errors, and other structural issues. When you *polish* the brief, you make it read smoothly and look nice on the page. For example, in the polishing phase you'll check for formatting issues such as spacing, margins, and orphaned headings (i.e., headings at the bottom of a page with no text underneath). You can also use the polishing phase to clean up sentences and paragraphs to make your writing more cohesive. For example, you may check for the following:

- Appropriate transition words and phrases to connect ideas
- Strong topic sentences at the start of each paragraph
- Proximity between subjects and verbs in sentences
- Avoiding overuse of certain phrases

Both editing and polishing can be accomplished with the assistance of AI-powered tools like Microsoft Word's built-in Editor or the Grammarly app. These tools are helpful, but they aren't foolproof. For example, editing apps sometimes miss correctly spelled but misused words like "statue" instead of "statute." Therefore, you'll want to conduct your own check as well. Also, be careful when accepting suggested changes or allowing an app to revise your brief without checking it yourself. The app could "help" by rewriting (incorrectly) your legal terms of art or Bluebook citations.

Exercises

1. *Overcoming roadblocks.* Imagine you have to write a brief that is due in thirty days. Identify the roadblocks that you anticipate encountering during this time frame. The roadblocks can be internal (e.g., writer's block) or external (e.g., traveling for a wedding). For each roadblock, identify at least one strategy you could use to minimize or overcome it.
2. *Creating a checklist.* The most effective checklist is one that you create based upon what you know about yourself as a writer and feedback that you have received on your writing. For this exercise, create an editing and polishing checklist to use on your next writing project. To get started, you can refer to the author's checklist in this book's appendix.

III. Writing clearly and concisely: The ACE approach

At this point in your legal writing career, you've likely heard this advice many times: "Write clearly and concisely." And it's good advice. After all, in crafting a solid legal document of any kind, you want the reader to understand it without having to wade through needless words. This advice, however, is more of an end state than a process. You want your writing to be clear and concise, but how do you achieve that goal?

This chapter offers a paradigm for honing your writing: the ACE approach. This paradigm helps you focus on the fundamental goals of good legal writing:

- Accuracy: Am I precisely and truthfully explaining the law and facts?
- Clarity: Can the reader understand my message the first time reading through my document?
- Efficiency: Am I conveying my message concisely and avoiding unnecessary words and details?

Each component of this paradigm is explained in detail below.

A. Accuracy

A threshold requirement for any type of legal writing is accuracy. Persuasive techniques and clever turns of a phrase mean nothing if you're unable to accurately explain both the law and the facts before the court. Failure to write accurately carries a range of consequences. If a court believes a brief is deliberately misleading, the responsible lawyer(s) could face sanctions and bar discipline. Even when inaccuracies result from rushed or sloppy work, a lawyer can lose credibility and damage their reputation. Of course, inaccurate work also impacts the client. Misstatements of facts and law can quickly torpedo legal arguments, even those otherwise well written.

To avoid inaccuracy in legal writing, advocates can take several approaches. Although lawyers occasionally mislead the court on purpose, those instances are far outweighed by unintentional mistakes. Taking the time to properly edit and proofread your legal brief can go far in avoiding misstatements. Go back and check all citations to the record to ensure that your statements of fact are accurate. After spending hours drafting a brief, an advocate could easily misremember a certain factual detail.

When editing for accuracy, check all pinpoint citations to statutes, regulations, and case law, too. Even when you're writing about a familiar area of law, you can accidentally transpose words or misstate a legal standard. For example, one type of conflict in Model Rule of Professional Conduct 1.7 is defined as "a significant risk that the representation of one or more clients will be materially limited by the lawyer's responsibilities…." Even experienced ethics lawyers sometimes state this as "a material risk that the representation of one or more clients will be significantly limited by the lawyer's responsibilities." Depending on the issue at hand, the difference between "significant" and "material" could be the key to resolving the conflict.

At times, the pursuit of persuasion itself can lead to inaccuracy. As discussed further in Chapters 9 and 10, word choice plays a powerful role in affecting a reader's perception. However, advocates must still be careful not to be so creative as to mislead. For example, let's say that a critical fact before the court is that the opposing party did not pay a bill. Perhaps you want to highlight that fact using more descriptive verbiage than "did not pay." As you ponder the alternatives, you come up with "declined to pay" and "refused to pay." Each of those phrases are a bit more vivid than "did not pay," but they also suggest that the party's nonpayment was intentional. If the facts in the record reflect that the nonpayment was unintentional, then using "decline" or "refuse" would be misleading.

Likewise, when explaining the law, advocates must be conscientious. At this point in your legal writing career, you've likely been admonished not to quote too heavily from legal authorities. Generally speaking, this is good advice. But when you paraphrase, you must ensure that you've accurately rephrased the legal standards articulated in the case, statute, or other source. The same holds true when selectively quoting language. Even when you've properly used brackets and ellipses to indicate alterations to a quotation, you should double check to ensure that the meaning itself hasn't been altered by the changes.

Writing accurately isn't hard to do, but it does require time and effort.

B. Clarity

Clear writing is understandable writing. Put differently, a reader should be able to understand your message without having to backtrack and reread sentences, paragraphs, or sections of your brief. To be certain, some areas of law are complex, as are some fact patterns. Your reader may want to go back through parts of your brief to ensure their own understanding. What you want to avoid, as the writer, is introducing more complexity through your writing style.

1. Words

Achieving clarity starts with word choice. You've likely heard the admonition to avoid "legalese." What qualifies as legalese can be subjective and varies by area of practice. For instance, one could define the verb "bequeath" as legalese because it seldom appears outside of legal writing and could be replaced by a more widely used synonym, like "pass down." However, if you're a trusts and estates lawyer, the word "bequeath" is commonplace. Moreover, writing a will without the word "bequeath," although doable, may seem strange. The traditional definition of "bequeath" is to give someone personal property through a will, so it may benefit the client to use the precise term.

As this example illustrates, specialized legal terms of art may be unavoidable, even if they aren't part of one's everyday vocabulary. But other terms do generally qualify as legalese. One example is using "said" as a modifier, as in "said property." Often, "said" can be replaced by a more familiar word like "this" or "that":

> Ms. Janssen parked her car along Allegre Avenue. A driver exceeding the speed limit subsequently struck said car.
>
> Ms. Janssen parked her car along Allegre Avenue. A driver exceeding the speed limit subsequently struck her car.

The table below provides other examples of legalese that can be easily replaced without losing meaning.

Legalese and Alternatives

Heretofore	Up to this point
Forthwith	Immediately
Henceforth	Going forward
Inter alia	Among other things
Arguendo	For argument's sake

The last two terms are Latin phrases that often appear in legal writing. It's possible for an advocate to use these words without detracting from a brief's readability. It all depends on context. Bear in mind that repeating Latin phrases throughout a brief, especially when intermixed with other legalese, risks affecting the brief's clarity.

Another key to writing clearly is to avoid nonstandard word usage, even when the words or their use are technically correct. For instance, the words "admission" and "admittance" can often be used as synonyms without confusing or distracting the reader. In certain contexts, though, "admission" is the expected word, as in admission to a university or to the practice of law. Indeed, the two words are not exact synonyms, as "admittance" means physical entry into a place, e.g., admittance into a private party. Thus, although writing about "admittance" to a university is not exactly wrong, it's nonstandard to a degree that a reader may be distracted by its use.

2. Sentences

When editing individual sentences for clarity, structure is key. A simple sentence structure typically works best. Placing subjects, verbs, and objects close together improves readability. Take the examples below:

1. Ms. Janssen, having just exited her car, was startled by a deafening sound.
2. Having just exited her car, Ms. Janssen was startled by a deafening sound.
3. Having just exited her car, a deafening sound startled Ms. Janssen.

In the first example, the subject (Ms. Janssen) and the verb (was startled) are separated by a modifier (having just exited her car.) The second example places the subject and verb close together. Doing so conveys the message more quickly and clearly; thus, the second example is preferable.

You may have noticed that both the first and second examples contain passive voice construction. When a sentence is written in the passive voice, the subject (Ms. Janssen) is receiving an action (was startled), not performing an action. Editing the sentence to avoid the passive voice requires changing the subject to "a deafening sound" so the subject can perform the action. However, in looking at the third example, you may have noticed that this creates another structural problem. "Having just exited her car" is now a misplaced modifier, as it is now modifying the subject "a deafening sound" when it should be modifying "Ms. Janssen." Thus, the second example remains the best choice.

As this example demonstrates, adhering too rigidly to legal writing "rules" can sometimes impede readability. Avoiding passive voice can often make your writing more concise and therefore more efficient. However, sometimes sentence clarity suffers as a result. Moreover, revising a sentence to eliminate passive voice also requires changing the sentence's subject. In the example above, the writer may want to emphasize Ms. Janssen as the subject, rather than the deafening sound. Thus, the passive voice construction can be a deliberate and effective choice.

Other legal writing "rules" that can impede readability include never splitting an infinitive and never ending a sentence with a preposition. Although grammar purists may chafe at the thought, breaking these rules can make your writing sound more natural. Here's an example of splitting an infinitive:

> Ms. Janssen had to quickly jump out of the way of the speeding car.

The infinitive is "to jump," and placing "quickly" in the middle splits the infinitive. To avoid the split infinitive, a writer could revise the sentence to read:

1. Ms. Janssen had to jump quickly out of the way of the speeding car.
2. Ms. Janssen quickly had to jump out of the way of the speeding car.
3. Ms. Janssen had to jump out of the way of the speeding car quickly.

The first revision is still readable, although not quite as natural sounding as the original sentence. Same for the second revision. The third revision is the least preferable; "speeding car quickly" is a confusing way to end this sentence. In addition, the third revision fails to keep related parts of the sentence together—"jump" should be kept close to "quickly." As this example illustrates, avoiding the split infinitive can create more problems than it ostensibly solves.

Ending a sentence with a preposition likewise can sound more natural than the alternative. Here's an example:

1. Ms. Janssen had many problems to deal with.
2. Ms. Janssen had to deal with many problems.
3. Ms. Janssen had many problems with which to deal.

The first version sounds like something a person would say in ordinary conversation. Writing this sentence in a legal brief would be acceptable, even though it ends in the preposition "with." The second version avoids placing the preposition at the end, and this version is also acceptable. However, it changes the location of the word "problems," therefore shifting emphasis away from that word. The third version is awkward and therefore best avoided.

Sometimes, sentences are hard to read because they say too much. If you find that your sentences tend to be long and meandering, try to write only one main thought per sentence. One way to check is to look for commas, semicolons, and conjunctions like "but" or "and." Often, you can swap in a period and break a sentence in two to make your message clearer. Here's an example of a sentence with more than one thought:

> Ms. Janssen parked her car along Allegre Avenue, and then a driver exceeding the speed limit struck her car, requiring Ms. Janssen to quickly jump out of the way to avoid being hit.

Breaking this sentence into shorter sentences can make the content easier to understand. Here's a revision:

> Ms. Janssen parked her car along Allegre Avenue. A speeding driver then struck her car. Ms. Janssen had to quickly jump out of the way to avoid being hit.

In this revision, each individual sentence is easier to read than one long sentence. Like all writing advice, however, the key is balance. Writing only short sentences in a brief can result in a choppy rhythm that is unpleasant to read.

Interspersing short sentences with longer sentences creates a more conversational flow. It also allows you to use the short sentences to emphasize key information. Readers pay attention to short sentences. Really.

Overall, achieving the goal of clear writing requires interrogating each sentence. Ask if the construction of the sentence helps or hinders its readability. When it comes to rules like splitting infinitives or ending sentences with a preposition, understand that writers can usually diverge from these rules without negative consequences. However, if you know that your court is a stickler for these rules, you'll have to adjust your strategy accordingly.

3. *Paragraphs and sections*

As explained further in Chapter 10, Advanced Persuasive Writing Techniques, readers tend to pay more attention to the beginnings of paragraphs (topic sentences) and the beginnings of sections (point headings). In addition to drawing attention, topic sentences and point headings can increase a brief's clarity. At the paragraph level, each topic sentence should state a main point, and each sentence in that paragraph should relate back to that point. Adding unrelated content to a paragraph muddles its meaning. One way to check for strong topic sentences is to create a topic sentence outline. Copy/paste just the first sentence of each paragraph into a separate document. Can you clearly discern your argument from the topic sentences alone?

The same advice applies to point headings. Well-crafted headings can serve as a visual signpost to make your brief more readable. As with topic sentences, the content under the point heading should relate to the heading. You can also create a point heading outline (or simply look at your brief's table of contents) to determine whether your point headings effectively convey the main points of your argument.

Often, both point headings and topic sentences are written as conclusory statements. The conclusion forecasts the argument, and the content below supports the conclusion. Starting with a conclusion is another way to increase your writing's clarity. You provide the reader with the destination, then explain how to get there. By repeating the conclusion at the end, you can bookend your paragraph or section with its key points.

C. Efficiency

The last component of the ACE approach is efficiency. An efficient writer conveys information using as few words as possible. At a practical level, writing efficiently allows an advocate to stay within court-mandated word or page limits. Efficient writing also contributes to the persuasive power of an appellate brief. As discussed in Chapter 9, a persuasive writer considers the external influences on the decision-maker who reads a brief. Busy judges must balance personal and professional obligations, and as an advocate, you have a narrow window for delivering your message. Doing so quickly and concisely reduces the reader's cognitive load, thus enhancing your brief's persuasiveness.

Guidelines for efficient writing echo several concepts already discussed in this book. For instance, avoiding legalese and conveying only one thought per sentence both contribute to efficiency. On a large scale, curating your arguments and eliminating irrelevant details from the Statement of the Case allow a brief to be more concise. In pursuit of efficiency, you can also rely on three simple writing tips to cut down on verbal bloat: Avoid the passive voice, avoid nominalizations, and avoid expletives.

1. Avoid the passive voice

As explained above under Clarity, a sentence written in the passive voice has its subject receiving an action instead of performing an action. Here are some examples:

1. The verdict was handed down by the jury.
2. The closing argument was delivered by the lead counsel.
3. The decision of the court below was made in error.

In each sentence above, the subject (verdict, closing argument, decision) is receiving an action, not performing one. Revising these sentences to change the passive voice to the active voice requires changing the subject, as follows:

1. The jury handed down the sentence.
2. The lead counsel delivered the closing argument.
3. The court below erred in its decision.

In these examples, eliminating the passive voice results in fewer words. In most instances, switching to the active voice makes a sentence shorter and therefore more efficient. Placing the actor up front also makes the sentence livelier. In general, reading active, vivid sentences engages the reader more than slogging through a series of passive-voice sentences.

You may have noticed also that changing the subject of the sentence shifts the emphasis. For instance, revising the first example shifts emphasis from the verdict to the jury. Knowing that choosing passive over active voice shifts the emphasis, as a writer you can use that technique to draw attention to key information. You may decide that the shift in emphasis is more important than trimming a few words. This is an instance of deliberately choosing passive voice for persuasive value.

An advocate may deliberately choose passive voice construction in a few other instances. For instance, sometimes the actor in a sentence is unknown:

> On July 6, 2023, Mr. Doddy was murdered in a mansion.

In the example above, the murderer may be unknown. Therefore, passive voice construction is preferred over a wordier, awkward active voice construction like the following:

> On July 6, 2023, an unknown person or persons murdered Mr. Doddy in a mansion.

At other times, the actor in a sentence is unimportant in the context of your overall argument:

> On September 15, 2023, Ms. Paloma was acquitted of Mr. Doddy's murder.

In this example, the contextual focus of this sentence may be the parties and the acquittal itself rather than the jury who decided the verdict.

Despite these examples of beneficial passive voice construction, a good default rule is to avoid passive voice construction. Efficient, concise writing should be an overriding goal. Deviating from the active voice should be a choice that you make deliberately and purposefully.

2. *Avoid nominalizations*

A nominalization is a verb, adjective, or adverb that is turned into a noun. In legal writing, problematic nominalizations are almost always nouns that are substituting for a verb. Below you'll find a few examples that crop up in legal writing:

Legal Writing Nominalizations

Nominalization	Verb
Allegation	Allege
Justification	Justify
Decision	Decide
Violation	Violate
Protection	Protect

Nominalizations decrease efficiency in two ways. For one, because a nominalization usually replaces a verb, it requires another verb to make it work in the sentence. Here are some examples:

1. The government *made an allegation* of fraud.
2. The defendant *provided a justification* for his actions.
3. The court *rendered a decision* in favor of the plaintiffs.

The revisions below uncover the verb that's hidden in the nominalization:

1. The government *alleged* fraud.
2. The defendant *justified* his actions.
3. The court *decided* in favor of the plaintiffs.

As you can see, using the verb instead of the nominalization shortens the sentence.

Nominalizations also decrease efficiency by diluting the message. In addition to adding more words, nominalizations take away the action in a sentence. In turn, this creates a sense of detachment between the actor in a sentence and the action performed. Rather than delivering a message in a crisp and concise package, nominalization-filled writing covers the message in layers of fluff. Take this example below:

> After the plaintiff's counsel delivered his argument on the motion, the judge issued a declaration that the court would take a fifteen-minute recess. The judge made her return to the bench after only ten minutes, providing her decision that resulted in a denial of the plaintiff's motion. The plaintiff's counsel then made a statement that she would file an appeal of the decision.

Although the point of this paragraph is simple, the abundance of nominalizations obscures the message. Compare this revision:

> After the plaintiff's counsel argued on the motion, the judge declared that the court would take a fifteen-minute recess. The judge returned to the bench after only ten minutes and denied the plaintiff's motion. The plaintiff's counsel then stated that she would appeal the decision.

The revision has fewer words, to be sure (forty-five instead of sixty-three). But also, using verbs instead of nominalizations tells the reader what each person is doing in a straightforward way. In this sense, avoiding nominalizations also increases the clarity of your writing, another component of the ACE paradigm.

To check for nominalizations in your writing, search your brief for words ending in -ion. Although some nominalizations do not end in -ion, many of them do. Once you find the -ion word, check to see if it's a noun that's covering up a verb. Then, revise the sentence to uncover the hidden verb. If doing so makes the sentence shorter and clearer, then make the change.

As with passive voice, sometimes nominalizations have their place in legal writing. Perhaps you strategically decide to use nominalizations to deemphasize a message that's unfavorable to your client's position. Or perhaps revising the sentence to omit the nominalization actually makes it longer or more awkward. All this is fine. What you want to avoid is the unconscious utilization of nominalizations in your writing. That is, you want to avoid unconsciously using nominalizations in your writing.

3. *Avoid expletives*

The word "expletive" has multiple meanings. Perhaps you're most familiar with this Merriam-Webster dictionary definition: "an exclamatory word or phrase *especially*: one that is obscene." If we were to use only that definition, then the advice would be clear. Do not use obscene exclamations in your legal writing unless you're quoting the record verbatim.

But expletive also carries this dictionary definition from Merriam-Webster: "a syllable, word, or phrase inserted to fill a vacancy (as in a sentence or a metrical line) without adding to the sense...." In other words, expletives are extra words that do nothing to promote the meaning of a sentence. Thus, avoiding these types of expletives helps to promote efficiency in your writing.

In legal writing, expletives typically reside at the start of sentences and take the form of the words "it," "that," or "there," followed by a "to be" verb. Here are some examples:

1. It is the judge who decides the sentence.
2. There are three theories that support the Appellant's position.
3. There is another definition for the term "material" provided in the statute itself.

Each sentence above starts with an expletive. The phrases beginning the sentences (it is, there are, there is) take the form of an expletive as described above. Importantly, the phrases "fill a vacancy… without adding to the sense." Each of these sentences is easily revised to eliminate the expletive:

1. The judge decides the sentence.
2. Three theories support the Appellant's position.
3. The statute itself provides another definition for the term "material."

The first two revisions simply chop off the expletive and reword the sentence so it makes sense grammatically. The third revision incorporates another step, which is to change the passive voice construction to active voice.

As with passive voice and nominalizations, the default guidance is to eliminate expletives, with some caveats. Sometimes, you'll encounter something that looks like an expletive but has no realistic alternatives:

> It's a widely held belief that juries don't always decide cases based on the law.

Let's say you come up with these possible revisions:

1. A widely held belief exists that juries don't always decide cases based on the law.
2. That juries don't always decide cases based on the law is a widely held belief.
3. Many people believe that juries don't always decide cases based on the law.

Are any of these alternatives better than the original? The first two revisions suffer from awkward sentence structure; they don't sound natural. And the first two revisions don't cut down on the number of words. The third revision is a tad bit shorter, but is it any better to start a sentence with "many people believe" instead of "it's"?

Therefore, when it comes to expletives, the overall guidance is to search and destroy. Scan your document for "it is," "there is," "there are," and "that is" (or their contractions, if you use contractions in your writing). Interrogate the sentence to see if chopping off the expletive makes the sentence more efficient without compromising its meaning or clarity. If your revised sentence sounds worse than the original, then leave it be.

Exercise

Revise the passage below for clarity and efficiency, using the ACE techniques described above. You don't have to revise the parentheticals following the citations.

> When privilege is selectively waived by an organization, it is seeking a form of protection of its privilege while still engaging in cooperation with the government in the performance of its investigation. Advocates of selective waiver make assumptions that the government lacks access to the underlying facts of internal investigations and that government investigations are more reliable as opposed to internal investigations, and said assumptions are faulty. *See Upjohn Co. v. United States*, 449 U.S. 383, 402 (1981). These are assumptions that are at odds with the plain text of procedural rules. Fed. R. Civ. P. 26(a)(1) (plaintiff's right to initial disclosures). Organizations should have no expectation, especially in the absence of express confidentiality agreements between organizations and the government, to retain confidentiality with respect to subsequent litigation by third-party litigants suing over similar subject matter. *See Permian Corp. v. United States*, 665 F.2d 1214 (D.C. Cir. 1981) (distinguishing selective waiver from attorney-client privilege in non-confidential government investigations).

IV. Maintaining a professional tone

When editing your brief, you should always read it for tone. If possible, have another person read it. The goal is to be both persuasive and professional. As you check your brief for a professional tone, keep the following points in mind.

- *Know your audience.* Typically, a legal writer thinks about writing for the decision-maker — the court. However, a legal brief has multiple audiences, including your client, the opposing party and their counsel, other lawyers, and the public. Think about these audiences, especially if you're tempted to write something unflattering about another person.
- *Consider your level of formality.* What constitutes formal writing varies among lawyers and judges. At one time, using contractions would be considered too informal for legal writing. Nowadays, you can find

contractions in U.S. Supreme Court opinions (especially those authored by Justice Elena Kagan). Using contractions can be a double-edged sword; they tend to make writing more readable, but they can also make some judges unhappy.

A similar dilemma arises with the singular "they" pronoun. Using the pronoun "they" to refer to single individuals allows you to avoid the awkward "he or she" construction. "A lawyer must follow their conscience" is easier to read than "A lawyer must follow his or her conscience." However, this usage may grate upon grammar purists who insist that "they" is always plural. In addition, a singular "they" can sometimes create confusion. For example, if a brief refers to a nonbinary individual using their preferred pronoun "they," then it might confuse a reader also to refer to other individuals as "they." As with contractions, the best advice is to know your audience and tread carefully.

- *Don't make it personal.* Caring about your client's legal matters and demonstrating empathy are usually assets in the practice of law. However, failure to maintain professional distance between yourself and your work can invite problems. Judges don't like briefs that focus on the parties and the lawyers rather than the factual disputes and legal precedents. As discussed in Chapter 3, an advocate should avoid non-germane accusations of ethical violations against opposing counsel. Likewise, an advocate should refrain from accusing the lower court of incompetence or bias.

  Even when a brief doesn't contain outright accusations, word choice can imply dishonest or unethical behavior. Take, for example, the word "specious." Lawyers sometimes use that word in briefs to refer to an opposing party's argument: "The Petitioner's argument is specious." But consider the Merriam-Webster dictionary definition of specious: "having a false look of truth or genuineness." In essence, using this term implies that the opposing party and counsel are being untruthful. Other terms to avoid include "ridiculous," "disingenuous," "frivolous," "two-faced," "incompetent," and "biased." Avoid using these terms unless you have a factual basis for the assertion and the assertion is relevant to your client's argument.

- *Use humor carefully.* Many lawyers have a way with words and enjoy demonstrating their wit. Used deftly, a bit of humor could help grab the reader's attention or establish a narrative theme. A drawback of expressing humor in writing, however, is the lack of other cues to signal the writer's humorous intent, such as facial expressions and body language. Therefore, a passage that reads to you as wry could come across as snarky.

Another consideration is the appropriateness of humor in context. Take, for instance, the Montana Supreme Court's opinion in *State v. Belanus.*[2] Up front, the court points out that the Defendant/Appellant opened his brief with an "expletive-laden" quote from Mike Tyson's character in *The Hangover*. This was, as the court notes, a "peculiar choice" in a sexual assault case. Although the lawyer may have been attempting humor, the subject matter warranted a more serious tone.

Also think carefully about using puns. Some judges enjoy sprinkling puns into their opinions. In *Western World Insurance Co. v. Markel American Insurance Co.*,[3] then-Judge Gorsuch referred to a claim as a "lingering specter of a lawsuit." The underlying facts involved a person who was injured by falling down an elevator shaft in a haunted house. Although the puns and allusions make the opinion entertaining to read, one must also consider the context. Certainly, if the claimant in question had lost his life, references to ghosts and specters would have been inappropriate.

Consider also that judges may have more leeway than lawyers when it comes to using humor and puns in their writing. Judges are in a position of authority and sometimes have lifetime appointments. Likewise, lawyers who are more established and have built up their credibility may be able to get away with humor more readily than a recent law-school graduate.

- *Avoid bias.* A contemporary appellate advocate should pay attention to potentially biased language. This has nothing to do with one's position on politics or social issues. Biased language reduces an advocate's effectiveness by diminishing credibility and clouding the legal issues. Sometimes, writers use biased language unintentionally. For example, the saying "off the reservation" is commonly used to mean breaking from convention. However, it traces its origins to the forcible removal of American Indians to reservations in the 1800s. Now, perhaps you could write that saying into a brief without offending any reader. But why take that risk when a less offensive phrase could accomplish the same purpose?

  Intentionally using biased language creates another host of issues. In addition to raising concerns about credibility and professionalism,

2. 240 P.3d 1021 (Mont. 2010).
3. 677 F.3d 1266 (10th Cir. 2012).

including biased language in a brief indicates an attempt to sway a court's decision using considerations other than relevant facts and law. Courts disfavor this tactic, to put it mildly.

One way to avoid bias in legal writing is to be aware of the origins and meanings of idiomatic phrases. In addition to "off the reservation," other phrases with insensitive origins include "bury the hatchet," "peanut gallery," and "low man on the totem pole." A brief online search will yield dozens of articles with more examples and explanations.

Another method to avoid bias is to include information relating to race, national origin, sex, and other categories only when relevant to the legal issues before the court. Nowadays, most writers exclude non-germane descriptions of sex or gender, even though terms like "lady lawyer" were commonplace just a few decades ago. Likewise, think carefully before including descriptors like "immigrant," "elderly," or "unemployed" when describing parties, witnesses, or court personnel.

Discussion Questions and Exercises

1. Find an example of a brief that was written unprofessionally in some manner. You can look online for "worst appellate briefs" or "benchslaps." What made the brief unprofessional?
2. What else can advocates do to avoid bias when writing appellate briefs?

V. Citing authorities and avoiding plagiarism

In legal writing, providing citations with appropriate frequency and correct formatting can go a long way toward increasing your brief's persuasiveness. In most instances, appellate courts aren't swayed by novelty and creativity. Rather, the court seeks reassurance that your argument is well grounded in existing legal precedent. Citing legal authorities—e.g., constitutions, statutes, regulations, or case law—can provide that reassurance. When it comes to citation frequency, a helpful default rule is to provide a citation whenever you quote, paraphrase, or refer to content from a legal authority or secondary source.

In addition to enhancing credibility, citations also allow you to avoid plagiarism in your legal writing. Chapter 3 discusses the ethical issues of using another lawyer's writing in your brief. As explained in that chapter, originality in legal briefs is not expected, or required, to the same degree as it would be in academic writing. Nonetheless, wholesale copying without proper attribution demonstrates, at best, a lack of attention to detail. At worst, non-attributed copying represents a form of intellectual dishonesty. The solution is straightforward: format direct quotations using quotation marks, ellipses, and brackets, as needed, and properly cite the source.

In appellate briefs, proper citations to the record are also critical. Perhaps you have heard this oft-quoted passage from *United States v. Dunkel*: "Judges are not like pigs, hunting for truffles buried in briefs."[4] This quote could apply equally to hunting for facts. Every fact provided in a brief requires an accurate citation to the record.

When it comes to where to place your citations, courts are split regarding textual citations versus footnotes. For decades, legal writing expert Bryan Garner has championed footnotes, arguing that the interruption created by textual citations reduces readability.[5] Although some judges agree, others prefer to keep citations in the text to avoid the "up and down" of going between main text and footnotes. As with many things in legal writing, this debate can evoke strong opinions.

Whether you fall in the pro- or anti-footnote camp, you should pay heed to the wisdom of Bluebook rule B1.1: "Footnotes should only be used in non-academic legal documents when permitted or required by local court rules."[6] Textual citations are traditional, and judges generally expect to find citations in the text. And yes, textual citations can disrupt the flow of your writing. Although some disruption is unavoidable, you can mitigate the issue by keeping long string citations to a minimum, as recommended in Chapter 9.

Finally, when it comes to citations, ensure that your formatting is immaculate. Build enough time into your writing process to check citations. Moreover, do not assume that every court uses Bluebook formatting. For example, California state courts use the California Style Manual, which requires placing the date of decision immediately after the case name and eliminates the comma following the case name, e.g., *Marbury v. Madison* (1803) 5 U.S. 137. In the federal system, the U.S. Court of Appeals for the Fifth Circuit uses the abbreviation "ROA." instead of "R." when citing the record on appeal. As explained in Chapter 7, you should consult not only the applicable state or federal rules but also local rules, style guides, manuals, and court websites for up-to-date guidance.

---

4. 927 F.2d 955, 956 (7th Cir. 1991).

5. *E.g.*, William Glaberson, *Legal Citations on Trial in Innovation v. Tradition*, N.Y. Times, July 8, 2001, sec. 1, p. 1, https://www.nytimes.com/2001/07/08/us/legal-citations-on-trial-in-innovation-v-tradition.html.

6. The Bluebook: A Uniform System of Citation 3 (21st ed. 2020).

VI. Conclusion

This chapter has explored the essential elements of good legal writing, from developing an effective writing process to refining your writing's clarity and concision. Good legal writing is easy to read and to understand. Moreover, a skilled legal writer maintains a professional tone, avoids bias, and cites sources scrupulously. The next few chapters build upon this chapter's foundation, providing insight into both the science of persuasion and advanced techniques you can use to increase the persuasive value of your appellate briefs.

Discussion Questions

1. What are the advantages and disadvantages of using textual citations versus footnotes? Considering the arguments discussed earlier, why might some judges prefer one style over the other?
2. Select a judicial opinion from a jurist whose writing style you admire. Analyze a passage from the opinion and identify specific legal writing fundamentals from this chapter that are demonstrated in the passage. How does the jurist's use of these fundamental writing skills contribute to the opinion's effectiveness?

Chapter 9

The Science of Persuasion: Modern Theories and Strategies

In this chapter, you will learn to:

- Understand the psychology of persuasion
- Conceptualize persuasion as an interactive process
- Employ tactics to maximize your writing's persuasiveness

I. Introduction

Think about the last time you were persuaded to do something you were not originally inclined to do. Perhaps a friend convinced you to try a new restaurant that you had planned to avoid. What got you to change your mind? You may have considered that your friend had made good recommendations in the past, and so you trusted their judgment. Or your friend may have emailed you a list of five-star reviews. Maybe your friend just waited until you were really hungry to make the suggestion, knowing that you would say yes in your famished state.

The point is that the process of persuasion is complex and multidimensional. What works in one situation is not guaranteed to work in another. Using the example above, some people are more likely to follow a trusted friend's opinion, whereas others are better convinced by hard evidence, e.g., online reviews. Still others may be influenced by environmental considerations like timing and hunger. If you find yourself trying to convince a friend to try a new restaurant, you should start by considering what technique would work best on your friend.

Similarly, when it comes to persuasive legal writing, no one-size-fits-all solution exists. At some point in your law school career, you likely learned the "rules" about structuring arguments, downplaying bad facts, and crafting point headings. However, you may not have learned why these techniques are effective.

Rather than provide hard-and-fast rules, this chapter introduces you to theories of persuasion and tools that you can deploy as the situation calls for them. We begin with conceptualizing persuasion as an interactive process influenced by factors both within and outside of your control. Next, we examine each component of this process, drawing upon disciplines ranging from psychology to economics. Understanding how each part of the persuasion process works allows us to formulate strategies for making our written and oral advocacy as persuasive as possible.

II. Conceptualizing the persuasion process

In your quest to become an effective appellate advocate, it makes sense to focus on the words — what you say and what you write. The message, however, is just one component in the persuasion process. No message exists in a vacuum. Indeed, a message exists only as a form of communication between the messenger and the recipient. In appellate advocacy, we can characterize the messenger as the advocate and the recipient as the decision-maker. Messages are created by people, for people. Understanding how people make decisions is essential for understanding how to craft an effective message.

But it's not enough to consider the advocate, the decision-maker, and the message. The external environment plays a critical role in the shaping and comprehension of your arguments. The environment can include something as simple as the temperature of a judge's chambers, or as complex as the political landscape in which a decision is being made. For purposes of this chapter, we will refer to the environment simply as the context.[1]

1. This four-part persuasion model for legal advocacy reflects the work of Carl Hovland and his Yale Attitude Change Model, a landmark study in the 1950s that examined the science of influence. C.I. Hovland, I.L. Janis, & H.H. Kelley, Communication and Persuasion (1953).

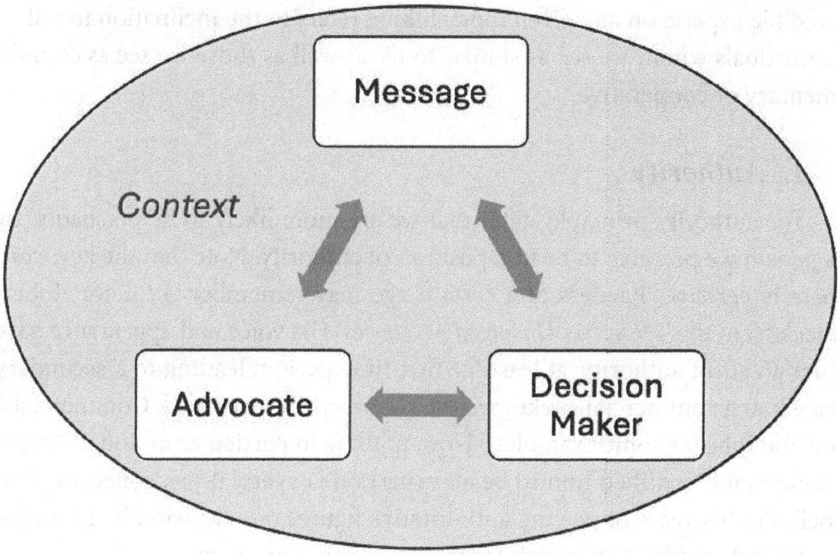

The rest of this chapter discusses each component of this four-part persuasion process. We start by analyzing the role of the messenger, or advocate, in the persuasion process. Next, we'll examine the characteristics of the Decision-Maker and the science behind how people make decisions, big or small. We then look at the Message itself, suggesting ways to tailor your writing for optimal influence. The chapter concludes with a reminder that the external environment, or Context, always plays a role in determining the effectiveness of our persuasive messages.

A. The advocate

Any message begins with the messenger. Whether you're writing a lengthy appellate brief or a one-page letter to a client, you are always a part of your message. And as such, you are an inextricable part of the persuasion process.

Think back to the example at the start of this chapter—about a friend convincing you to try a new restaurant. Remember the times you have found yourself in the same or a similar situation. In going along with your friend's suggestion, how much of your decision was based on objective evidence, and how much was simply based on trusting your friend? If your answer was based more on trust, then you're not alone.

When it comes to persuasion, the credibility and likeability of the messenger cannot be discounted. Renowned psychology and marketing expert Dr. Robert Cialdini includes authority and liking among his seven principles of persuasion.[2] Authority refers to the tendency to believe those we deem to be credible experts on any given topic. Liking refers to the inclination to follow individuals whom we see as similar to us, as well as those we see as complimentary or cooperative.

1. Authority

The authority principle states that we are more likely to be persuaded by a person we perceive to be in a position of authority. Note that the key word here is *perceive.* Readers of a certain age may remember the actor Robert Stack from the TV series *Unsolved Mysteries.* His voice and appearance gave him an air of authority, at least for that time period, leading to a secondary career as a commercial spokesperson. (Look up "Robert Stack Commercials" on YouTube for some examples.) Now, nothing in particular in Robert Stack's background qualified him to be an expert on lawyers, Pepsi, coffee, or Taco Bell. But his years of playing authoritative figures on television lent him the perceived credibility to vouch for these and other products.

This principle extends to appellate advocacy. Social scientists have found that in practice before the U.S. Supreme Court, the current U.S. Solicitor General will prevail more often than any other type of attorney.[3] To serve as the attorney who represents the entire U.S. government before the Supreme Court lends a person a great deal of authority, and in turn, credibility.

Even if you're not the Solicitor General, the authority principle of influence can increase your persuasive power as an appellate advocate. The building blocks of credibility coincide with the fundamentals of good lawyering. In your writing and speaking, you want the audience to perceive you as having some degree of expertise in your topic. When it comes to appellate briefs and other court documents, proper citations to legal authority can go a long way toward establishing credibility. The reader may infer that you have put a good deal of time and thought into researching the law and applying it properly. Of course, good writing also increases credibility. Typos and other errors indicate a brief that was constructed in a careless or hasty manner.

When it comes to oral argument, presenting yourself professionally can enhance your authority. Think carefully about your speaking style. If you tend to speak quietly, or quickly, or timidly, you may consider working with a speaking coach or consulting one of the many books or videos on speaking authoritatively. Keep in mind that the goal is not to change your voice or sound like a different person. Rather, you're striving to sound like a more authoritative

---

2. Robert B. Cialdini, Influence: The Psychology of Persuasion (rev. ed. 2007).

3. *See* Morgan L.W. Hazelton & Rachael K. Hinkle, *What Social Science Can Teach Us Regarding Briefing*, 28 J. Legal Writing Inst. 305, 318–19 (2024).

version of yourself. Chapter 11, Mastering Oral Argument: From Preparation to Delivery, has some other tips for enhancing your speaking style.

2. *Liking*

In the context of persuasion, the liking principle encompasses distinct yet overlapping concepts. First, we tend to be more influenced by people that we find *likeable*. Second, we are more easily persuaded by people whom we perceive to be *like us*. Likeability can include both superficial characteristics and more profound behaviors. It may be no surprise in our image-obsessed culture that people perceived as physically attractive are often deemed more persuasive. Perhaps you have heard of the halo effect, where all sorts of positive qualities are attributed to a person based solely on their physical attractiveness. (Fans of the Tina Fey comedy *30 Rock* may remember "The Bubble," an episode where Liz Lemon's boyfriend Drew is treated as an expert tennis coach, motorcyclist, and doctor based on his handsomeness.) Unfortunately, these superficial aspects of likeability play upon biases, both conscious and unconscious. In addition, reliance on physical appearance for likeability often reinforces negative aspects of culture like sexism and ableism.

When it comes to lawyering, however, an individual's behaviors carry more influence than appearance. Something as simple as displaying good manners can make a person more likable and, in turn, more influential. A likable person extends courtesy to everyone they deal with, including court staff and judicial assistants. Even indirect contact, e.g., through court filings, provides opportunities for courteous behavior. An attorney can extend courtesy through cooperation, following court rules and agreeing to opposing counsel's requests for extensions, for example.

Beyond likeability, the liking principle encompasses the notion that, consciously or not, we are more likely to follow a person we deem to be similar or familiar to us. Have you ever heard this: "They're from [fill in the town, university, or employer], so they must be a good person"? Chances are the speaker is from the same town, went to the same university, or works for the same employer. Repeated contact with a person also increases liking through familiarity. The more you appear before a certain court, the more you can benefit from familiarity (assuming you make a positive impression each time). Social science research supports this: "As attorneys appear before a court repeatedly, they not only obtain important insight, but also gain the court's trust."[4]

4. Hazelton & Hinkle, *supra* note 3, at 317.

3. *Strategies for advocates: Increasing authority and likeability*

You can employ several strategies for increasing your **authority** as an advocate. Although at this stage in your career you may not consider yourself an expert, remember that the goal is to be *perceived* as an expert. To increase authority, you can:

- Ensure arguments are fully supported by legal authority with properly formatted citations.
- File documents free of grammar and spelling errors.
- Dress professionally, with a level of formality appropriate to the situation.
- Prepare thoroughly for oral arguments and speak with authority.

When it comes to **likeability**, it's important to remember that the goal isn't to be liked by everyone. As the aphorism goes, no one can please all of the people all of the time. Rather, the goal is to present yourself in a way that makes it easier for people to like you if they are so inclined. A simple way is to be as courteous as possible when interacting with judges and court personnel. Although we commonly think of courtesy as displaying good manners in face-to-face interactions, a courteous advocate can also be one who does the following:

- Meets deadlines
- Agrees to reasonable requests for extensions by opposing counsel
- Follows formatting rules
- Avoids intemperate language in briefs or oral argument

When it comes to the second component of liking, similarity, some factors may be beyond your control. Perhaps you're in the same age range as a judge; perhaps you went to the same law school or grew up in the same city. Or perhaps not. At times, you can use your knowledge of the court and its judges to make strategic choices. For example, if you know the court tends to be more (or less) formal or conservative, you can use that knowledge when deciding what to wear or how to present yourself.

If you appear frequently before the same court, you can take advantage of familiarity, another aspect of liking. Being a familiar name or face to a judge could prove advantageous — but only if your name or face has a positive association. As you may have guessed, this circles back to likeability. Courtesy, civility, and professionalism, whether in the short or long run, can go far in establishing your likeability and influence.

Discussion Questions

1. Consider a time when someone persuaded you. It can be as simple as a commercial or online review of a product. To what extent did the messenger, or advocate, play a role in the persuasion process?
2. In addition to the suggestions above, what other ways can you think of to increase your authority and likeability?

B. The decision-maker

Although the persuasion process begins with the advocate, the outcome of this process depends on the decision-maker. Therefore, our discussion of the persuasion process continues with how to better understand the key audience for our persuasive writing and oral advocacy.

Nearly every type of legal writing involves either persuading someone to make a decision or memorializing a decision that has been made. Obvious examples include appellate briefs or trial-level briefs accompanying motions. In those instances, the decision-makers are judges, and the advocate/lawyer is requesting them to take certain action.

Less obvious examples include documents like client advice letters. The recipient — the client — is the decision-maker; they must decide whether to accept or reject the lawyer's advice. Thus, even though advice letters are meant to convey objective legal analysis, they are still persuasive in nature. The lawyer must persuade the client that the lawyer is credible and their reasoning is sound.

Given that the decision-maker is the focus in appellate advocacy, understanding how people process information and make decisions can prove advantageous in maximizing persuasiveness. Decision science has emerged as an academic discipline in the last few decades, combining psychology, neuroscience, and behavioral economics.[5] Below are some key concepts from decision science as they relate to the art (and science) of legal writing.

---

5. *See What Is Decision Science?*, Ctr. for Health Decision Sci., Harv. T.H. Chan Sch. of Pub. Health, https://chds.hsph.harvard.edu/approaches/what-is-decision-science/ (last visited Sept. 7, 2024); Leigh Buchanan & Andrew O'Connell, *A Brief History of Decision Making*, Harv. Bus. Rev. (Jan. 2006), https://hbr.org/2006/01/a-brief-history-of-decision-making.

1. Fast and slow thinking

Before making a decision, a person has to process the information relevant to the choice at hand. Quite often, the act of processing information is so quick it seems automatic. Think about the last time you took a bite of food. Did you stop to examine the substance on your fork, think about whether it was food or not, analyze whether it was safe to eat, and figure out how to get it into your mouth? Likely not; rather, you took a bite without consciously thinking about it.

In truth, your brain actually was processing information and making decisions before you ate that bite, but it was doing so in a manner that was effortless and imperceptible. This is the type of thinking that Nobel-prize winning psychologist Daniel Kahneman has labeled System 1. In his bestselling book *Thinking, Fast and Slow*,[6] Kahneman defines System 1 as automatic and effortless. In System 1, our thinking is unconscious and more emotional than rational.

Of course, not all thoughts and decisions can be effortless and automatic. When our brains have to slow down and concentrate on processing information, we shift into what Kahneman calls System 2 — slow thinking. When we are in System 2, our thinking is not only slow but deliberate, rational, and effortful. Indeed, we can think of System 2 as being difficult compared to System 1. Imagine the process of parallel parking a car on a city street versus parking in the familiar garage or driveway of your home. Unless you have worked as a valet in the past, parallel parking likely requires much more effort and concentration than parking in your usual spot. In fact, it may even provoke anxiety. This is characteristic of System 2; the effort involved in being deliberate and vigilant can also be stressful.

According to Kahneman, the ability to make decisions often relies on System 2 working in conjunction with System 1. Even when making a weighty or complex decision, if we are able to process and understand information using our effortless System 1, we are more likely to trust it. However, when we have to shift away from effortless System 1 and strain our minds to make sense of information by relying primarily on System 2, we are more likely to be wary and suspicious. It follows that a person who feels wary and suspicious is less likely to be receptive to another person's efforts to persuade.

For maximum persuasion, then, an appellate advocate should create an effortless experience for the decision-maker. Even when discussing complex facts and legal doctrines, an advocate should explain them in an easy-to-digest manner. Concrete tips to do so are provided below, under Strategies for

---

6. Daniel Kahneman, Thinking, Fast and Slow (2011).

Advocates. You can also follow the advice found in Chapter 8, Fundamentals of Good Legal Writing.

2. *Mental shortcuts and cognitive biases*

Do you feel like you have to process more information on a daily basis than you did one, five, or ten years ago? Well, it's not just a feeling. Studies show that we are browsing, reading, and listening to more content with each passing year. For example, a 2009 New York Times article reported that individuals were consuming 34 gigabytes of data each day.[7] Per legal practice management software company MetaJure, in 2015, its customers "were creating or receiving more than 70 documents every day."[8] Culturally, we have developed slang to describe this phenomenon: "information overload," "drinking from a firehose," or even "information explosion."

To manage this high volume of information without becoming paralyzed in our decision-making, our brains rely on shortcuts and rules of thumb. Another term for this is *heuristics*, i.e., "mental shortcuts that can facilitate problem-solving and probability judgments."[9] Using heuristics is a method to process complex information. When faced with novel or complicated information, our brains default to transforming the information into something easier to deal with. This allows us, at a subconscious level, to turn hard decisions into easier ones, and to default to the easier decision when possible. Although heuristics allow us to make a multitude of daily decisions in an efficient manner, they can also lead to systematic errors in thinking that psychologists refer to as cognitive biases. In other words, relying on our gut feelings may not always lead to the right answer.

Estimating probabilities provides an example of cognitive bias. Here's an example: You toss a coin six times and keep track of whether it lands on heads (H) or tails (T). Which sequence is more likely?

Choice 1: H T H T T H
Choice 2: H H H T T T

7. Nick Bilton, *Part of the Daily American Diet, 34 Gigabytes of Data*, N.Y. Times, Dec. 10, 2009, sec. B, p. 6, https://www.nytimes.com/2009/12/10/technology/10data.html.

8. *Surprising Statistics about Lawyer Information Overload*, MetaJure (Apr. 25, 2016), https://metajure.com/surprising-statistics-lawyer-information-overload/.

9. *Why Do We Take Mental Shortcuts? Heuristics, Explained*, Decision Lab, https://thedecisionlab.com/biases/heuristics (last visited Sept. 7, 2024).

They are both equally likely (three heads, three tails). However, most people think the first is more likely, because it looks more random. The random-looking sequence fits the gut feeling of what a random coin toss should look like. This example demonstrates how relying on a mental shortcut can lead to erroneous thinking.

Another example of a cognitive bias that can influence decision-making is loss aversion. Human beings tend to feel a greater emotional impact when losing something than when gaining something. To illustrate, imagine you have two choices. Choice 1, I will give you $5. Choice 2, I will give you $10, then you have to give me $5. Which option do you prefer? The net result is the same, but most people will prefer Choice 1, which is framed solely as a gain, to Choice 2, which involves giving something up.

As legal writers, we want to avoid relying on bias in our writing. Certainly, judges want to avoid relying on bias in decision-making; however, it can be hard to avoid. When faced with complex information, decision-makers often revert to mental shortcuts, including cognitive biases, to make decisions. This inclination can be exacerbated by external influences such as fatigue and emotional stress.

What's the takeaway? Everything you say (and write) matters. How you present choices will influence how a decision-maker will think about them. Put another way, even if you're not thinking about how you're presenting information, you're still influencing your decision-maker, just inadvertently. Doing so means that you may be influencing a decision-maker in a manner that's detrimental to your client's position. Later in this chapter, we examine specific ways to craft your argument that account for the cognitive biases your reader may be experiencing.

3. *Cognitive load and decision fatigue*

Cognitive load theory deals with the amount of information our brains can process at any given time. Have you ever had so many apps running on your laptop that it starts to slow down? Our brains go through a similar process when we are dealing with a lot of information. Simply put, cognitive load theory tells us that our brains have a finite capacity when it comes to accurately processing information. Related to cognitive load is decision fatigue, sometimes referred to as ego depletion. Decision fatigue is a psychological phenomenon surrounding a person's ability or capacity to make decisions. The theory is that a human's ability to make decisions can get worse after making many decisions. This fatigue applies to all decisions, not simply the large or more difficult ones.

Decision fatigue of this nature could apply to any scenario where sequential decisions must be made. It's likely you have experienced decision fatigue after a long day at school or work, where you have had to think hard about various legal topics and make decisions regarding your own day or a client's case. At the end of that long day, you may find yourself more likely to resort to a default choice for dinner rather than venture out to a new restaurant. Decision fatigue may also underlie the well-worn advice to get a good night's sleep before making any important decision.

Putting together the possible influences on a decision-maker's thinking, we can draw a few conclusions:

- Keeping the decision-maker in a state of effortless thinking (System 1) will make them less anxious, less suspicious, and more receptive to our message than if they have to engage in deliberate, effortful thinking (System 2).
- Presenting an argument in an overly complex manner can lead the decision-maker to rely on mental shortcuts and cognitive biases, which can create errors in reasoning.
- Creating or exacerbating decision fatigue can lead the decision-maker to resort to default thinking and impaired reasoning.

4. *Strategies for advocates: Persuading the decision-maker*

Knowing that your reader/decision-maker is likely to experience the effects described above, as an advocate you can make strategic choices to present your arguments in a way that minimizes cognitive load and decision fatigue. The strategies below apply to both written and oral advocacy.

a. Use natural, conversational language

Even when writing (or speaking) about the law, you should strive to communicate simply and fluently. Doing so allows the reader to stay largely within the effortless System 1 way of thinking, shifting into System 2 only when necessary to process complex legal topics. As discussed above, this tactic may help the reader stay more relaxed and open to your message. In addition, using easy-to-understand language and sentence structure can help you avoid contributing to the reader's cognitive load.

To be certain, appellate briefs should strike an appropriately professional tone. However, it's possible to achieve that tone while writing conversationally. As discussed in more detail in Chapter 8, perhaps the best advice for writing professionally is to be respectful when describing lawyers, judges, and parties in your appellate brief. Word choice plays a role as well. Although conversational writing prefers using simpler words over "legalese," an advocate can also avoid casual jargon or idiomatic expressions (unless deliberately used for emphatic or rhetorical purposes).

Now, some lawyers believe that writing about complex subjects in a complex manner is a way to showcase the author's expertise. One might think that a reader who has trouble understanding a document would mentally defer to the author's superior knowledge. Interestingly enough, research has shown that readers actually perceive an author to be *less* intelligent if their writing is difficult to understand.[10] Indeed, the consistency of this research prompted one scholar to offer this advice: "Write clearly and simply if you can, and you'll be more likely to be thought of as intelligent."[11]

Complicated Language	Simple Language
As referenced hereinafter	As stated below
In the process of	While, during
Aside from the fact that	Regardless, nonetheless
At the point in time that	When
On or about the date in question	On, when
In the event that	If
Until such time as/that	Until

b. Pay attention to formatting

Another way to help the reader avoid cognitive load and decision fatigue is to make your briefs visually appealing. Many judges, lawyers, and scholars have written about best formatting practices, and from their advice we can glean some conventional wisdom. Chapter 7 provides specific advice on formatting briefs, covering topics like typeface, headings, and white space.

---

10. Daniel M. Oppenheimer, *Consequences of Erudite Vernacular Utilized Irrespective of Necessity: Problems with Using Long Words Needlessly*, 20 Applied Cognitive Psych. 139, 142 (2006).

11. *Id.* at 153.

Sometimes, legal writing conventions create their own challenges to achieving fluency. For example, string citations and block quotations can create a visual interruption. Take, for example, this excerpt from the petitioner's brief in *Bostock v. Clayton County*:

> Rather, the Court has consistently upheld a classification-based, rather than a class-based, approach in applying the statute. As the *Manhart* Court explained, Title VII requires "a focus on fairness to individuals rather than classes" and that focus is "unambiguous." 435 U.S. at 708-09 (emphasis supplied); *see also, e.g., Phillips v. Martin Marietta Corp.*, 400 U.S. 542 (1971) (per curiam); *Manhart*, 435 U.S. 702; *Connecticut v. Teal*, 457 U.S. 440, 455 (1982); *Price Waterhouse*, 490 U.S. 228; *Int'l Union, United Auto., Aerospace & Agr. Implement Workers of Am., UAW v. Johnson Controls, Inc.*, 499 U.S. 187, 192, 197 (1991) ("Johnson Controls"); *Oncale*, 523 U.S. 75.[12]

When the reader transitions from the text to the string citation, reading becomes more effortful (and therefore more likely to cause a shift to System 2 thinking). Because the citation is written in "Bluebook language," not natural language, the reader must slow down and expend more mental energy to make sense of it. This effort can increase cognitive load, thereby disrupting the message and fatiguing the reader. Or, perhaps worse, the reader may skip over the citation to avoid the effort altogether.

A similar phenomenon may occur with block quotations. For one, a block quotation, by its very nature, contains fifty or more words written or spoken by another person. Their language may disrupt your efforts at keeping your message natural and conversational. Additionally, block quotations are often formatted as a chunk of single-spaced text. Reducing the white space in the quotation makes it more difficult to read, leading to the same cognitive load concerns described above.

Armed with this information, advocates can make strategic choices regarding string citations and block quotations. Sometimes they are unavoidable. But, when alternatives are available, you should use them.

c. Be selective when presenting facts and arguments

When it comes to the content of your writing, you'll want to avoid unnecessary details. For example, when writing a statement of facts, do you need to

12. Brief for Petitioner at 16, Bostock v. Clayton Cnty., 590 U.S. 644 (2020) (No. 17-1618).

include all dates, addresses, names, etc.? It can tire the reader who is trying to sort important information from irrelevant information. The same advice applies to arguments. When presenting multiple arguments, place the most compelling argument first unless a different order is dictated by logic. Consider whether to present all possible arguments or to focus on the strongest ones. You want to take the burden off the reader to choose the best argument.

You also want to consider the role of mental shortcuts when presenting choices. For example, when you ask an appellate court to reverse a lower court, you are asking the court to disagree with a decision. For most people, agreeing with the status quo is an easier default position than disagreeing. With that in mind, think of how you can frame the decision differently. Perhaps you can emphasize that reversing the lower court will actually allow the appellate court to *agree* with case law precedent. (Framing is discussed further below in section C, The Message.)

Discussion Questions

1. Think of a situation where you experienced decision fatigue. What factors exacerbated it? What did you do to overcome it?
2. This chapter identified several cognitive biases, such as loss aversion. Look up a list of cognitive biases. Which other biases could come into play in legal decision-making? As an advocate, what strategies could you use to deal with these biases?

C. The message

The third component of the persuasion process is the message. In achieving a client's goals, it's not enough for an advocate to understand themselves and the decision-maker. A successful advocate must craft a compelling message, one which is designed to convey the advocate's arguments with maximum persuasive force.

In appellate advocacy, the message is the appellate brief itself and, to a lesser extent, the oral argument. Given that the goal of this book is to teach effective brief writing and oral advocacy, you may wonder why the message is not the first component in the persuasion process. The answer is simple: to be effective, a message must be designed for the decision-maker. To use an analogy, think of a dressmaker. They could design and create the most beautiful dress in the world, made of luxurious materials in eye-catching colors. However, if the dress is not properly tailored to fit the intended wearer, then the dress has failed to serve its purpose.

In the same vein, the discussion below will provide tools for you to tailor your message to best fit your appellate advocacy objectives. Doing so requires understanding the needs of the decision-maker as discussed above, along with any unique contextual circumstances. We start by examining the concept of legal writing "rules" and the theories that support them. Next, we closely examine additional concepts from decision science and other disciplines that help us craft compelling and forceful arguments.

1. *The "rules" of persuasive writing*

As noted at the start of this chapter, lawyers often focus on the message itself when developing their advocacy skills. Legal writing courses typically provide rules to follow, such as:

- Do not write overly long sentences.
- Avoid legalese.
- Write persuasive point headings.
- Bury bad facts between good facts.

Reading through these rules, you likely realize that they are designed around how the written word affects the reader. Long sentences and legalese can increase cognitive load and reduce understanding and decision-making capability. Busy readers tend to skim, thereby relying on point headings more than text. Putting good facts up front can alter the lens through which the reader views the subsequent bad facts.

Thus, although these are generally good rules to follow, they are not intrinsically good. Instead, they are only as good as their ability to influence the decision-maker. Rather than automatically apply rules to your legal writing, we encourage you to examine the theories behind the rules. Some of these theories are outlined in the discussion above on the decision-maker. Below, we have described several other theories that come into play when crafting persuasive messages. These theories come from many disciplines — economics, policy-making, and storytelling, to name a few. Not every theory will be applicable to every persuasive document you write. But understanding these theories gives you the flexibility to deploy them as needed in any given situation.

2. *Strategies for advocates: Crafting a persuasive message*

Thus far in this chapter, you have learned ways to influence your reader by making your briefs easier to read. The advice below takes your writing strategy to the next level. By employing principles of priming, framing, and word choice, you can subtly persuade while staying within professional and ethical boundaries.

a. Priming and framing

Priming involves choosing *when* to present information to the reader. When you prime the reader, you choose to present certain information first in order to create an impression that colors the reader's perception of subsequently presented information. When properly primed, the reader will focus on certain information and even reject information that doesn't fit into their impression. Here's a simple word completion puzzle that demonstrates the power of priming:

Water -> Boat -> Fishing -> _AKE

Cookies -> Bread -> Oven -> _AKE

More likely than not, for the first puzzle you completed the word as "lake," and for the second you used the word "bake." In other words, your next, best guess was highly influenced by the prompts that preceded the puzzle.

Priming can also be used to stimulate emotions in a reader, which in turn influences decision-making.[13] An example of priming would be choosing to focus on graphic details in the statement of facts in an appellate brief. Reading about something emotionally stimulating such as a car accident tends to make people believe these events happen more often than they actually do. Thus, if you represent a client against a car manufacturer in a product liability case, you could use priming to your advantage by describing the underlying car accident early in the brief.

The priming effect also explains some frequently dispensed legal writing advice: introduce your theme early in the brief, and present facts from your client's perspective first. Chapter 10 discusses how to incorporate themes in the storytelling of a brief, but it makes sense to place the theme up front in your brief; doing so helps the reader view subsequent information through your carefully crafted lens. Presenting facts from the client's perspective first is a similar technique; the goal is to indirectly guide the reader to understand the relevant facts from your client's viewpoint, versus a neutral or opposing point of view.

---

13. Kathryn M. Stanchi, *The Power of Priming in Legal Advocacy*, 89 Or. L. Rev. 305, 310 (2010).

Exercise: Priming in a statement of facts

The excerpt below comes from *United States v. Hasan*, a case before the U.S. Court of Appeals for the Armed Forces.[14] Hasan was convicted of thirteen counts of murder and thirty-two counts of attempted murder as part of a highly publicized shooting at Fort Hood in 2009. The sentences below open the Statement of Facts. Can you identify how the author used priming to present the client's viewpoint?

> On November 5, 2009, Appellant went on a shooting rampage at the Fort Hood Soldier Readiness Processing (SRP) center. He murdered thirteen people—twelve U.S. Army soldiers and one Department of the Army civilian employee—and attempted to murder thirty-two others. Appellant only stopped shooting when he was shot and seriously wounded by law enforcement officers responding to the scene.

Framing involves choosing *how* to present information to a reader. A classic example is framing an eight-ounce glass with four ounces of water as either half empty or half full. Although both descriptions are factually accurate (and therefore, ethically permissible), one portrays an optimist's perspective and the other... well, you get the picture. In the context of appellate practice, an advocate can use framing techniques both when describing facts and when explaining decisions/outcomes.

Let's use a simple scenario to demonstrate how you can frame facts. A person ("the driver") is driving to work when they receive a call on their cell phone. A family member is calling in a panic because the driver's young daughter seems to be missing. The driver turns the car around and speeds home, asking questions of the family member all the while. Just short of reaching their home, the driver makes a wide turn and collides with another driver ("the claimant").

How might an advocate for the driver frame these facts? Most likely, an advocate would want to emphasize the facts that put the driver in a sympathetic light. The driver is a concerned parent who puts family first. When considering how to describe the driver's action, an advocate would choose words carefully. Was the driver "frantic" with concern? That word implies potentially erratic behavior—maybe not the best choice. "Worried" might work better here. (Word choice is discussed further, below.) Employing the priming technique, the advocate would place these sympathetic facts up

---

14. Appellee's Brief at 5, United States v. Hasan, 84 M.J. 181 (C.A.A.F. 2024) (No. 20130781).

front before providing the less sympathetic facts (speeding, using phone, wide turn).

Of course, an advocate for the claimant would take the opposite approach. From the claimant's perspective, the driver engaged in a series of careless behaviors (speeding, using phone, wide turn). Moreover, the claimant may want to emphasize that the driver disregarded everyone else on the road, thinking only of themselves and their own family.

Now, here we may run into a problem. Any time an advocate employs persuasive techniques like framing, they must do so within ethical boundaries. An advocate cannot make up facts or misrepresent the facts, including a misrepresentation by omission. Depending on the record before the court, an advocate for the claimant may overstep by writing "The driver raced down the road with complete disregard for anyone in their way, thinking only of themselves and their family the entire time." An advocate could effectively frame the facts by relying less on word choice and more on how facts are juxtaposed: "While driving twenty miles over the speed limit, the driver swung around a corner in a residential neighborhood, crashing into the claimant. The driver was on the phone with his family member the entire time." This description places unsympathetic facts in positions of emphasis — the beginning and end. Using the phrase "the entire time" implies that the driver was distracted throughout the entire sequence of events without having to state this explicitly.

The framing technique can also be used when presenting potential outcomes to a decision-maker. In broad terms, an appellate court has a range of choices for any given case, e.g., affirm, reverse, remand, vacate, or make no decision based on justiciability. The consequences of these choices may also vary, depending on the circumstances. An appellate court could potentially establish new law or enjoin enforcement of an existing law, for example. Advocates should consider how to frame choices and outcomes: broad or narrow, default or risky, etc.

An advocate can strategically frame these choices to the client's advantage. For example, is affirming the lower court a vote for the status quo? Would reversal be an opportunity to right a wrong? Understanding the particular panel of appellate judges can come into play (Chapter 12 discusses the role of judicial analytics.) Another factor to consider is the standard of review. An advocate would likely frame an issue quite differently if the appellate court is applying a *de novo* standard rather than abuse of discretion. The context, as discussed below, also comes into play. Certain decisions may be more politically fraught than others, for instance.

Exercise: Framing the issues

In this example, the parties disagreed over whether the State of Arizona recognized a real-property common-law cause of action called "boundary by acquiescence." How did the advocates take different approaches in framing the issues?

> ***Brief for Appellees/Petitioners:***
>
> Boundary by acquiescence is a rarely used equitable cause of action the elements of which vary among those states that recognize it.... There is no Arizona Supreme Court case affirmatively recognizing the cause of action of boundary by acquiescence or defining its elements.[15]
>
> ***Brief for Appellants/Respondents:***
>
> At the outset, there is no need for this Court to "affirmatively recognize" boundary by acquiescence for it to be a valid cause of action. When Arizona became a state, it adopted the common law to the extent it is not inconsistent with its statutes.... Boundary by acquiescence is a classic common-law claim, and [Appellees] have not cited any authority that it has been repealed by the legislature. Section 1-201 thus makes it unnecessary for this Court to "affirmatively recognize" the claim before it can be pled as a cause of action.[16]

b. Abstract vs. Concrete language

As previewed by the above discussion on priming and framing, word choice can be serious business for appellate advocates. Graphic or emotional language can be used to prime readers to view information through a particular lens. When it comes to framing, word choice can be used to narrow or broaden the scope of a legal issue. Even apart from priming and framing, word choice is a powerful tool for persuasion.

In some ways, an advocate's ability to persuade is similar to a magician's ability to craft an illusion. Both processes rely on focusing the audience's attention in a particular direction. A magician's sleight of hand works best when the audience looks away from the mechanics of the illusion, i.e., when

15. Petition for Review at 5, Beck v. Neville, 540 P.3d 906 (Ariz. 2024) (No. CV-22-0134-PR), 2022 WL 20014365, at *5 (internal citations omitted).

16. Respondents' Supplemental Brief at 7–8, Beck v. Neville, 540 P.3d 906 (Ariz. 2024) (No. CV-22-0134-PR), 2022 WL 20014366, at *7–8 (internal citations omitted).

their attention is misdirected toward a gesture, voice, or even another person on the stage. Similarly, an advocate crafts a persuasive story by drawing the reader's attention to certain details while downplaying others.

One technique for using word choice to your advantage is to deliberately choose either concrete or abstract language, depending on your persuasive goals.

Abstract	Concrete
Tall	Looming
Loud	Deafening
Bright	Dazzling
Quiet	Aloof
Happy	Joyous

In his book *Magic Words*,[17] Jonah Berger points out some distinctions between concrete and abstract language in the business context. Concrete language:

- Helps people better understand complex topics
- Makes information more memorable
- Effectively conveys emotion

Similarly, abstract language tends to work in the opposite direction. Because it is less specific, abstract language can be used to convey big-picture ideas without becoming too granular.

The same distinctions hold true in legal writing. Take the example above from *United States v. Hasan*. The author could have written that Hasan "went on a shooting spree" or "engaged in an active shooting." Instead, the author used the term "shooting rampage." Without a doubt, the word rampage provokes an emotional reaction. It allows the reader to better visualize what happens. It's memorable. In a similar manner, abstract language can be used to deemphasize information by making it less vivid and, thus, more forgettable.

Like many choices a writer makes, the benefits must be weighed against the drawbacks. Writing in a concrete, vivid manner can grab a reader's attention. However, language deemed to be too emotional can work against an advocate. Empirical studies of the U.S. Supreme Court demonstrate that justices are more likely to decide against a party whose brief contains emotional

---

17. Jonah Berger, Magic Words: What to Say to Get Your Way (2023).

language.[18] Determining when colorful language crosses the line into overly emotional language requires experience, both in writing and before your particular court. A trusted colleague's review of your draft can help greatly in this regard.

Discussion Questions and Exercises

1. Identify one of your favorite authors (fiction or nonfiction). What do you like about their writing? How do they use word choice to keep you engaged?
2. Think of a simple children's story, like *Goldilocks and the Three Bears* or *Little Red Riding Hood*. Now, rewrite a passage from this story using abstract, complicated language. What words or techniques did you find yourself relying on? How many of those are you currently using in your own writing?

c. The context

The final component of the persuasion process is the context. Although this chapter discusses context last, it surrounds every other component of the process and is therefore equally important for an advocate to consider. Indeed, understanding the environment in which you are filing an appeal can sometimes be the key consideration in determining how to shape a persuasive argument. The Rules of Professional Conduct inform lawyers that, in addition to legal advice, they are permitted to "refer ... to other considerations such as moral, economic, social and political factors that may be relevant to the client's situation."[19] Likewise, in formulating an appeal, advocates should consider the **moral, economic, social, and political** context of the decision to be made.

Clients are another component of context. Appellate arguments are unique because, in many instances, they seek an outcome that establishes a legal precedent. At times, a client may seek only to establish precedent regarding "law of the case," i.e., a ruling that is binding only within subsequent litigation of the client's legal matter. At other times, a client seeks to modify, extend, or reverse existing legal precedents in a manner that reaches far beyond the client's case. Thus, the **client's objectives** provide an important contextual factor. Understanding whether a client seeks a narrow or broad outcome will affect the nature of arguments the advocate makes.

---

18. Hazelton & Hinkle, *supra* note 3, at 323–34.
19. Model Rules of Pro. Conduct r. 2.1 (Am. Bar Ass'n 1983).

Finally, an advocate must consider the impact of **professional reputation.** As discussed in Chapter 3, Ethics and Professionalism in Appellate Advocacy, creating your professional identity is a critical part of practicing in an ethical manner. Whether you work on it proactively or not, your professional reputation will precede you. To be a credible advocate, you should take care to abide by the Rules of Professional Conduct and your jurisdiction's professionalism oath or creed.

III. Conclusion

This chapter has provided a comprehensive overview of the persuasion process. Rather than memorize a set of rules, you should think about persuasion as an interactive process that incorporates your status as an advocate, the characteristics of your decision-maker, the components of your message, and the surrounding context.

Discussion Questions and Exercises

1. Below is an excerpt from the Respondent's brief in *Mahanoy Area School District v. B.L.*.[20] Identify at least three persuasive techniques that the advocate employed (e.g., priming or framing). How do these techniques relate to the persuasion process (the advocate, the decision-maker, the message, and the context)?

> This case is about the free speech rights of young people outside of school—at church, during weekend protests, at home, or, as in this case, at a local convenience store with a friend on a Saturday afternoon. Outside of the school environment, young people have the right to find their voices without being unduly chilled, their parents have the right to manage their upbringing, and others have the right to hear what they have to say.
>
> Petitioner seeks to change that. It would take *Tinker v. Des Moines Independent Community School District*, 393 U.S. 503 (1969), where this Court has never gone. In its view, *Tinker*'s rule, which permits schools to punish speech if listeners might react disruptively, would become not just something young people must endure at school, but a con-

20. 594 U.S. 180 (2021).

stant feature of their lives. It would subject young people to *Tinker*'s vague "disruption" standard 24 hours a day, 365 days a year, deterring them from saying anything that school authorities might deem controversial, critical, or politically incorrect, and therefore disruptive. Petitioner's only limitation, that the speech be "directed" to the school and reasonably likely to reach it, is defined so broadly that it would encompass all speech to another student, no matter its content, and all content that is school related. For young people whose contacts are primarily classmates and for whom school affairs are a frequent topic, that is no limit at all.

2. The excerpt below is from Justice Neil Gorsuch's dissenting opinion in *Arizona v. Navajo Nation*.[21] In this excerpt, Justice Gorsuch provides both an analogy and a historical reference. How do these techniques accomplish his goal of persuading the reader that the majority reached an incorrect conclusion? Did you find these choices to be effective?

   Where do the Navajo go from here? To date, their efforts to find out what water rights the United States holds for them have produced an experience familiar to any American who has spent time at the Department of Motor Vehicles. The Navajo have waited patiently for someone, anyone, to help them, only to be told (repeatedly) that they have been standing in the wrong line and must try another. To this day, the United States has never denied that the Navajo may have water rights in the mainstream of the Colorado River (and perhaps elsewhere) that it holds in trust for the Tribe. Instead, the government's constant refrain is that the Navajo can have all they ask for; they just need to go somewhere else and do something else first. The Navajo have tried it all. They have written federal officials. They have moved this Court to clarify the United States' responsibilities when representing them. They have sought to intervene directly in water-related litigation. And when all of those efforts were rebuffed, they brought a claim seeking to compel the United States to make good on its treaty obligations by providing an accounting of what water rights it holds on their behalf. At each turn, they have received the same answer: "Try again." When this routine first began in earnest, Elvis was still making his rounds on The Ed Sullivan Show.

21. 599 U.S. 555, 598–99 (2023).

Chapter 10

Advanced Persuasive Writing Techniques

In this chapter, you will learn:

- A paradigm to help you write more persuasively
- How to harness the power of storytelling in your legal writing

I. Introduction

In Chapter 9, you learned how to employ certain techniques, like priming and framing, to take advantage of the psychology of persuasion. This chapter provides additional concepts to maximize the persuasive value of your appellate briefs. First, you'll learn another paradigm, this time to conceptualize the many persuasive writing techniques available to you as an advocate. Then, you'll learn how incorporating storytelling techniques can help your reader understand complex arguments and relate better to your clients.

II. The three Ps of persuasive writing

First-year law students, new to legal writing, sometimes struggle to conceptualize the idea of persuasive legal writing. Typically, these students will spend their first semester learning how to write so-called "objective" legal documents, like a legal memorandum. In the second semester, students are tasked with writing a "persuasive" document, like a trial- or appellate-level brief. With this assignment, legal writing professors often provide several admonishments:

- Don't distort the law or the facts.
- Don't start every sentence with adverbs like "clearly" or "obviously."
- Don't use dramatic language for emphasis.

It's no wonder that some students find this process confusing. In truth, the foundation of persuasive writing is *good* writing. Typos, grammatical errors, and verbose sentences will distract a reader from any persuasive polish that you have applied to your brief. If you were to choose only one focus for your legal writing, we would advise nailing down the fundamentals, including the ACE method described in Chapter 8, before working on persuasion.

When you're ready to focus on the persuasive value of your writing, Chapter 9, The Science of Persuasion: Modern Theories and Strategies, provides a good deal of writing-related tips and how they tie into the psychology of influence. In addition to those tips, we recommend looking for these three Ps when checking your writing:

1. Perspective: Are you telling a story from your client's point of view? Are you framing legal rules from your client's perspective?
2. Perception: Are you choosing words not only for their literal meaning but also for how the reader perceives their meaning?
3. Position: Are you taking advantage of traditional positions of emphasis to highlight or downplay information, as necessary?

A. Perspective

Turning first to *perspective*, the idea here is to present both facts and the law from your client's point of view. Another way to conceptualize this is to ensure that any discussion of the facts and law is consistent with the theme of your client's argument. Later in this chapter, the section on storytelling provides some ideas for presenting the facts from your client's perspective.

You can present the law from your client's perspective by framing the legal rules persuasively. Legal rules, whether derived from constitutions, statutes, regulations, case law, or some combination, follow recognizable structures.

Legal Rules: Common Structures

Structure	Definition	Example
Element-based	Each component of the rule must be proven or met to result in a given consequence.	The intentional tort of battery requires intent, contact, harm, and damages.
Factor-based	The factfinder has the discretion to weigh either all relevant circumstances (i.e., a totality of the circumstances test) or a number of enumerated circumstances to reach a conclusion.	In determining a sentence, a court may consider aggravating and mitigating factors such as the seriousness of the crime, the defendant's criminal history, and the defendant's remorse.
If/then or trigger test	The first part of the rule must be satisfied before proceeding to the next part of the rule or triggering a particular consequence of the rule.	When the Department of Veterans Affairs receives an application for benefits, this triggers the VA's duty to assist the veteran in obtaining evidence to support the claim.
Balancing test	This is a type of factor test where two factors are balanced against each other.	Federal Rule of Evidence 403 requires weighing the probative value of evidence against its prejudicial impact.
General Rule + Exception(s)	Many legal rules contain exceptions or exemptions. Depending on the legal issue, a full articulation of the rule may require explaining both the general (default) rule and the exceptions or exemptions.	Federal Rule of Evidence 801 makes hearsay evidence inadmissible. Federal Rule of Evidence 803(2) provides an exception for excited utterances.

A legal rule's structure will often dictate the manner in which an advocate can frame the rule persuasively. For example, in a criminal case, the government must prove all elements of a crime beyond a reasonable doubt. Thus, a prosecutor may frame a legal rule in a manner that focuses on the consequence of proving all elements:

> "The jury must find the defendant guilty of assault if the defendant intentionally placed the victim in reasonable apprehension of imminent harmful or offensive contact."

Conversely, the defendant may frame the rule in a manner that focuses on only one element:

> "If the defendant's conduct was unintentional, then the jury cannot find her guilty of assault."

An advocate can frame a rule from the client's perspective by choosing how broadly or narrowly to draw the rule. Within ethical boundaries, an advocate can use language like "only," "always," "never," and "unless" to outline a rule's contours.

Framing Rules Broadly or Narrowly — Examples

Rule	Broad Framing	Narrow Framing
If a tenant provides the landlord reasonable notice, the tenant may deduct the cost of certain repairs from the rent.	A tenant is entitled to deduct the cost of certain repairs from the rent once the tenant provides reasonable notice.	A tenant cannot deduct the cost of certain repairs from the rent unless the tenant provides reasonable notice.
If a lower court makes a discretionary decision at trial, then the appellate court will use an abuse of discretion standard of review.	Appellate courts may always reverse a lower court's discretionary decision if the lower court abused its discretion.	An appellate court will not disturb a lower court's discretionary decision unless the lower court abused its discretion.

Exercise: Writing rules from a client's perspective

Select a legal rule from an appellate assignment you're currently working on or from a previous assignment.

1. What is the rule's structure?
2. Write the rule from your client's perspective. What words did you choose to frame the rule persuasively?
3. Now, write the rule from the opposing party's perspective. What words did you change?

B. Perception

The second P of persuasion is *perception*. When writing from your client's perspective, paying attention to word choice is critical. Ordinarily, a writer can choose among multiple words without losing meaning or accuracy. Take, for example, the sentence below:

> The captain steered the ship to the east, where the sun was shining in the morning sky.

This sentence paints a simple picture. It's a sunny morning, and the captain is on the water. Depending on your client's perspective, this sentence may perfectly convey the image and emotion you want the reader to perceive. But what if you want to emphasize the sun's brightness? Perhaps it was so bright that it affected the captain's ability to see an object on the horizon. In that case, you may write something like this:

> As the captain steered the ship to the east, the brilliant morning sun burst into view.

Here, the key words are "brilliant" and "burst." Describing the sun as "bright" is ordinary and expected. Using "brilliant" is unusual, and the word itself is vivid. Similarly, the verb "shining" is commonly associated with the sun; a reader may skim over that word without much thought. "Burst into view" is a less typical way to describe the sun, and it also evokes a feeling of surprise.

As described in Chapter 9, choosing words that are concrete and vivid will make what you're writing about more memorable and emotionally resonant. On the other hand, strategically choosing bland or neutral language removes emphasis.

Another way to alter the reader's perception is through repetition. Used judiciously, repeating key language can reinforce an image or concept in the reader's mind. One technique is to selectively quote a phrase from a legal authority and then repeat that phrase when applying the law to your client's facts. Let's say you're writing a brief about parody and copyright law. You decide to quote this colorful phrase from a leading case, *Campbell v. Acuff-Rose Music, Inc.*:[1]

> This is not, of course, to say that anyone who calls himself a parodist can skim the cream and get away scot free.

When applying the law, you can include a callback to this quote:

> Here, the Appellee took the subject, composition, and color from the Appellant's artwork and produced a cheap copy. He skimmed the cream, claiming parody after the fact.

Another technique is to repeat the structure of a phrase or sentence for rhetorical emphasis. We can look at some famous speeches for examples of this technique:

> "I came, I saw, I conquered." — Julius Caesar
>
> "[G]overnment of the people, by the people, for the people, shall not perish from the earth." — Abraham Lincoln
>
> "Ask not what your country can do for you — ask what you can do for your country." — John F. Kennedy

In your writing, you can use this technique to draw the reader's attention to a fact, policy, or legal standard. Keep in mind that this technique is most powerful when it stands out in your writing. Overuse can nullify its persuasive effect.

Of course, you can always use repetition in its simplest form by repeating words or phrases throughout your brief. Now, some writers were taught to never repeat words in their writing. This leads to "elegant variation" — using synonyms for the sake of avoiding repetition. In legal writing, elegant variation can create confusion or misstate legal standards. For instance, in criminal law, "beyond a reasonable doubt" is a term of art with a specific meaning. It can't be replaced with "exceeding a sensible uncertainty" without changing its meaning and confusing the reader.

Even when elegant variation doesn't change the meaning of a legal phrase, it can detract from your writing's persuasive impact. Using an example from above, let's say you decided that "brilliant" was the perfect word to describe the bright sunlight from your client's perspective. Judicious repetition of "brilliant" throughout your brief serves to reinforce this image in the reader's mind. Like most things in life, balance is the key.

---

1. 510 U.S. 569, 589 (1994).

Exercise: Word choice and perception

Review the passage below. Now, assume you are representing Dr. Jamison. Your brief will argue that Dr. Jamison is immune from civil liability under your jurisdiction's Good Samaritan law. This law shields individuals from liability if they act reasonably and without compensation to aid a person having a medical emergency. Revise the passage to tell the story from your client's perspective, paying attention to word choice. Which words did you choose, and why?

> Dr. Jamison was out for an early-morning walk on January 3, 2024. He saw a person struggling in a partially frozen lake. Dr. Jamison ran to the lakeside and realized that the person was a girl who was about eleven years old. Dr. Jamison assumed a prone position on the ice and slowly moved forward until he could reach the girl and pull her from the ice. At this point, the girl was unconscious. Dr. Jamison called 911 and spoke to dispatch while performing CPR. When paramedics arrived, the girl was conscious. At the hospital, an ER physician discovered that Dr. Jamison's chest compressions cracked two of the girl's ribs and several vertebrae. The girl has now lost all sensation in her left leg.

C. Position

The final P is *position*. Understanding positions of emphasis in legal writing allows you to manipulate the structure of sentences, paragraphs, and arguments to maximize their persuasive value.

In the television series *Mad Men*, protagonist Don Draper was once told, "You only like the beginnings of things." Although this was meant as an admonishment regarding his infidelity, this saying could also apply to a cognitive bias called the primacy effect. When asked to recall information, people tend to better remember the information that's presented first. The primacy effect also supports the conventional wisdom related to the power of first impressions.

Because of the primacy effect, writers should place the most important information at the beginning of an argument, a paragraph, or a sentence. Thus, if you have alternate legal theories to support a particular position, put the strongest one first. Also, ensure that the first sentence of every paragraph you write (usually called the topic sentence) is written with care. In addition to summarizing the point of the following paragraph, topic sentences should be carefully crafted for their persuasive value. Consider also the optimal length for each paragraph. Shorter paragraphs allow a writer to create more topic sentences, therefore providing more opportunities to take advantage of the primacy effect.

The primacy effect also ties into the importance of point headings. As discussed in Chapter 7, readers (especially screen readers) are drawn to point headings. With that in mind, ensure that your point headings summarize the forthcoming argument in a complete sentence. Pay attention also to word choice, as discussed in section B, Perception, above.

Understanding the primacy effect also allows a writer to utilize its inverse. Knowing that information in the middle of a sentence, paragraph, or section is less likely to be remembered, you can use that middle position to deemphasize unfavorable information. For instance, in a statement of facts, you can sandwich less helpful facts between favorable facts to draw the reader's attention away.

Like many rules of legal writing, the primacy effect has exceptions. The beginning of a sentence can actually be a good place for unhelpful information when using dependent-clause construction. A dependent clause within a sentence is a clause introduced by a word like although, unless, despite, or while. By its nature, a dependent clause introduces information that is subordinate to the main clause of a sentence. Here's an example:

> Although the defense counsel did not object during the trial, depriving the defendant of a public trial is a structural error that requires reversal, even when not preserved below.

In this example, the defense counsel's failure to preserve an error through a timely objection is an unfavorable fact. However, placing it at the start of a sentence, introduced by "although," allows the writer to confront the unfavorable fact head-on before rebutting it. Dependent-clause construction is especially useful when writing a rebuttal to the opposing party's counterargument.

Exercise: Positions of emphasis

Review the word choice and perception exercise above. If you completed this exercise, you should have a draft paragraph that's written from the client's (the doctor's) perspective. Critically examine what you have written. Have you taken advantage of positions of emphasis within the paragraph? Have you used dependent clauses to deemphasize unfavorable information?

III. Telling a story with your legal writing

During a trip to Disney California Adventure Park, one of the authors noticed something as she was riding the theme park's distinctive Incredicoaster. As somewhat of a coaster enthusiast, she had visited many theme parks and enjoyed some thrilling rides. The Incredicoaster, however, provided something more than a 55-mile-per-hour launch and an inversion. It also came with a story, based on the Pixar movie *The Incredibles*. One character, baby Jack-Jack, runs away using his superpowers. Throughout the coaster, riders see other characters racing to find Jack-Jack and hear accompanying music and dialogue. A few times, characters are seen and heard luring Jack-Jack with a chocolate chip cookie. As riders exit the coaster after an exhilarating two-and-a-half minutes, they immediately run into a stand selling Jack-Jack's Cookie Num-Nums.

Now, the Incredicoaster could have been just a fun roller coaster. Instead, it was a narrative with all the components of a good story: theme, characters, conflict, and resolution. Coupled with the physical and emotional intensity of riding a roller coaster, the story was especially impactful. But perhaps most impressive was its power of persuasion. Passengers exiting the ride were perfectly primed to buy some hot, fresh Cookie Num-Nums.

If you're a Disney enthusiast, then you likely know that incorporating a storyline into every ride is what sets Disney parks apart from other theme parks. Experiencing immersive stories makes the rides emotionally resonant and memorable for park visitors. And these storylines don't happen by chance; the theme park "Imagineers" create storyboards for the rides long before they are built.

Can we analogize appellate briefs to Disney theme parks? Why not? In an appellate brief, the writer can take the reader for a ride, using the facts and law to lead the reader to conclude that the law favors the writer's client. Without facts and law, the appellate brief wouldn't exist. But, beyond this framework, an imaginative writer can use the facts and law to tell a memorable story. If the law is the brain of a legal brief, then the story is its heart.

This certainly isn't a new concept. Cultures around the world have used storytelling for centuries, not only to entertain but to educate as well. Native Hawaiians used storytelling, moʻolelo, to create a rich oral history and hand down cultural beliefs and values from one generation to the next.[2] In the Four Corners region, the oral tradition of Navajo elders combined with mod-

2. *See* Peter Keali'i Thoene, *Excavating the Scientific Truths in Hawaiian Moʻolelo*, FLUX Haw. (Oct. 11, 2021), https://fluxhawaii.com/the-science-behind-hawaiian-myths/.

ern medicine helped scientists to pinpoint the Hantavirus as the cause of a mystery disease.[3]

Regardless of subject matter, good writers can draw upon storytelling techniques to make their writing memorable and persuasive. As explained below, readers tend to remember information better when it's presented as a story. Moreover, incorporating a theme into your writing can make your clients and their arguments more relatable.

A. The power of narratives

Chapter 9 discusses how biases and heuristics affect how people process information. This chapter introduces another cognitive bias: story bias, sometimes called narrative bias. Story bias is a cognitive shortcut that allows us to process new, perhaps voluminous information into something our brains can more easily comprehend — a story. Our brains have a tendency to piece together seemingly random, unrelated information into a narrative.

If a writer doesn't pay heed to story bias, then it's possible for the reader to overlay an appellate brief with a story of their own. This could very well be a story that the writer did not intend. A better strategy would be to examine your facts and law to create your own story, one that puts your client in the best possible position. Even the simplest or driest of legal problems can give rise to the basic storytelling components, described further below.

B. Story components: Theme, conflict, and archetypes

Whether found in a feature film, novel, or comic book, all stories share certain characteristics. A good story will have a relatable theme, some form of narrative conflict, and characters that conform to particular archetypes. Incorporating these three components into the story of your appellate brief will create a narrative that is recognizable and relatable.

1. Theme

In a narrative, the theme is the unifying idea that explains what the story is all about. In turn, the story has to remain consistent with the theme. Have you ever had trouble watching a movie or television series because it seemed

---

3. James MacDonald, *Solving a Medical Mystery with Oral Traditions*, JSTOR Daily (Mar. 14, 2018), https://daily.jstor.org/solving-a-medical-mystery-with-oral-traditions/.

"all over the place"? If so, then it's likely the story failed to adhere consistently to an identifiable theme.

Many themes that commonly appear in modern literature and media have been in existence for centuries. These types of themes are sometimes dubbed "universal," based on how they describe enduring aspects of the human condition. Often, a universal theme will reflect common principles and values, such as fairness, integrity, and the importance of family.

Some examples of universal themes include:

- Seeking revenge
- Finding a lost love
- Starting as an underdog and emerging triumphantly
- Coming of age and losing one's youthful innocence

If you have any concerns about finding a theme within your legal writing, think for a minute about the sheer number of law-based television shows and movies, past and present. There's a reason audiences consistently return to legal procedurals—they generate relatable themes. Sometimes, the relationship between the parties provides the primary theme. A film like *Erin Brockovich* is an underdog tale, as reflected through its protagonist (who is at first underestimated by the lawyer who employs her) and the plaintiffs (who take on a large corporation, Pacific Gas & Electric). The theme can also arise from the nature of the legal conflict in the story. For instance, *The People vs. Larry Flynt* is about how the First Amendment protects everyone's right to free speech, even when the speech and the speaker are unpopular, outrageous, or offensive.

When coming up with a theme for your appellate brief, keep in mind that it should be (1) relatable and (2) articulable in one or two sentences. If your theme stretches into a paragraph, there's a good chance you're actually stating the theory of your case, i.e., the legal and factual basis for your argument. Although a workable theory is an important part of a legal argument, it isn't a substitute for a narrative theme.

Another way to test the validity of your theme is to preface it with the statement "This case is about...." See if adding that prefatory language accurately conveys what your case really *is* all about. If your thematic statement is valid, it could even make its way into your brief, as seen in the Introduction to the Respondent's brief in *Mahanoy Area School District v. B.L.*, discussed earlier in Chapter 9:

> This case is about the free speech rights of young people outside of school—at church, during weekend protests, at home, or, as in this case, at a local convenience store with a friend on a Saturday afternoon.

Exercise: Articulating a theme

In one or two sentences, articulate the theme for either (1) a legal argument that you're currently working on or (2) a law-related book, television show, or movie. What universal principles or values are reflected in the statement you've written?

2. Conflict

A compelling storyline incorporates conflict. The hero of the story has to endure some type of hardship or struggle in achieving a goal, even in the simplest of tales. Sometimes the conflict takes place between two human characters — a protagonist and an antagonist. At other times, the protagonist clashes with another foe, like the natural world (hence the popularity of weather-related disaster movies). Common types of story conflict are:

- Person versus person
- Person versus nature
- Person versus society
- Person versus technology
- Person versus themselves

A story can incorporate multiple types of conflict. The film *Titanic*, for example, was about more than a person versus an iceberg. The primary character, Rose, dealt with a daunting number of conflicts. She clashed with her parents, with her fiancé, with society's expectations, and with a freezing ocean. Importantly, Rose did not suffer through these conflicts for no reason. Rose was pursuing true love, embodied by the character Jack.

Conflict and theme go hand in hand. Sometimes, they overlap almost completely. For instance, a story may have a David-versus-Goliath theme that reflects the struggle of an underdog hero, and the conflict may take place between the underdog (David) and their antagonist (Goliath). Other times, the theme incorporates conflict in a subtler manner. Going back to *Titanic*, a primary theme is about the enduring nature of true love. To demonstrate the theme, Rose must journey through her many sources of conflict while remaining steadfast in her love for Jack.

In legal writing, an obvious source of conflict arises between the parties on each side of the "v." A lone plaintiff suing a faceless corporation embodies both a relatable type of conflict and an understandable theme. Depending on the situation, however, the story of your appellate brief may give rise to different types of conflict. For example, in a criminal appeal arguing ineffective assistance of counsel, the primary conflict may be between the defendant and their trial lawyer rather than between the defendant and the government.

Appellate briefs must be persuasive, and both the theme and conflict can assist in that goal. Just as a persuasive story incorporates a relatable theme, it should also incorporate relatable conflict. The reader should understand the nature of the conflict, both intellectually and emotionally. This may require you to think broadly about how you articulate conflict in your legal writing. Take, for example, a music composer suing an artificial intelligence company for using their music without permission. If you articulate the conflict as "musician versus artificial intelligence," the reader may have trouble relating. On the other hand, if your conflict is framed as "human being versus technology that threatens to replace all of our jobs," the reader will likely find it more accessible.

Exercise: Sources of conflict

Similar to the last exercise, choose either a brief you're working on or a law-related movie, television show, or novel. Identify the various conflicts arising within the storyline. Can you articulate these conflicts broadly enough to be relatable to a wide range of audiences?

3. Archetypes

Another component of storytelling, archetypes, are the types of characters you frequently encounter in literature and other media, both classic and contemporary. Psychiatrist Carl Jung popularized the idea of archetypes as a means to understand what he termed the "collective unconscious," or an understanding of the world that is common across all human cultures. In psychology, some of the Jungian archetypes include The Mother, The Shadow, and The Self.

Universal archetypes make stories more relatable to their audience because such archetypes can be understood irrespective of someone's particular culture, upbringing, or experiences. Some archetypes, like The Ingenue, The Sage, and The Trickster, occur in many types of stories—drama, comedy, tragedy. Other archetypes are specific to particular genres. If you like war movies, then you have probably seen these archetypes over and over: The Country Bumpkin, The Wisecracking New Yorker, and The Sergeant Who is About to Retire After This One Last Mission.

One benefit of using archetypes in storytelling is that it can make a story accessible to many types of people. A judge reading an appellate brief may have trouble relating to a billionaire tech entrepreneur. But if you cast this person as a pulled-himself-up-by-the-bootstraps embodiment of the American dream, the judge can recognize the archetype and better understand the person's perspective and motives.

However, relying too heavily on archetypes in legal writing does have drawbacks. For one, casting a party or client into an archetype could cross over as oversimplifying them into a stereotype. In turn, this risks turning your brief's narrative into a collection of trite story tropes. In addition, real-life people are often too complex to neatly fit into a classic archetype. Lastly, using archetypes to describe parties can inadvertently make your writing biased, given that many archetypes reflect roles relating to sex, gender, and status.

Thus, you should be mindful when incorporating archetypes into your brief's narrative. Check your brief to see if your writing is inadvertently relying on stereotypes. Sometimes, portraying someone as an archetype (e.g., the client as The Hero) can increase your story's persuasive value. But you want to be aware of and avoid the risks described above.

Exercise: Telling a story from a different perspective

Using a simple children's story, rewrite the story but from a different character's perspective (e.g., rewrite *Goldilocks* from the bears' perspective). How did you change the theme, conflict, and archetypes to express the new perspective?

IV. Conclusion

In this chapter, you've learned that the art of legal writing is not just about conveying information but also about crafting a narrative that resonates with the audience. By embracing the principles of perspective, perception, and position, you can enhance your arguments and maximize their persuasive effect. Employing storytelling techniques such as themes, conflict, and archetypes allows you to transform dry legal briefs into engaging narratives.

As an appellate advocate, you have the power to give voice to your client's story. Understanding the power of narratives empowers you to tell these stories with creativity and empathy.

Discussion Questions

1. Consider a recent legal opinion or brief you've read. How did the author use storytelling techniques to convey their argument? What was effective, and what could be improved?
2. How do the three Ps (Perspective, Perception, and Position) intersect with storytelling in legal writing? Provide examples of how each one can be used to enhance a narrative's persuasive impact.
3. Consider a complex legal concept or doctrine. How could you use storytelling techniques to explain it more effectively to a non-expert audience?
4. Reflect on your own writing style and habits. How can you incorporate more storytelling techniques into your legal writing to enhance its persuasive value and better engage the reader?

Part 4

Oral Argument in the Modern Era

Chapter 11

Mastering Oral Argument: From Preparation to Delivery

In this chapter, you will learn:

- The overall purpose and goals of oral argument
- Theories of face-to-face persuasion
- Considerations for arguing in person, virtually, or in a hybrid setting
- Advice for putting your best self forward, no matter your comfort level with public speaking

I. Introduction

In modern appellate practice, oral argument can look very different from how it did even a decade ago. Nonetheless, it remains a fundamental part of appellate advocacy and a true test of an advocate's skills. Oral argument is about more than showcasing legal expertise; it's an opportunity for face-to-face persuasion, dialogue, and connection. This chapter explores the art of oral argument, delving into the latest research from psychology and social science, and providing practical advice to improve your presentation skills. From traditional in-person arguments to video and hybrid proceedings, this chapter highlights the considerations and strategies you need to succeed.

Whether you're a seasoned pro or a nervous newbie, this chapter gives you the tools needed to overcome performance anxiety and present your best self to the court. By the end of this chapter, you'll be equipped with the tools and confidence to make a persuasive case for your client.

II. The role of oral argument in your appellate strategy

Appellate oral argument serves a critical purpose in the legal process: to provide a forum for lawyers to persuade judges to adopt their interpretation of the law and facts. For lawyers, the goal is clear: to convince the judges to rule in their client's favor, whether that means upholding or reversing the lower court's decision. Likewise, judges have specific goals when it comes to oral argument. For judges, oral argument can be a chance to engage in a thoughtful discussion of the case's complexities, testing the lawyers' arguments and probing the boundaries of the law.

Effective oral argument is a dialogue, not a monologue. It's an opportunity for lawyers to engage with the judges, respond to their concerns, and address the counterarguments. Judges, in turn, seek to understand the lawyers' positions, identify potential weaknesses, and clarify ambiguities. Through this exchange, both lawyers and judges aim to distill the essence of the case to arrive at a just and well-reasoned decision. Understanding the court's goals for oral argument will better equip you to navigate the process, starting with the decision to request oral argument.

A. When to request oral argument

Nowadays, most cases are decided without oral argument. In the federal courts, over 80 percent of appeals are decided on briefs alone.[1] Nonetheless, oral argument can be a critical component of appellate advocacy. This is especially true in situations where the court can benefit from hearing from the parties in person, such as when the complexity of the issue merits an interactive dialogue. This section will explore the scenarios where oral argument is essential.

---

1. *Appellate Courts and Cases—Journalists' Guide*, ADMIN. OFFICE OF THE U.S. COURTS, https://www.uscourts.gov/statistics-reports/appellate-courts-and-cases-journalists-guide (last visited Sept. 9, 2024).

1. *Complex or novel issues*

Imagine you're representing a client in an appeal where the issues are so complex that you worry the court might miss something if the judges read only your briefs. Oral argument provides you a chance to speak directly with the court, clarify nuances, and address potential misunderstandings. When dealing with complicated facts or law, oral argument is your opportunity to guide the court through the intricacies of the case. Or, if you're dealing with an issue of first impression in your jurisdiction, oral argument is your chance to shape the court's understanding of this novel legal question. Through oral advocacy, you can help ensure that any resulting precedent is carefully reasoned and well-founded.

2. *Split in authority*

In cases where a split in authority exists among different jurisdictions, oral argument presents a critical opportunity to guide the court in adopting a particular approach. By acknowledging and addressing the conflicting precedents, you can help the court navigate the divergent authorities and reconcile the differences. This may involve highlighting the strengths and weaknesses of each position, identifying the underlying policy considerations, and demonstrating how your proposed approach aligns with the court's prior decisions or broader legal principles. Through effective oral argument, you can facilitate the court's decision-making and shape the development of the law.

3. *Far-reaching consequences*

When a case has far-reaching implications, oral argument offers a crucial opportunity to illuminate the potential consequences of the court's decision. By thoughtfully addressing the impact on diverse stakeholders—including individuals, businesses, communities, and broader societal interests—you can help the court grasp the decision's significance and potential ripple effects. Discussing these implications can inform the court's deliberations, ensuring that its ruling is not only legally sound but also mindful of the potential consequences and sensitive to the needs of those affected.

4. *Close cases*

In close cases, oral argument can tip the scales. When the legal issues are finely balanced, judges may rely heavily on the advocates' expertise and understanding of the case.[2] Almost invariably, the lawyers are more familiar

2. Michael Duvall, *When Is Oral Argument Important? A Judicial Clerk's View of the Debate*, 9 J. App. Practice & Proc. 121, 124–25 (2007).

with the facts and law and are thus able to guide the judges through the complexities. Moreover, oral argument offers judges an opportunity to test their own thinking, probe weaknesses in their colleagues' views, and build consensus on the panel. Through their questions, judges may be seeking not only clarification but also attempting persuasion — trying to convince their fellow judges to adopt their perspective on the case.[3] By anticipating and addressing these dynamics, skilled advocates can leverage oral argument to shape the court's decision-making process and secure a favorable outcome.

B. Waiving oral argument in appellate cases

When preparing for an appeal, you might assume that oral argument is always necessary and well advised. But the truth is that sometimes waiving oral argument makes more sense. According to Federal Rule of Appellate Procedure 34(f), the parties may agree to forgo oral argument and allow the court to decide the case on the briefs. In fact, sometimes skipping oral argument altogether can provide a strategic advantage.[4]

Take, for instance, cases where the briefs are straightforward and concise, leaving little room for further clarification. Or cases that involve uncomplicated issues, where the law is settled and oral argument wouldn't add much value. Perhaps the arguments are weak, and oral argument would only highlight the weaknesses. In these situations, waiving oral argument can save clients the cost and expense of preparing for oral argument.

Time-sensitive cases are another good example. If a speedy resolution is crucial, waiving oral argument can help expedite the decision. And if the appellate court has a history of deciding certain types of cases without oral argument or has indicated a preference for written submissions, it may be wise to follow the court's lead.

Before deciding, take a step back and assess the strength of the case. Consider the appellate court's dynamics and how they might impact the decision to waive oral argument. Evaluate the potential impact on the case's outcome and consider whether waiving oral argument aligns with your client's goals. If you do decide to waive oral argument, make sure to consult with your client and formalize the waiver with the court. Also, keep in mind that in some circumstances the court may order oral argument, notwithstanding your client's desires or your objectives.

---

3. *See id.*

4. Be aware that the Federal Rules also allow a three-judge panel to unanimously decide that oral argument is unnecessary. FED. R. APP. P. 34(a)(2).

By strategically waiving oral argument in circumstances as described above, lawyers can better advance their clients' interests while efficiently managing resources. If you do opt for oral argument, however, you can take advantage of the psychology of face-to-face persuasion, as discussed in the next section.

III. The dynamics of face-to-face persuasion: Theories and insights

Effective oral advocacy relies on more than just knowledge of the law; it also depends on the art of persuasion. Face-to-face interactions offer unique opportunities for persuasion as they allow for nonverbal cues, emotional connections, and lively exchanges. This section explores the science behind face-to-face persuasion, drawing on research from psychology, sociology, and communication studies.

In-person interactions offer a unique set of persuasion opportunities that leverage nonverbal cues, physical presence, and real-time feedback. One relevant theory is the *mere exposure effect*, which shows that people tend to develop a preference for things simply because they are familiar with them.[5] This connects to the *liking principle* discussed in Chapter 9, The Science of Persuasion: Modern Theories and Strategies. Rather than being a faceless name attached to a brief, you can become real, human, and perhaps even familiar through oral argument. Over time, the exposure effect can intensify if you frequently appear in the same court before the same judges. To enhance this effect, you can strategically use eye contact, nodding, and other nonverbal cues to build rapport and establish a connection with the judge. This mirroring technique, which involves subtly imitating a conversation partner's body language and speech patterns, can create a sense of rapport and build trust.

Another key aspect of face-to-face persuasion is the role of proximity and physical space. The *proximity principle* suggests that people are more likely to be influenced by those who are physically close to them.[6] In appellate oral argument, you're required to stand at a podium rather than walk right up to the judges. However, the oral argument allows you to occupy the same physical space as the judges deciding the appeal, something that a brief alone doesn't

---

5. *Why Do We Prefer Things That We Are Familiar With? The Mere Exposure Effect, explained*, The Decision Lab, https://thedecisionlab.com/biases/mere-exposure-effect (last visited Sept. 9, 2024).

6. *See* Cynthia Vinney, *What is the Proximity Principle in Psychology?*, VeryWellMind (updated Aug. 4, 2022), https://www.verywellmind.com/what-is-the-proximity-principle-in-psychology-5195099.

allow. Indeed, this is a good argument for choosing to argue in person rather than virtually, when you have the option to do so.

Although as an oral advocate you'll convey your arguments principally through the words you choose, when it comes to persuasion it's not just what you say but how you say it. Scientists use the term *paralinguistic cues* to refer to the acoustics of speech, such as tone, volume, and pitch.[7] One experiment found that sounding confident—which typically translated to a higher pitch and volume—made the speaker's message more effective.[8] This held true even when the listener knew the speaker was deliberately trying to sound confident.[9] In many ways, this research confirms some tried-and-true public speaking advice, like "Speak up!" When arguing virtually, this research also underscores the importance of using a good microphone and a quiet setting.

The research into face-to-face persuasion tells us not only what works but also what doesn't work. A lack of eye contact, nervous gestures, and a quiet voice could potentially undermine an oral advocate's efficacy. Still, it's important to remember that even the most well-founded scientific research should be used as a guide, not taken as an imperative. Ultimately, presenting your authentic self will work better than trying to adopt a persona. (This will be further explored later in this chapter.) You should also keep in mind that many notions of what makes a speaker sound or look confident are rooted in cultural norms and societal expectations. Thus, when a peer, judge, coach, or friend critiques your speaking skills, you should listen with an open mind but also understand that their idea of an effective lawyer may be influenced by race, gender, or class.

IV. Oral argument: Practice and procedures

This section will break down the details when it comes to planning for and executing an oral argument. Understanding the logistics, like courtroom layout and time limits, can help you prepare and avoid surprises. This section also compares traditional, or in-person, oral arguments with the virtual or hybrid proceedings becoming more prevalent in the modern courtroom.

7. Karinna Hurley, *How "Paralinguistic Cues" Can Help You Persuade*, Sci. Am. (Jan. 23, 2020), https://www.scientificamerican.com/article/how-paralinguistic-cues-can-help-you-to-persuade2/.

8. *Id.*

9. *Id.*

A. Logistical preparation

A traditional oral argument takes place in person, usually in a courtroom. Although courtroom layouts may vary, typically the parties sit at tables on either side of a lectern, and whoever is speaking stands at the lectern facing the panel of judges. Facing the bench, the custom is for the appellant to sit at the table to the left of the lectern and the appellee at the table to the right. The lectern will have a microphone and space for you to place your notes or any electronic devices. The courtroom will usually have some mechanism for keeping track of time, such as a wall-mounted clock, a lectern clock, a colored light, or some combination of these.

Beyond these essential details, courtrooms will vary in terms of their style, decor, lighting, and dimensions. Although these may seem like superficial details, they could be relevant to your preparation. For example, if the lectern in a particular courtroom is farther away from the bench than you're used to, then you may need glasses or other vision enhancement to better see the judges' faces. Considerations like flooring materials (e.g., carpet versus tile), aisle widths, and inclines can impact an advocate who uses a wheelchair or other mobility device. Even temperature plays a role; shivering (or sweating) based on unexpected climate control conditions can rattle even the most experienced orator.

You'll also want to know about the environment outside the courtroom. Some considerations include parking logistics, restrooms, vending machines (or other places to get a drink or snack), and areas to speak with your client or co-counsel in private. Whenever possible, investigate an unfamiliar courtroom in advance to eliminate uncertainty and plan for contingencies.

To be best prepared, you'll also want to learn what type of technology is present in the courtroom.

- Depending on the type or location of the clock, you may consider using your own timekeeping device as a supplement.
- The type of microphone at the lectern could affect your delivery. A traditional lectern mic will be on a stand or have a flexible neck that you can adjust for your height. These types of mics are usually unidirectional, meaning you should speak straight into the mic from about six inches away for the best sound.
- Although less common, your courtroom may have a boundary mic at the lectern. A boundary mic looks kind of like a speaker and is relatively flat. These types of mics are

omnidirectional, so you can speak as you usually do, and they should pick up your voice just fine.

- Your courtroom will likely have at least one camera. You can find out ahead of time if your oral argument will be livestreamed (as many are nowadays) or if some oral argument participants will be remote. Hybrid court proceedings are discussed more below.

To throw an additional wrinkle in your preparation, remember that many appellate courts routinely hold oral arguments off-site as a matter of educational outreach. Thus, it's possible you may find yourself arguing at an alternative venue, like a law school or high school, at some point in your career. The usual advice — to find out as much as you can about parking, technology, and other logistics to avoid being caught off-guard on argument day — still applies.

Another critical component of your preparation will be familiarization with the rules governing oral argument procedures. Federal Rule of Appellate Procedure 34 does not prescribe time limits in the federal courts; each court sets time limits by local rule. For example, the Federal Circuit limits oral argument to fifteen minutes per side for cases argued before a panel, thirty minutes for cases heard en banc.[10] The appellant will argue first and may reserve a portion of time for rebuttal. The appellee argues second, followed by the appellant's rebuttal, if applicable. In some instances, a lawyer representing a party who has filed a brief as amicus curiae (friend of the court) may participate in oral argument with the court's permission.[11]

B. Substantive preparation

Thus far, this section has discussed an important part of oral argument preparation — understanding the courtroom, the procedures, and other logistical concerns. Your attention should turn next to the intellectual heart of your oral argument. Your substantive preparation will include researching the judges, anticipating their questions, selecting arguments to present, organizing them for maximum effect, and planning for contingencies. Concurrently, you'll be preparing the materials that you'll bring to court on argument day.

---

10. U.S. Court of Appeals for the Federal Circuit Clerk's Office, Guide for Oral Argument 5 (Feb. 2024), https://cafc.uscourts.gov/wp-content/uploads/OralArguments/OralArgumentGuide.pdf [hereinafter Guide for Oral Argument].

11. Fed. R. App. P. 29(a)(8).

1. *Researching judges*

Most courts of appeal are made up of multiple judges who will hear cases in a group of three, called a panel, unless the court is hearing the argument en banc. Depending on the jurisdiction in which you're arguing, you may or may not know in advance which judges will make up the panel for your oral argument. In Division One of the Arizona Court of Appeals, for example, the parties and their lawyers will know before oral argument which panel will hear the case.[12] In contrast, lawyers arguing before the Federal Circuit will learn the names of the judges on their panel on the morning of the argument.[13]

If you can learn in advance which judges will be hearing your argument, take some time to learn about them. Review their past decisions, opinions (including concurrences and dissents), and any relevant publications. This will help you understand their perspectives and tailor your argument accordingly. Chapter 12, Technology's Evolving Role in Contemporary Appellate Practice, discusses how legal analytics can assist in this type of research. In addition, you can probably review video or audio of past oral arguments in front of your panel. Some courts post these to a YouTube channel; others post the video or audio files on the court's website. Even if the videos you review deal with cases in a different area of law, you can likely get a sense of the judges' oral argument style. For example, some judges like to ask long, multi-part questions, while others say little. At the very least, reviewing videos can demystify the experience of appearing for the first time in front of an unfamiliar court or panel.

2. *Choosing arguments to present*

As you prepare for oral argument, you must strategically select which arguments to prioritize during your limited time before the judges. Sometimes, the court provides guidance by requesting specific issues be addressed or, in rare instances, sharing draft opinions that reveal the court's concerns and leanings.[14]

When left to your discretion, focus on the arguments that will resonate most with the judges. Emphasize your strongest points and be prepared to elaborate on them. Given the time constraints—often, just ten to twenty minutes per side—you must prioritize your most compelling arguments and

---

12. *E.g.*, Arizona Administrative Office of the Court, Arizona Appellate Court Cases: Court of Appeals Division One: Court Calendar, https://www.azcourts.gov/appellatecourt-cases/COA1/Calendar (last visited Sept. 9, 2024).

13. Guide for Oral Argument, *supra* note 10, at 8.

14. *See* Mark Hummels, *Distributing Draft Decisions Before Oral Argument on Appeal: Should the Court Tip Its Tentative Hand? The Case for Dissemination*, 46 Ariz. L. Rev. 317, 320 (2004).

sacrifice weaker ones. This targeted approach ensures you effectively allocate your time.

3. *Organizing your argument*

With your key arguments selected, it's time to organize them for maximum impact. When sequencing your main points, consider the strength of each argument and the time constraints. Chapter 5's discussion of organizing arguments within an appellate brief can provide some guidance in this regard.

Next, consider the large-scale structure of your oral argument. While no rigid rules govern appellate argument organization, certain conventions guide the typical structure. You can follow the outline below to structure a clear and logical oral argument.

a. Introduction

In many ways, the introduction is the most important part of your oral argument. Like the Introduction section of a brief, the first few moments of your oral argument provide a chance to preview your theme and your argument. Moreover, in those moments you're also making a first impression on the judges and establishing your rapport and credibility.

Oral advocates take different approaches to the introduction, but a standard formula is provided below. Your introduction should contain the following components:

- A greeting. The most formal would be the traditional greeting, "May it please the Court." Depending on the court, you may be able to use a slightly less formal greeting, such as "Good afternoon, Judges."
- An introduction of yourself and your client. "I'm Mary Marks, and I represent the Appellant, XYZ Corporation."
- A concise statement of the requested relief. "This Court should reverse the district court's decision granting summary judgment for ABC Corporation."
- A brief roadmap of the key points you'll cover. "The district court's decision should be reversed for two main reasons..."
- (Optional) A statement of your theme: "This is a case about [insert theme]." The statement of the theme can either precede or follow your requested relief and roadmap.

Example:

> May it please the Court, I'm John Jacobs, counsel for the appellant, Myrna Long. This is a case about a company who

> took away my client's job and a judge's decision that took away her day in court. The lower court erred in granting a motion to dismiss my client's claim of wrongful termination, and this Court should reverse the lower court for these two reasons....

b. Argument

In the body of your argument, you'll present your main points. Your argument should follow your roadmap and provide clear signals to the judges when you transition from point to point. You can use language like, "Turning to my first point," or "This brings me to my second point," to refer to your roadmap.

You can present your arguments in a fashion similar to how you wrote them in your brief, but keep in mind that the court is listening rather than reading. Thus, you'll want to use simple language and explain the law in a straightforward manner. Remember that the judges have already read your brief, so you don't need to reiterate all the facts or legal principles, especially if they're complicated. Instead, you can highlight the key facts and principles that best support your client's position.

Although your oral argument may use simplified language, it still needs to follow the basic principles of argumentation discussed in Chapter 5. Your argument should focus not only on the law but on how the law applies to your client's specific facts. In presenting both law and facts, you should provide citations. Whether you provide a full citation when referring to case law is a discretionary choice. A well-known case cited by both parties could potentially be referred to by name alone, whereas you may choose to provide a full citation for a recently decided case that wasn't in your brief. When pointing out key facts, provide a quick citation to the record on appeal.

c. Conclusion

In oral arguments, conclusions tend to be brief. Often, you'll be answering judges' questions or presenting your arguments right up to the finish line. Therefore, it's totally acceptable to conclude with a simple sentence.

Example:

> "For these reasons, my client respectfully asks the Court to reverse the lower court's decision and remand for further proceedings."

If time runs out:

> "I see my time is up, Your Honor. May I have a moment to conclude?" and then, if the court permits it, state your one-sentence conclusion.

Of course, if you're out of time, you can also simply say, "I'll stop here, Your Honor. Thank you."

d. Rebuttal

After the appellee's primary argument, the appellant can use their reserved time to deliver a rebuttal. This is an opportunity to address and rebut the appellee's primary points, for example, by offering an alternative interpretation of the law or clarifying any misconceptions relating to the record. An effective rebuttal addresses only the arguments raised by the appellee. Judges can tell when an appellant is using the rebuttal merely to reiterate their earlier argument.

In rebuttal, you don't need to provide a full introduction. As a courtesy, you can say "May it please the Court" as you start, but you don't need to reintroduce yourself, your client, or your theme. Instead, you can go straight into your rebuttal argument. If possible, you can provide a brief roadmap if you plan to address more than one point during the rebuttal. Keep in mind, however, that the few minutes you reserved for rebuttal will fly by, especially if the judges have questions. When your time is up, conclude your rebuttal as you did your opening argument.

Example:

> "During rebuttal, I'll address the appellee's argument regarding [insert issue]. Our position remains that [insert main argument]. The appellee's argument fails to consider [insert key point]."

4. *Anticipating questions*

Perhaps no aspect of oral argument is as intimidating as dealing with questions from the bench. During oral argument, judges will jump in with questions to clarify your points, challenge your arguments, or explore new ideas. As an advocate, you can't control this aspect of oral argument, but you can make certain predictions to reduce some of the uncertainty.

As a preliminary matter, you must mentally prepare yourself for interruptions. Judges can ask questions at any point in your argument, so be ready to pivot. To properly answer a judge's question, you may have to deviate from the sequence of arguments you had planned. As you have already read in this chapter, it helps to think of oral argument as a dynamic conversation. A good conversation partner is an active listener who can be flexible and adapt as the conversation changes directions. With adequate preparation and rehearsal, you can use your communication skills both to argue your main points and to engage in a lively dialogue with the bench.

As you gain experience, you'll come to welcome the judges' questions as an opportunity to tailor your argument on the spot. Whether by answering questions while you're at the lectern or listening to the questions posed to opposing counsel, you can gain valuable insight into which arguments are landing best with the court—and which ones are better left on the page.

At a basic level, you should have a disciplined approach to answering questions. Practice this approach every time you rehearse your argument in front of a mock panel. When a judge asks you a question:

- Immediately stop talking.
- Listen attentively and actively. Try not to think ahead to what you want to say before the judge has finished asking the question.
- Pause for a moment, if necessary, to gather your thoughts.
- Clarify the question if needed, but avoid the appearance that you're trying to stall while you think of an answer.
- Respond concisely and clearly, avoiding unnecessary elaboration.
- Don't say "Thank you" or "That's a good question" before responding.

Although every case is unique, oftentimes you can predict broadly what types of questions you might encounter during oral argument. Questions tend to fall into categories based upon the judge's purpose in asking the question.

Depending on the nature of the appeal, judges might ask:

- Clarifying questions about the facts or relevant law
- Questions about legal standards, such as the standard of review or burden of proof
- Questions about the policy implications of their decision
- Hypothetical questions to explore new ideas or test the boundaries of your proposed interpretation of the law
- Questions that seem off-topic (but might be connected to a larger point)
- Softball questions to help you out or to help convince another judge to buy into the point that you're making
- Questions asking you to concede a point of fact or law to narrow down the issues that the court must decide

Here are some best practices for answering questions professionally:

- Stay calm and composed.
- Focus on the question asked, and avoid getting sidetracked or going down rabbit holes.
- Do not ask your own questions back to the judge unless you're asking for a clarification.
- Do not tell the judge that you will get to their question later. Even if the question makes you address an argument out of your planned sequence, you must answer it immediately.
- If you don't know the answer to a judge's question, don't make something up. You can truthfully answer that you don't know. In some instances, such as when a judge asks you to apply a legal authority that you're unfamiliar with, you can offer to file a supplemental brief with the court's permission.
- When you have finished your answer, you can pause briefly to see if the judge has a follow-up question. Depending on the situation, you can sometimes ask, "Did I answer your question, Your Honor?" However, you don't want to do this for every question. Many judges will give you a verbal or nonverbal cue that you can return to your argument.
- Smoothly transition back to your primary argument by saying something like: "That brings me to my next point," or "Returning to my __ argument, ..."

As you can tell from this discussion about preparing for oral argument, you'll want to ensure that on argument day, you have a set of useful and organized materials to bring with you to the lectern. The next section goes over some suggestions for putting together your argument materials.

5. *Preparing your materials*

Organize your notes and supporting materials in a way that makes sense for your argument. At a minimum, you'll want to include:

- A clear and concise outline of your argument, including the introduction, roadmap, and conclusion
- Key excerpts and summaries of legal authorities, such as case law and statutes, along with full citations
- Relevant record excerpts

You'll notice that the list above doesn't include a full script of your argument. Instead, you should create a bullet-point outline of your main points. This will make it easier to stay on track when the judges' questions cause you to deviate from your planned roadmap.

A traditional way to organize your materials would be in a hard copy format. Many advocates like to use a three-ring binder with transparent plastic pockets on the front and back covers. You can put your bullet-point outline into one or both cover pockets, and then organize case law summaries, record excerpts, and other supporting materials inside the binder, separated by tabbed dividers. Of course, this is just one suggestion; the best method is whatever works best for you. Other materials to consider would be legal pads, file folders, or even loose-leaf paper. Just be sure that whatever you use can stay organized even if you drop it on the floor (yes, this does happen) and will fit on the lectern comfortably.

If hard-copy materials seem a bit quaint, you could use an electronic device like a tablet instead. An electronic device allows you to refer to a large volume of material in a compact form. You can choose from numerous notetaking and organization apps to help arrange your outline and supporting materials in an easy-to-access format. Using a tablet at the lectern also helps you avoid leafing through or shuffling papers during your argument, which could be distracting.

However, electronic devices have some drawbacks. For one, a technical mishap could render your notes inaccessible or unusable. The device could crash, the battery could die, or an ill-timed drop or spilled beverage could destroy it altogether. Even short of such a disaster, electronic devices affect your presentation style. Just as frantic shuffling of pages on the lectern could be distracting, aggressive swiping through a tablet could also draw unwanted attention. If you decide to use a tablet or other electronic device, be certain to rehearse with the device and bring a backup (hard copy or digital).

V. Oral argument: Virtual and hybrid proceedings

The previous section covered the basics of traditional appellate oral arguments, meaning arguments that take place in a courtroom with all personnel present in person. In recent years, oral argument practice has transformed significantly. The COVID-19 pandemic accounted for many of these changes, as it forced courts to adapt and innovate to accommodate social distancing requirements and travel restrictions. This period of adaptation also led to improvements in remote video conferencing hardware and software that allowed courts to hold virtual and hybrid hearings in lieu of meeting in person.

Although the pandemic has receded, virtual and hybrid hearings remain prevalent in the legal system and are likely here to stay. Courts, counsel, and parties realized that virtual hearings allow for reduced costs, reduced delays, and better access for those who live in remote areas. The convenience that technology provides, however, comes with trade-offs. This section explores how virtual hearings work and best practices for lawyers who conduct appellate oral argument in either virtual or hybrid proceedings.

A. Virtual oral arguments

Virtual oral arguments are also known as remote or video arguments. This format allows lawyers to present arguments via video conferencing platforms, eliminating the need for in-person appearances. This section discusses how to prepare for and deliver an oral argument if you're doing so from your home or office rather than in a courtroom.

1. *How virtual oral arguments work*

Although virtual arguments are technology-driven, the general format remains the same in terms of the order of arguments, time limits, and the ability of judges to ask questions. Above all, even if you're arguing from a home office, you're still considered to be in court, so the typical rules regarding dress code, courtesy, and timeliness will apply.

Different courts require different video conferencing platforms, so you should be prepared to install the platform used by the court in which you're appearing. For convenience's sake, this section will refer to best practices using the Zoom platform. Keep in mind that the advice in this section generally applies to any video conferencing platform, including Microsoft Teams, GoTo Meeting, and Webex.

If you're arguing virtually, you'll want to consult any local rules or guidance your court has published concerning virtual appearances. At a minimum, the court will issue requirements regarding:

- The required video conferencing platform
- Any recommendations about early check-ins or testing
- Any requirements to log in early
- Whether a passcode is required

Your court may publish additional requirements regarding virtual hearings, such as:

- Whether a virtual background is required
- Whether advocates are required to stand while presenting
- Information about preferred equipment (e.g., preferred microphones or headphones)
- Any prohibitions on virtual appearances, such as prohibiting advocates from appearing while inside a vehicle

2. *Best practices for virtual oral arguments*

For virtual hearings, the paramount advice is to do what the court tells you to do. Familiarize yourself with the court's rules and for best results, consider any "suggestion" of the court to be the equivalent of a mandate. Here are some additional best practices for conducting an effective and error-free virtual oral argument.

a. Video considerations

- Connectivity: Always test your video before participating in any virtual court hearing. You'll want to ensure that your internet connection is stable to avoid freezing, glitching, or dropping the video call. A direct connection between your laptop and internet router, if possible, is more reliable than a wireless connection.
- Lighting: Ensure that you have adequate lighting so that your face and body are visible and illuminated on screen. If you're in a poorly lit space, the light from the laptop screen can give you an eerie glow. Lighting doesn't have to be complicated. Ring lights (the bright ring-shaped fixtures used by YouTube influencers) are a popular option, but not suitable for every person. Staring into a bright, harsh ring might be

uncomfortable or distracting. Almost always, you can achieve good lighting by turning on whatever overhead light you have in your workspace, then placing a small lamp either directly behind your laptop screen or monitor, or slightly to its left or right. The key is to avoid harsh shadows by using the smaller lamp to fill them in. In cinema or theater, this type of light is called a "fill light" for that very reason.

- Background: Ensure your background is distraction-free. If you're arguing from your office, the usual office-type background (books, shelves, knick-knacks) is probably fine, as long as the background is tidy and doesn't contain anything overly reflective or eye-catching. If you're working from home, investing in a portable backdrop — the kind used by portrait photographers — can shield your private space from public view. Using a virtual background or the "blur" feature is acceptable, although it can cause parts of your body to disappear depending on what's behind you and what you're wearing. Don't place a mirror or anything reflective behind you, as it may pick up images outside of the camera's range. (You probably don't want your dog's butt-scooting, for example, to be featured during your argument.) Lastly, do not turn on an overhead ceiling fan if the fan is within the frame. A rotating fan directly above the speaker's head is more distracting than you'd expect.
- Personal appearance: As previously stated, you should dress for a virtual argument as you would dress for an in-person court appearance. This means wearing appropriate professional attire on your entire body, not just from the waist up. Solid colors work better on video than stripes or patterns, and muted colors such as navy or charcoal work better than pure white or black. Avoid wearing reflective jewelry around the face and neck area. If you wear glasses, be aware that the lenses may reflect the screen and obscure your eyes. If you want to avoid this, you can tilt your glasses slightly forward so they aren't parallel to the screen, or you can invest in non-reflective lenses. You can also adjust your laptop to ensure that the built-in camera is at a height and angle to best capture your features while minimizing glare. In terms of positioning your body in front of the camera, the court will likely allow you either to sit or stand when arguing remotely, so you should practice both to see what you prefer.

b. Audio considerations

- Microphone: If you're able to present from a quiet space, the microphone that's built into your laptop or other device should be adequate. An external microphone that connects to your laptop can help if you need higher quality amplification, e.g., if you have a naturally quiet speaking voice. If you frequently argue virtually, you may consider investing in a higher quality microphone; you can look into what podcasters and radio hosts use to produce the best sound. For most advocates, however, a simple setup will work just fine.
- Speaking style: When using an external microphone that's close to your mouth, your normal speaking style should be adequate for good sound quality. As discussed above, a built-in laptop mic should also be fine if you can talk in your normal speaking voice without too much background noise. Remember that Zoom and other platforms have live-captioning ability, so be sure to speak slowly and clearly enough for the captions to accurately state what you have said.
- Background noise: Keep in mind that even the best microphone can't compensate for arguing in a space that isn't audio friendly. Sound waves will bounce around a room that's large, empty, or lacking any type of fabric like window treatments or carpet. When possible, argue from an office or room that's adequately furnished and not too large. Do your best to control the environmental noises in your workspace. If you work from home, consider boarding your dogs and canceling the gardener on oral argument day. Larger cities often have shared office space available to rent by the hour, in case your home environment is too noisy.

  Even if you're presenting from a traditional office space, take precautions. A sign on the door that states "virtual hearing in progress" can prevent knocking or other interruptions. To cut down on background noise, you can also adjust the settings on your video conferencing platform. Zoom and other platforms allow you to enable a noise suppression feature, usually under advanced audio settings.

c. Presentation style

- Modifying your style: As discussed above under theories of face-to-face persuasion, simply occupying the same space as another person allows you to employ the proximity principle, paralinguistic cues, and other tactics related to physical presence. Speaking over video diminishes the face-to-face effect but doesn't eliminate it entirely. With that said, you'll have to take deliberate steps to replicate the benefits of in-person argument when speaking over video. Replicating eye contact is crucial. Just like a television news anchor, you'll have to simulate direct eye contact by looking directly into the camera lens as you speak. But you'll also have to occasionally look at the judges to see how they are responding to your argument and if they have questions.

  You should also be conscious of your on-camera behavior when the opposing side is arguing. In a cavernous courtroom, you may be able to get away with a lifted eyebrow or drifting concentration while the opposing counsel speaks. When you're tightly framed in a Zoom meeting, however, every small expression is on display. Lastly, you'll want to record yourself arguing and study the recording to see if you're making any distracting gestures while speaking. Hand gestures and body positioning that may come across effectively in person could seem exaggerated or aggressive when viewed on camera.

- Materials: Arguing virtually allows for more flexibility in organizing and arranging materials. You're not limited to the surface area of a lectern, so you can spread your materials out. Nonetheless, exercise caution: Perhaps you decide to skip the step of distilling your argument into a succinct outline because you know you have the extra space. Or perhaps you decide to refer to your notes on your laptop screen in a window next to your Zoom window. But neither of these practices is advised. In particular, the practice of reading notes on your screen often backfires because it's quite noticeable when an advocate is reading from a screen rather than engaging with the audience. On balance, the best practice is to use the same method for creating and using written materials in a virtual argument as you would for an in-person argument.

In addition to the best practices described above, a little common sense goes a long way. Virtual arguments are flexible enough to allow the counsel and court to be in different time zones, so ensure you plan accordingly if you're arguing from out of town. Have a backup plan available (laptop, tablet, phone) in case your primary means of connecting falls through. By following these best practices, you can make a good impression and ensure that the court focuses on your argument and your client's position, rather than on any technology-related issues.

B. Hybrid proceedings

Hybrid oral arguments, where some court personnel are remote and others are present in the courtroom, present a unique set of challenges. Advocates must adapt to a blended environment and engage with both in-person and remote participants. For the most part, the advice above regarding virtual hearings applies to hybrid oral argument as well, especially if you're the one arguing remotely. If you're the one in the courtroom, however, you'll have some additional considerations, depending on the nature of the hybrid proceeding.

Some hybrid proceedings take place in a courtroom with all judges present and one or both opposing counsel appearing remotely. If you're in person, you can present your oral argument in a traditional fashion, without the worry of accounting for videoconferencing technology; however, you should still act as if the remotely appearing attorney is present in the courtroom. For instance, when the remotely appearing attorney argues, you should listen attentively and courteously, just as you would if they were in person.

Because of the versatile nature of hybrid proceedings, it's also possible that some judges on the panel will be in the courtroom, while one or more judges will be appearing remotely. If that's the case, then your challenge will be to engage equally with all judges on the court, including those that are appearing by video. In a hybrid proceeding of this nature, the court may alter its rules regarding questioning. For example, rather than the traditional free-for-all style of questioning, where any judge can jump in at any time, the court may instead allot a period for judges to take turns asking questions.

Whether you find yourself arguing in a 100 percent virtual courtroom environment or a hybrid scenario, the key is to be flexible. Some awkward moments will likely occur, and some technological glitches are bound to arise. If you have thoroughly prepared and practiced your argument, then a few bumps in the road shouldn't knock you off your course. If anything, demonstrating an ability to handle small frustrations with a cool head can help your professional reputation. The next section provides additional tips for putting your best foot forward on oral argument day, regardless of the setting.

VI. Presenting your best self during oral argument

It's natural to feel nervous when arguing before an appellate court. Many lawyers, even those with considerable experience, deal with performance anxiety or the fear of public speaking. Fortunately, with preparation, practice, and a few shifts in mindset, you can overcome these obstacles and present your best self. This section provides some straightforward advice for tackling performance anxiety and delivering a persuasive argument while still being yourself.

A. Projecting confidence

The first line of attack against performance anxiety is thorough preparation. Know your argument inside and out, both the facts and the law. Rehearse your argument several times, ideally in front of a panel of mock judges. Anticipating questions and refining your responses will help you feel more in control, which should boost your self-assurance.

Even if you're quite nervous, you can use body language and voice control to project a different image. Empowering yourself starts with taking on an assertive posture. In her widely viewed TED Talk, psychologist Amy Cuddy argues that merely standing in a "power pose" can lift your confidence.[15] Even if you're sitting, you can sit tall, lifting your chest and drawing your shoulders back if you're able to do so. This type of open posture also allows you to breathe more easily while you speak.

And yes, remember to breathe. You'd be surprised how often performers of all types—musicians, actors, athletes—forget to breathe when they are nervous. Breathing deeply from the diaphragm also allows your breath to support your voice, allowing for your voice to be resonant rather than breathy or squeaky. Also, pay attention to your rate of speaking and your use of pauses. Although some speakers slow down when nervous, the more common reaction is to speed up. Nervous speakers also tend to omit a natural pause when

15. Amy Cuddy, *Your Body Language May Shape Who You Are*, TED (June 2012), https://www.ted.com/talks/amy_cuddy_your_body_language_may_shape_who_you_are?subtitle=en.

moving from sentence to sentence or thought to thought. You can listen to a recording of yourself or ask an objective listener for feedback.

Facial expressions can be another area of concern for public speakers. Worrying excessively about facial expressions is counterproductive; it's sufficient to ensure that your expression is professional and matches the nature of your argument. For example, a person who tends to smile a lot when nervous should work on not smiling when arguing about a serious topic. A professional facial expression is one that's free of exaggerated emotional responses, like frowning or eye rolling. In cultures where eye contact is associated with confidence (such as most Western cultures), you'll want to make eye contact when speaking directly with a judge and periodically throughout your argument.

Some speakers also worry about hand gestures, especially those who tend to use lively gestures in their everyday speech. When arguing from a lectern, you can always just rest your hands on the surface and forgo hand gestures altogether. If you'd like to use hand gestures, then keep in mind that gestures look most natural when the hands move in the space in front of your body and between your elbows and shoulders, rather than above, below, or to the side. If you're working on toning down your hand gestures, you can observe broadcast journalists on local or national news programs to see how they use minimal gestures to accentuate their words.

Above all, remember that oral argument is a conversation, not a performance. Simply keeping that concept in mind can help you argue in a more natural and confident manner. Focus on communicating your arguments rather than trying to impress.

B. Authenticity matters

When presenting an oral argument, be the best version of yourself, not someone else. Trying to adopt a different persona or alter your voice and speech patterns to fit a stereotype can come across as insincere. For a highly publicized example, look up Elizabeth Holmes, the founder of now-defunct biotech company Theranos. Perhaps to compensate for being a young woman in Silicon Valley, Ms. Holmes dressed in a black turtleneck like Steve Jobs and adopted an unnaturally deep voice and affected mannerisms. Even before Theranos collapsed amid allegations of fraud, Ms. Holmes drew attention for her style of speaking and dress.[16]

---

16. *See, e.g.*, Tierney Bricker, *Why Elizabeth Holmes Still Fascinates: That Voice, the $1 Billion Dollar Lie & an 11-Year Prison Sentence*, E! News (June 3, 2023), https://www.eonline.com/news/1024870/the-deep-voice-the-black-turtleneck-and-the-1-billion-lie-why-no-one-can-stop-talking-about-elizabeth-holmes.

Now, in many ways, the negative attention on Ms. Holmes was at least partly due to the male-dominated nature of the technology industry. Perhaps any attempt on her part to fit in would have been met with harsh criticism. But the takeaway here is that her inauthentic manner of presenting herself drew attention away from her message. You don't want to make the same mistake.

In the context of oral advocacy, authenticity means using your natural voice and mannerisms rather than trying to emulate someone else. Of course, this can be a fine line to tread. The section above provided tips for standing, gesturing, and speaking more confidently, given that most speakers have room for improvement. But this advice is geared toward making your natural speech and movements as polished and persuasive as possible, rather than trying to turn into a different person altogether. Remember, your uniqueness is your strength.

C. Speaking like a pro: Advice from other disciplines

If you're seeking to further refine your oral advocacy skills, you may consider taking lessons from other public-facing disciplines. Many acting schools and coaches provide private lessons and group classes specifically designed for lawyers.[17] If you'd rather not pay the premium associated with these types of classes, you could take basic stage acting classes from a local theater or community college. Acting classes allow you to work on many skills that cross over into oral advocacy, such as stage presence, breath control, and body language.

Improvisational comedy, simply known as improv, can also reinforce public speaking skills. If you're unfamiliar with improv, look up The Groundlings, Second City, or the television show *Whose Line Is it Anyway?* to see what it's all about. The unscripted and collaborative nature of improv comedy is analogous to the spontaneous dialogue that occurs between an advocate and a judge during oral argument. Taking an improv class can help you with active listening skills as well as thinking and speaking on your feet.

If you prefer self-study, you can identify well-known speakers you admire and then watch their speeches and performances on YouTube or other streaming platforms. For example, you could study Oprah Winfrey's 2018 Golden Globes acceptance speech, which was lauded for her masterful use of rhetoric

17. *See, e.g.*, Debra Bruno, *Inside DC's Acting School for Lawyers*, The Washingtonian (Jan. 7, 2020), https://www.washingtonian.com/2020/01/07/inside-acting-for-lawyers-school/.

and engagement with the audience.[18] Once you have found some examples to watch, study how the speakers use skills like timing, variances in pitch and volume, eye contact, and body language to enhance their message.

VII. Dealing with challenges

The courtroom is a high-pressure environment, and lawyers may face various challenges that can impact their oral argument performance. In most circumstances, challenges present some elements you can control and others that are outside your control. This section discusses two common challenges that advocates face, along with some practical advice for doing what you can to manage them.

A. Extreme anxiety

Performance anxiety is a common experience for many lawyers. While some degree of nervousness is normal, extreme anxiety can negatively impact your argument. In the context of this discussion, anxiety is extreme if it causes you to alter your behavior in a maladaptive way. For example, a lawyer's anxiety would be extreme if the lawyer avoids requesting oral argument even when it would be in the client's best interest. Anxiety can also be extreme when it causes debilitating symptoms like fainting or severe nausea.

If you're struggling with extreme performance anxiety, consider seeking help from a medical professional or therapist, or perhaps both. They can help you develop coping strategies and recommend therapies or medications to manage your anxiety. Nowadays, the stigma around seeking professional help for anxiety has diminished greatly in the legal profession. Moreover, many actors, musicians, and other performers are open about using medical therapies like beta blockers to calm nerves before taking the stage.

In addition to seeking professional help, you can employ several other strategies to manage anxiety:

- Prepare thoroughly, knowing the facts, law, and court procedures inside and out.

18. *E.g.*, Emily Canal, *Oprah Winfrey Nailed Every Public Speaking Lesson You Could Learn in Her Golden Globes Speech*, Inc. (Jan. 8, 2018), https://www.inc.com/emily-canal/oprah-winfrey-golden-globes.html.

- Rehearse your argument, timing yourself and seeking feedback.
- Focus on the message you're conveying and its effect on the listener, rather than on your own anxiety.
- Visualize success: Imagine yourself delivering a confident and effective argument.
- Engage in mindfulness meditation exercises to quell negative self-talk.
- Take care of yourself, get plenty of rest and exercise, and eat nutritious meals.
- Avoid using alcohol or drugs (other than those prescribed) within twenty-four hours of oral argument.
- Seek out support groups to share both concerns and coping strategies with an empathetic audience.

B. Addressing biases

Although oral argument can be a valuable opportunity to engage in face-to-face persuasion, the very nature of in-person dialogue introduces bias to the process. Numerous studies have demonstrated that appellate advocates may face different treatment based on race, gender, or other characteristics. For example, a 2017 study of U.S. Supreme Court oral arguments revealed that the Court interrupted women lawyers both earlier and more frequently than men.[19] Moreover, if the person evaluating the advocate's performance holds stereotyped views regarding what an effective advocate looks or sounds like, any deviation from that perceived norm may be viewed unfavorably.[20]

If you find yourself experiencing this type of bias in the courtroom, first and foremost you should understand that it isn't right. Indeed, the Model Code of Judicial Conduct, Canon 2, Rule 2.3, states in part:

> (A) A judge shall perform the duties of judicial office, including administrative duties, without bias or prejudice.
>
> (B) A judge shall not, in the performance of judicial duties, by words or conduct manifest bias or prejudice, or engage in

---

19. Rachel Stabler, *All Rise: Pursuing Equity in Oral Argument Evaluation*, 101 Neb. L. Rev. 439, 457 (2023).

20. *See id.* at 460–63.

> harassment, including but not limited to bias, prejudice, or harassment based upon race, sex, gender, religion, national origin, ethnicity, disability, age, sexual orientation, marital status, socioeconomic status, or political affiliation, and shall not permit court staff, court officials, or others subject to the judge's direction and control to do so.

Although it can be difficult to address this type of conduct during oral argument, you can report violations of your jurisdiction's version of Rule 2.3 to the appropriate commission on judicial conduct.

Of course, some forms of biased treatment are quite subtle. Or in some cases, you may be disinclined to report for various reasons. Remember that you deserve to be treated with respect just as much as the court does. Judges should be treated with professional courtesy, but bad behavior shouldn't be tolerated. Learning to argue with poise and confidence on behalf of your clients may also help you use that confidence to stand up for yourself, when necessary.

Because judges are in a position of authority in our legal system, we sometimes forget that they, too, can experience bias and discriminatory treatment. Anecdotally, some appellate judges have reported being treated differently by lawyers based on characteristics like gender or disability. For example, on a three-judge panel where one judge is a woman and two are men, the woman may notice that male lawyers make less eye contact with her or are more willing to talk over her questions.

As an advocate, consider not only the biases you may encounter but also the biases you may harbor. You can reflect on your potential biases, solicit feedback from other lawyers and judges, and seek out opportunities for professional and social interaction with diverse groups of judges and other lawyers. Recognizing and dealing with bias in the courtroom can help promote a more inclusive and equitable legal system.

VIII. Conclusion

This chapter has provided a comprehensive guide to appellate oral argument. Whether you're stepping up to the lectern in a 100-year-old courthouse or arguing in front of a laptop from your home office, you're now equipped to excel in the modern era of oral argument.

Effective oral advocacy is built on a foundation of skills that require consistent practice and refinement. To further hone your skills, you can study publicly available oral arguments from the world's top advocates. Many courts have YouTube channels where you can watch live or archived arguments. The website Oyez.org provides audio-only recordings of U.S. Supreme Court oral arguments dating back to 1955 (the year the Court installed a recording system).[21] If you enjoy listening to TED Talks, former U.S. Acting Solicitor General Neal Katyal provides meaningful advice in his talk "How to win an argument (at the U.S. Supreme Court, or anywhere)."[22] Study these resources and use them as inspiration.

In addition to the resources described above, be sure to consult this book's Appendix. You'll find a comprehensive oral argument checklist to aid in your preparation. Refer to it regularly and use it to guide your practice.

While oral argument can be intimidating, remember that persistence, preparation, and a commitment to learning are the keys to success. Approach each argument with confidence, professionalism, and authenticity. Your clients and the court expect nothing less.

Discussion Questions

1. Which theory of face-to-face persuasion resonates with you the most, and why?
2. Imagine you are arguing a case in a virtual setting. How would you adapt your style to persuade the judges effectively?
3. What strategies could you use to build rapport with the judges and establish credibility during oral argument?
4. What are your strengths and weaknesses as an oral advocate, and how will you work to improve your skills?
5. What steps will you take to ensure you're presenting your best self during oral argument, regardless of your comfort level with public speaking?

---

21. *About Oyez*, OYEZ, https://www.oyez.org/about (last visited July 30, 2024).

22. Neal Katyal, *How to Win an Argument (at the U.S. Supreme Court, or Anywhere)*, TED (July 2020), https://www.ted.com/talks/neal_katyal_how_to_win_an_argument_at_the_us_supreme_court_or_anywhere?subtitle=en.

Part 5

Special Considerations in Modern Appellate Advocacy

Chapter 12

Technology's Evolving Role in Contemporary Appellate Practice

In this chapter, you'll learn:

- A lawyer's ethical duties regarding legal technology
- Advice for selecting legal technology for your law practice
- How legal analytics can enhance an appellate practice
- The role of artificial intelligence in appellate advocacy

I. Introduction

Writing about technology may seem like an act of folly, given how quickly it evolves. That's why this chapter takes a different approach. Rather than delving into the specifics of rapidly changing tools and platforms, it focuses on the enduring principles that guide lawyers' use of technology.

The legal technology discussion starts with the ethical considerations, exploring how to select technology that aligns with your professional obligations. Next, this chapter examines legal analytics, an established tool that provides valuable insights into case outcomes, judicial behavior, and litigation strategies.

Finally, this chapter ventures into one of the most transformative areas of legal technology: artificial intelligence, specifically generative AI. This chapter discusses its potential to assist lawyers, the parameters for its use, and the pitfalls to avoid. In addition, this chapter provides best practices for using generative AI to assist in drafting legal documents.

Although this chapter refers to specific technology and tools by name, these references are for illustrative purposes only; they are not endorsements. While the information here was accurate when it was written, the nature of technology and the associated firms and brands will change over time. But the underlying principles discussed in this chapter, such as ethical considerations and best practices, will remain relevant. By focusing on principles rather than specific tools, this chapter aims to provide a foundation to navigate the ever-changing landscape of legal technology with confidence and integrity.

II. The ethics of using legal technology

As explained in Chapter 3, Model Rule of Professional Conduct 5.3 makes lawyers ethically responsible for work they delegate to nonlawyers. This responsibility extends to any type of nonlawyer assistance, including legal technology providers. For example, a solo practitioner who is selecting an email platform must carefully assess the provider to ensure that confidential client communications are reasonably safe from a data breach or leak.[1] Further, this ethical responsibility applies to all types of legal technology, from practice management software to online legal research platforms.

Although lawyers have been using legal technology for decades, the widespread availability of generative artificial intelligence has prompted newfound ethical concerns. For example, in 2023, a couple of New York lawyers made national news for filing a brief in federal court written by ChatGPT, a generative AI program.[2] The brief included citations and quotes from nonexistent cases provided by ChatGPT.[3] Apparently, the lawyers failed to research the limitations of this type of AI; one of the lawyers involved stated, "It just never occurred to me it could be making up cases."[4]

1. Model Rules of Pro. Conduct r. 5.3(a); r. 1.6(c) (Am. Bar Ass'n 1983) [hereinafter Model Rules].

2. *See* Molly Crane-Newman, *NYC Judge Scolds Lawyer for Using ChatGPT to Write Brief Full of 'Legal Gibberish'; Attorney Swears Robot 'Duped' Him*, N.Y. Daily News (June 8, 2023), https://www.nydailynews.com/2023/06/08/nyc-judge-scolds-lawyer-for-using-chatgpt-to-write-brief-full-of-legal-gibberish-attorney-swears-robot-duped-him/.

3. *Id.*

4. *Id.*

In this case, the lawyers failed not only to properly supervise as required by Model Rule 5.3 but also to meet their duties of diligence, competence, and candor. In his order imposing sanctions, Judge P. Kevin Castel noted that "there is nothing inherently improper about using a reliable artificial intelligence tool for assistance," but he scolded the lawyers involved for "abandon[ing] their responsibilities when they submitted non-existent judicial opinions ... [, and] then continu[ing] to stand by the fake opinions after judicial orders called their existence into question."[5]

Although AI played a role in this case, the lawyers' shortcomings related to a lack of diligence, oversight, and candor rather than the choice to use ChatGPT. Therefore, the takeaways are fairly mundane, although still quite important: Do not cite cases you have not read. Check your work. Read court documents before signing and filing them. Come clean and admit your mistakes.[6]

Indeed, lawyers may potentially breach their ethical duties if they do *not* use cutting-edge legal technology. As stated above, the duty of competence in Model Rule 1.1 encompasses the duty of technological competence. Comment 8 to Model Rule 1.1 requires lawyers to "keep abreast of changes in the law and its practice, including the benefits and risks associated with relevant technology." Among the many benefits associated with legal technology is the ability to streamline tasks and save time, thereby lowering a client's fees. If a lawyer were to forgo technology and do everything the old-fashioned (read: slow) way, then the lawyer wouldn't be able to charge the client for that time without running afoul of Model Rule 1.5's prohibition on unreasonable fees.

In addition to saving time, legal technology can enhance a lawyer's practice in a multitude of ways. Practice management software provides a suite of applications for communicating with clients, storing electronic files, and maintaining billing records. Legal research platforms are continually evolving to provide brief-writing, cite-checking, and contract-drafting assistance alongside traditional research functions. As discussed later in this chapter, legal analytics and generative AI can help with strategic decisions and document drafting.

Ultimately, the question isn't whether lawyers should use legal technology. Rather, it's how to best use technology while maintaining high ethical standards. The next section goes over some considerations to keep in mind when choosing among the many legal technology vendors in the marketplace.

5. Mata v. Avianca, Inc., 678 F. Supp. 3d 443, 448 (S.D.N.Y. 2023).

6. Notably, the court in *Mata* imposed Rule 11 sanctions based on the lawyers' bad faith, which included "acts of conscious avoidance and false and misleading statements to the Court." *Id.* at 449.

III. Selecting legal technology for your practice

Lawyers have many options when it comes to technology. For purposes of this discussion, technology includes not only applications and cloud computing but also hardware such as phones and laptops. If you're in a position to select software and hardware for an entire law practice, then you'll certainly want to consider your ethical obligations alongside factors such as cost, warranties, training, and ease of use. Even if you're not in that position, you still have individual choices to make about how you use technology to manage your work. Something as simple as storing work-related passwords in a password manager on your personal phone could potentially jeopardize practice-related data.

When assessing legal technology, a paramount consideration must be confidentiality. Model Rule 1.6(c) requires lawyers to take reasonable measures to safeguard confidential client information, including communications. When it comes to using applications, lawyers must be especially careful to ensure that vendors have safeguards in place to protect information from data breaches or leaks. The American Bar Association has issued several formal ethics opinions in the last decade to address this ethical obligation. Formal Opinion 498, issued in 2021, analyzed issues relevant to a virtual law practice.[7] Regarding technology and confidentiality, the opinion made the following suggestions:

- Read and understand the terms of service for hardware and software.
- Use and train staff on the use of strong passwords, virtual private networks (VPNs), encryption, and antivirus software.
- Understand the risks associated with WiFi networks, especially those that are unsecured and publicly available.

As noted above, a lawyer must make reasonable efforts to ensure protection of confidential information when engaging a third-party vendor or using a cloud storage system. Thus, although no system is entirely foolproof, a lawyer must exercise at least a reasonable level of competence and diligence in vetting law practice-related technology. If you find yourself in this situation, keep in mind that you can acquire technological competence through education, training, and association with individuals who possess the requisite level of expertise.

7. ABA Comm. on Ethics & Pro. Resp., Formal Op. 498 (2021).

Even when legal technology provides ironclad protection against breaches and leaks, an untrained user can make decisions that put confidential information at risk. For example, a law firm employee may decide, for the sake of convenience, to use personal devices (phones, tablets, or laptops) rather than workplace devices to access confidential client information. This practice is problematic for a few reasons. Personal devices may lack the robust security measures of workplace-issued devices, making them more vulnerable to hacking and data breaches. Similarly, using personal accounts for work purposes can blur the lines between personal and professional data, increasing the likelihood of accidental sharing or exposure of confidential information. In addition, employees may be putting their personal information at risk, especially if they work for a government agency. If the agency is subject to open records laws, those laws will likely apply to work-related communications even when stored on personal devices.

Ethical use of legal technology also requires training employees to avoid socially engineered data breaches. One of the most widespread methods of unauthorized access is a phishing attack, which can compromise even the most secure technology. Phishing attacks rely on tricking users into divulging sensitive information or clicking on malicious links. Training employees to detect phishing attempts is crucial. This includes educating them on:

- Identifying suspicious emails and attachments
- Verifying sender authenticity
- Avoiding clicking on unfamiliar links
- Reporting potential phishing attempts

Another legal tech consideration is choosing between the free and paid versions of apps. For example, anyone can create a free Gmail account. Gmail also offers, for a fee, email accounts for workplaces that range in size from a handful of employees to hundreds. Paid versions of email and data storage apps, like Dropbox, typically offer advanced data encryption, access controls, and activity monitoring to ensure compliance with industry-specific regulations. While free versions may seem appealing, the risks associated with reduced security features can far outweigh any cost savings.

As you can see, selecting and using legal technology requires a two-pronged approach. First, you must exercise competence and diligence in vetting and engaging legal tech providers. Second, you must ensure that you and those you work with understand how to use technology properly to avoid ethical violations, especially regarding confidential information. Fortunately, several resources exist for lawyers to educate themselves. The American Bar Association's Law Practice Division has a Legal Technology Resource Center that provides helpful guidance on selecting legal technology.[8] Your state or local bar association likely provides similar services to members.

IV. Using legal analytics in appellate advocacy

The previous section examined the general obligation to use legal technology in a competent manner while safeguarding client confidences. With regard to appellate advocacy, certain types of legal technology are especially useful in enhancing a lawyer's practice. A law-related subset of data analytics, legal analytics, has the potential to optimize a lawyer's strategic decisions based on information about courts, judges, and their track record of decision-making.

Using legal analytics in appellate practice carries with it several benefits. For one, legal analytics enable a lawyer to make legal decisions and strategies based upon objective, quantifiable information. As you know from reading Chapter 9, even the most experienced decision-makers are susceptible to the influence of cognitive biases. One way to guard against bias is to check any qualitative decision against the data that legal analytics can provide.

Legal analytics tools also allow lawyers to process and analyze large amounts of data much more efficiently than a person could do alone. If you think about it, tracking down all past decisions of a single judge on a single appellate court could be incredibly time-consuming. Publicly available sources of information, such as PACER, don't always provide the specific information lawyers are looking for. And even if all the information is readily available, sorting and processing it can be time-consuming. However, a legal analytics platform can deliver this information to a lawyer in a manner of seconds.

And the information yielded through analytics can be incredibly useful. For one, tracking past cases and outcomes through a single court can allow for predictive modeling, which forecasts future results based on similar facts. In turn, this type of modeling can allow both lawyers and their clients to make informed decisions regarding case strategy. In addition, legal analytics can reveal trends and patterns in legal decisions. For instance, a lawyer may be able to track the trends in a particular type of dispute when it comes up before a particular appellate court. Given that the U.S. legal system relies on stare decisis, understanding the trends created by past decisions is a skill highly relevant to modern appellate practice.

---

8. *Legal Technology Resource Center*, Am. Bar Ass'n, https://www.americanbar.org/groups/law_practice/resources/legal-technology-resource-center/ (last visited Sept. 9, 2024).

Understanding legal analytics can also provide lawyers and their firms a competitive edge. As you've likely already experienced in your practice, lawyers tend to adopt new trends and technology at a slow pace, arguably slower than that of the general American public. In other words, lawyers are almost never among the early adopters of any specific technology. In this sense, law firms can attain a competitive advantage in the legal marketplace by not only adopting legal analytics but also explaining to clients its advantages and disadvantages.

In a similar manner, individual lawyers or soon-to-be law graduates can also stake out a competitive edge based on tech savvy. Lawyers with a good deal of work experience often embrace the idea of adapting the practice of law to keep up with technology. However, they're also usually reluctant to personally follow through. If you're a junior lawyer in your legal office, you may be able to distinguish yourself through your knowledge of legal tech, especially legal analytics. Of course, it can be personally frustrating to lead the charge when it comes to analytics, especially when the same people who herald it are also likely intimidated by it. Nonetheless, when it comes to legal technology, a willingness to be an early adopter can pay off in the long run.

Although lawyers stand to benefit from legal analytics, using this technology also carries with it some risks:

- Data quality issues: Inaccurate or incomplete data can lead to flawed insights and decisions.
- Overreliance on data: Relying too heavily on analytics may lead to overlooking important subtleties and context that data can't capture.
- Lack of transparency: Complex algorithms can make it difficult to understand the reasoning behind analytics-driven decisions.
- Bias in data and algorithms: Biases in data or algorithms can perpetuate existing inequalities and lead to unfair outcomes.
- Dependence on technology: Technical issues can hinder access to critical tools and insights. The same can happen when a firm is locked into using a specific vendor, whether by contract or because of high switching costs.
- Ethical considerations: Lawyers must ensure that analytics-driven decisions align with their ethical obligations.
- Security and confidentiality: As with all technology, lawyers must ensure that analytics tools protect confidential client information and are reasonably secure from breaches or leaks.

As with anything law-related, your job is to balance the potential risks against the potential reward. The following sections provide a more detailed description of legal analytics and its relevance to appellate lawyers.

A. Legal analytics overview

Legal analytics is a rapidly growing field that leverages data analysis and artificial intelligence to provide insights into legal outcomes, trends, and patterns. Over time, advancements in technology and the increasing availability of legal data have fueled the development of legal analytics. Today, legal analytics involves the analysis of large datasets, including court decisions, briefs, and other legal materials, to identify trends, predict outcomes, and inform strategic decisions. Many lawyers and firms now utilize legal analytics tools to gain a competitive edge in appellate practice, with some reports suggesting that nearly 70 percent of lawyers in firms of all sizes use legal analytics in some form.[9] By harnessing the power of data, legal analytics empowers lawyers to make more informed decisions, anticipate potential outcomes, and craft more effective legal strategies.

Although individual platforms may take different approaches to legal analytics, we can look at Lex Machina as an example to illustrate how legal analytics works.[10] The analytics process begins with data collection. Sorting through various sources, like court filings, dockets, records, and judicial opinions, Lex Machina aggregates large amounts of litigation data. The collected data is then processed and organized into a format that can be analyzed efficiently. Similar to other AI tools, Lex Machina uses natural language processing and machine learning algorithms to analyze the data, extracting relevant information like case facts, judge and attorney profiles, and case outcomes.

To make this processed data useful to users, Lex Machina presents it through interactive dashboards, charts, and reports. In addition, users can look for insights like decision-making trends associated with different judges or courts, attorney and firm performance, and the effectiveness of different legal arguments. Through an interactive platform, users can search and filter

---

9. 2024 *Survey: The Impact of Legal Analytics*, Lex Machina (Jan. 2024), https://pages.lexmachina.com/rs/098-SHZ-498/images/2024%20Legal%20Analytics%20Survey.pdf?version=0.

10. This book doesn't endorse any particular legal analytics platform. However, Lex Machina has a good deal of publicly available information explaining how it operates. For a helpful graphic illustrating the analytics process, visit https://lexmachina.com/how-it-works/ (last visited Sept. 9, 2024).

data based on various criteria, similar to using a legal research platform like LexisNexis or Westlaw.

Lex Machina also uses human expertise to augment machine-driven data processing. While automated systems excel at handling large datasets, human review and oversight are essential for ensuring data accuracy and relevance. By incorporating legal experts into the analytics process, Lex Machina's platform can provide insights that might otherwise be missed by automated systems alone.

Perhaps the most promising feature of legal analytics is its ability to predict outcomes. With the ability to swiftly process large amounts of data and sift through trends, analytics platforms can help lawyers apply predictive analytics to their own cases. These analytics can help lawyers foresee outcomes like the probabilities of prevailing on certain claims or potential settlement ranges.

Thus, legal analytics can be a powerful tool for making informed decisions, saving clients time and money, and providing legal advice that's backed by quantitative data. Moreover, lawyers and firms that use legal analytics can gain a competitive edge in the legal services market. Firms can use trends and insights in newsletters, blogs, and other marketing materials. Lawyers can also look up which firms have previously represented prospective clients to get an idea of potential competitors.

Of course, lawyers must also consider the drawbacks. When it comes to legal analytics, a primary concern would be relying too much on the processes behind the collection, sorting, and analyzing of data. A failure at any point could compromise the reliability of the output, such as trend analysis and outcome prediction. In a broader sense, relying too much on legal analytics to craft strategies and advice could cause lawyers to overlook the human aspect of representing clients. Sometimes, clients have personal or professional reasons for pursuing a "suboptimal" course of action. Data alone cannot inform those types of decisions.

Moreover, lawyers' ethical obligations regarding legal technology apply equally to legal analytics. In selecting a platform, a lawyer must exercise due diligence. In particular, a lawyer must determine whether any confidential client information provided to the platform is kept encrypted and secure from breaches and leaks. In addition, lawyers must ensure they have the requisite competence to properly assess and use legal analytics tools. Lawyers should understand how to place data-driven insights and predictive modeling into the full array of considerations that go into properly advising clients.

B. Using legal analytics in appellate practice

As you've discerned from the overview above, legal analytics can be a powerful tool for appellate practitioners. Predictive analysis is a fundamental part of legal writing. As an appellate advocate, strategic decisions like selecting appellate issues for the brief or requesting oral argument are largely based on your best prediction of how that decision could help or harm your client's case. Without analytics, advocates must focus on the limited data sets of their own experience, observations from other lawyers, and anecdotal evidence. With analytics, advocates can quickly assess high volumes of data to make informed decisions. This section discusses the beneficial uses of legal analytics in appellate practice.

1. Identifying trends and patterns

Legal analytics can help you identify trends and patterns in judicial decisions. For example, platforms like Westlaw Edge[11] allow you to search by judge and then dissect information about the types of appeals they have heard, how frequently the judge affirms, reverses, or remands different types of cases, and how often the judge is subsequently affirmed or reversed by a higher court. You could also study similar data related to particular courts, law firms, or attorneys. When analytics are combined with a legal research platform, you can easily move between the data and the underlying cases and opinions to gain further insights.

Legal analytics also allows you to follow issue-specific trends. For example, you can look up a specific issue, like qualified immunity, and then see how various federal and state courts have decided cases involving that issue.

2. Assessing case strength

Legal analytics can also help you evaluate the strength of your case. Analytics platforms can assist you in comparing your case to similar cases, i.e., cases where the legal issues and facts are analogous. Analyzing how your court has ruled in analogous cases can help you gauge the likelihood of success. You can also use analytics to determine which factors, such as legal issues or procedural history, have most influenced the court's decisions.

And if you and your client are concerned about prevailing in court, you can also turn to analytics for information about settlements and verdicts. For example, Lexis+ can provide analytics as specific as dollar amounts for set-

---

11. *Westlaw Edge Litigation Analytics*, THOMSON REUTERS, https://legal.thomsonreuters.com/en/products/westlaw-edge/litigation-analytics (last visited Sept. 9, 2024).

tlements in your jurisdiction. This data can help you and your client make strategic decisions and potentially save both time and legal fees. Analytics can also help by providing graphics, like charts, to visually explain to clients their likelihood of success on the merits.

3. *Crafting effective arguments*

Legal analytics can inform your argumentation strategy by helping you craft persuasive language for a particular judge. LexisNexis has a tool called Context® that allows you to identify the specific language a judge has used in their own rulings and opinions.[12] You can then choose to use similar language in your brief as a persuasive tactic. Legal analytics tools can also illustrate which sources your judge tends to cite most frequently. If you determine that your judge has their own favorite jurist, you can consider mirroring some of that jurist's language or rhetoric.

Of course, this section provides just an introduction to some of the benefits of legal analytics for appellate practitioners. By the time this book lands in your hands (or on your device), it's likely that the application of legal analytics to appellate advocacy will have evolved even further. The rapid pace of change in the ability to analyze large amounts of data has been influenced in large part by advances in machine learning and the advent of generative artificial intelligence tools like ChatGPT. The next section describes in greater detail how lawyers can incorporate AI tools into appellate practice in a responsible and ethical manner.

V. The role of artificial intelligence in appellate practice

The buzz around AI can be deafening, and the debate is multifaceted. Some decry the end of the practice of law as we know it. Others extol the exciting changes to come. Both viewpoints have some merit. And technology is regularly touted as the harbinger of doom for lawyers. So far, however, technology has not proved to be lawyers' kryptonite, and AI is likely not the death knell for lawyers.

Many, especially those who are developing AI systems, have touted the technology's ability to, among other things, review contracts and other legal documents, draft memoranda, assist with legal research, prepare witness testi-

12. *Context: Predictive Data Analytics for Legal Language*, LexisNexis, https://www.lexisnexis.com/en-us/products/context.page (last visited Sept. 9, 2024).

mony outlines, and review electronically stored information (ESI) for discovery. Lawyers and courts are assessing their value. And many see AI as having the potential to ensure that self-represented litigants are afforded access to justice as never before.

Here's what ChatGPT, a popular AI-powered chatbot, has to say about why law students should learn to use AI systems:

> Law students should learn to use AI systems because these technologies are increasingly becoming integral to the legal profession. Here are a few reasons why:
>
> 1. Efficiency: AI can handle routine tasks like document review, legal research, and drafting, which can significantly speed up legal processes. Learning how to use these tools can help law students become more efficient and effective in their work.
> 2. Competitiveness: Familiarity with AI tools can make law students more competitive in the job market. Many law firms and legal departments are adopting AI technologies, and knowledge of these tools can be a valuable asset.
> 3. Enhanced Legal Research: AI can assist in identifying relevant case law and legal precedents more quickly and comprehensively than traditional methods. Understanding how to leverage these capabilities can improve the quality of legal research.
> 4. Cost Savings: AI can reduce the cost of legal services by automating repetitive tasks. Being able to use these tools can help future lawyers offer more cost-effective services to clients.
> 5. Innovation: AI is driving innovation in the legal field, from predictive analytics to contract management. Law students who are well-versed in AI are better positioned to contribute to these advancements.
>
> However, there are also risks and challenges associated with AI in the legal practice:
>
> 1. Bias and Fairness: AI systems can perpetuate or even exacerbate biases present in the data they are trained on. This could lead to unfair outcomes if not properly managed and monitored.
> 2. Confidentiality and Security: Using AI involves handling sensitive client information, which raises concerns about data privacy and security. Law students and practitioners need to understand how to safeguard this information.

3. Quality Control: Relying too heavily on AI could lead to a loss of critical thinking and judgment. It's important to ensure that AI tools complement, rather than replace, human oversight and expertise.
4. Legal and Ethical Issues: The use of AI in legal practice raises new ethical questions, such as the transparency of AI decision-making processes and accountability for errors made by AI systems. Law students need to be aware of these issues and understand the regulatory landscape.
5. Job Displacement: While AI can increase efficiency, there is a concern that it might displace certain legal jobs, particularly those involving repetitive tasks. Understanding how to adapt to these changes is crucial for future lawyers.

   In summary, while AI presents exciting opportunities for the legal profession, it also brings significant risks that need to be managed carefully. Law students who are adept at using AI and aware of its implications will be better prepared for the evolving landscape of legal practice.

Not bad for a general explanation. And actually, using a generative AI system to help prepare a speech on the overall topic can be useful and efficient. But a lawyer should not rely solely on generative AI, even for this purpose. AI systems have weaknesses, including confidentiality concerns, biases, and hallucinations. For those reasons and others, lawyers should always pull back the curtain and make sure the AI system's generated information is accurate.

A. Technology's impact on the practice of law

All technological advances come with a promise of positive changes, but they also carry a price. By analogy, the automobile has saved untold numbers of lives, but it also has caused countless deaths. When the automobile arrived on the scene, society began the process of maximizing its benefits while minimizing its risks. That balance is the key to successful integration of any technological advance into the practice of law. And when it comes to AI, today's lawyers must find ways to leverage its benefits while controlling for its risks. No doubt, AI will lead to new and novel legal issues. Indeed, it already has.

Rising to such a challenge is nothing new for lawyers. From early on, the legal community has looked for ways to make legal research easier. One need only look to the text preceding opinions from the U.S. Supreme Court to see an early research tool, though one based on human intelligence and not AI.[13] In the late 1700s, the Supreme Court began including a syllabus with each opinion. The syllabus precedes and summarizes every opinion, but it is not part of the opinion, a point the Supreme Court has made markedly clear.[14] In *Detroit Timber*, the government made the mistake of citing the syllabus (or headnote) as controlling authority. The Supreme Court commented, "[T]he headnote is not the work of the court, nor does it state its decision.... It is simply the work of the reporter, gives his understanding of the decision, and is prepared for the convenience of the profession in the examination of the reports."[15]

And the syllabus can be wrong, as one former Reporter of Decisions for the Supreme Court has discussed.[16] In 1886, the then Reporter of Decisions wrote the following in the syllabus for *Santa Clara County v. Southern Pacific Railroad Co.*:

> The court does not wish to hear argument on the question whether the provision in the Fourteenth Amendment to the Constitution, which forbids a State to deny to any person within its jurisdiction the equal protection of the laws, applies to these corporations. We are all of opinion that it does.[17]

The problem: The *Santa Clara* opinion does not address this issue at all, though many have cited it for that proposition based just on the syllabus.

So why discuss this ancient history? Like the Supreme Court's syllabus, AI is a tool for lawyers. And like the Supreme Court's syllabus, it is subject to human and artificial error: human when it comes to bias and artificial when it comes to hallucinations.[18] One even might say the *Santa Clara* Reporter was hallucinating when he wrote the syllabus.[19]

---

13. *See, e.g.*, Chisholm v. Georgia, 2 U.S. 419 (1793).

14. United States v. Detroit Timber & Lumber Co., 200 U.S. 321, 337 (1906).

15. *Id.*

16. *See* Frank D. Wagner, *How Not to Write a Syllabus*, 15 Scribes J. Legal Writing 153, 154–57 (2013).

17. Santa Clara Cnty. v. S. Pac. R.R. Co., 118 U.S. 394, 396 (1886).

18. In the context of legal research outputs by generative AI, "hallucinations" refer to false or inaccurate information generated by the AI that is not based on actual legal authority, precedent, or facts. Generative AI produces hallucinations because it is trained on patterns in data and may mistakenly generate information that resembles but is not actually based on real-world facts, due to limitations in its training data, algorithms, or understanding of context.

19. Frank D. Wagner, a later Reporter, has defended his predecessor and shown that the Santa Clara Reporter had the then Chief Justice's blessing to discuss corporate personhood in the syllabus, even though the opinion did not discuss it. *See* Wagner, *supra* note 16, at 154–57. Between the two, they pulled a rabbit from an empty hat, and a long-standing precedent was made.

Late in the 1800s, Westlaw began indexing opinions, creating value for the legal researcher with what have become Westlaw's West Topic and KeyNumber systems.[20] Likewise, LexisNexis developed its own system of categorizing cases, which revolutionized legal research. Shepard's® became the go-to source for determining how other courts had treated an opinion. But these tools are not a substitute for reviewing and analyzing the opinions themselves.

The hardware associated with legal technology has also evolved rapidly over the last century. On April 2, 1973, about four years after Neil Armstrong took a giant leap for mankind, legal research took a giant leap forward when LexisNexis introduced the first digital tool to search full case opinions.

Starting in the 1980s and 1990s, personal computers, word processing software, fax machines, and the internet became commonplace in every law office, and "the benefits and risks associated with relevant technology" joined the mix along with them.[21] The likelihood of mistakes and inadvertent disclosures increased. During this time, for example, many a lawyer learned the hard way about the risks associated with the "track changes" function in word processing software.

After fifty years of using technology to practice law, the concept is hardly novel. Indeed, technology has been a driving force behind the practice of law since LexisNexis's first foray in 1973. Nowadays, lawyers can use cell phones or tablets to do work that used to require a desktop computer. The cloud has replaced floppy disks and hard drives. E-discovery has taken over traditional paper document reviews. And courtroom technology has far surpassed the overhead and slide projectors of bygone days. Though routine today, the idea of virtual video hearings was practically unheard of a decade or so ago.

No lawyer can avoid the implications of AI. Even everyday applications like Word and Excel incorporate some level of AI technology. Predictive text models and AI-driven grammar and spelling tools are standard features. Internet search engines have used AI since its earliest iterations. And legal research engines, such as Westlaw, LexisNexis, and many newcomers to the market, have released AI-focused research tools. Today, it is virtually impossible to do legal research without using AI. Indeed, law libraries no longer maintain full copies of the office reporters and digests necessary to conduct effective research. Everyone coming into contact with the law inevitably will come into contact with AI.

---

20. *See Conducting Legal Research—Expanding Primary Sources*, Univ. of Fla. Levin Coll. of Law, Lawton Chiles Legal Info. Ctr., https://guides.law.ufl.edu/legalresearch/headnotes (last visited Sept. 9, 2024).

21. Model Rule 1.1 cmt. 8.

As new technology has come online, lawyers have been expected to become competent to work with it and with technology professionals. For example, AI is just the most recent technology whose use raises issues regarding the role of the court and of forensic experts in ensuring that evidence is unaltered. Although using technology to alter evidence is not a new or novel issue, AI-created "deep fakes" have made detection significantly more difficult.[22]

B. AI, defined

AI, in fact, means many things. And the concept is expanding. A key issue for lawyers today is understanding generative AI. The Arizona Supreme Court developed this definition:

> "Generative AI" means AI technology that can create new content through machine learning based on data input. Large Language Models (LLM's) are a type of Generative AI that have been trained on vast amounts of data, which they use to understand prompts and produce content such as, but not limited to, text, images, videos, or sounds. ChatGPT, Microsoft Copilot, and Perplexity are examples of LLM's.[23]

The key is the creation of new content. Generative AI can take a question (also known as a prompt) and draft a document based on its LLM training. Westlaw and LexisNexis now include drafting tools that use generative AI technology. And law firms are using AI to create first drafts of memoranda and other documents.

Generative AI also can sort through a large amount of data, including documents, videos, and photos, and generate summaries, timelines, and the like. In large document cases, judges are expecting lawyers to leverage AI and other search tools to simplify ESI discovery. This type of generative AI requires training to be effective. And large law firms have begun to have groups of lawyers specialize in testing and training these AI tools. Courts are experimenting with AI to improve case processing and responses to public inquiries.

As the above should suggest, AI is a growing presence in almost all aspects of the practice of law. And the above does not address the progressively pervasive use clients are making of AI systems. Increasingly, lawyers will need to understand AI systems to counsel clients and litigate their issues.

---

22. *See, e.g.*, In re Estate of Nunz, 36 N.Y.S.3d 346 (Sur. Ct. 2015).

23. Ariz. Jud. Branch Admin. Code, pt. 1, ch. 5, § 1-509.

C. The lawyer's responsibility

At bottom, it is the lawyer's job to understand the available AI tools—their value and their risks—and then use them accordingly. Just as a lawyer should not blindly rely on a syllabus, a lawyer should not assume that AI has correctly cited a primary source. With that in mind, lawyers must consider certain issues when using technology, chief among them competence, confidentiality, and bias.

1. Establishing competence

Section II of this chapter discussed the ethical duty of competence, including technological competence. Today, Westlaw, LexisNexis, and various newcomers continue to revolutionize legal research with AI-based services. And these companies are using a time-tested means of growing a market for new legal technology: they are making the services available for free to law schools and students. Law students should take advantage of the opportunity and learn everything they can about AI, both its benefits and risks.

In reality, clients (and legal employers) will demand that new lawyers become competent with AI. Law schools are rising to the challenge, as must every new lawyer. AI will redefine many aspects of legal practice over the next five years and will shape its trajectory for at least the next thirty to forty years. By staying ahead of this curve, lawyers can meet their duty of technological competence while providing top-notch services to their clients.

2. Protecting confidentiality

When it comes to AI, the same confidentiality concerns that accompany all legal technology apply to its use. In addition to the best practices described in Part II above, lawyers should take precautions when using generative AI. The platform operates based on user input, or prompts. Lawyers using AI to generate legal documents may create prompts that contain information related to a client's representation. Therefore, a paramount concern is how, where, and for how long the user-provided information is stored.

The gold standard is a software system that does not upload, store, or use user inputs. Most do not meet that gold standard. The next step down, and the most common, is a software system that will hold the user's input in a temporary, sequestered manner. "Sequestered" means that "the vendor protects the confidentiality of user input or prompt data."[24] Even if a vendor claims to

24. *Id.*

protect user data, however, lawyers must take reasonable steps to ensure the accuracy of this claim before providing confidential information.

Of course, non-sequestered systems are a no-go when it comes to client information. Because a non-sequestered system doesn't take steps to safeguard user-provided data, lawyers should never input confidential information in such a system. To learn more, lawyers should review the user agreements for any software used in delivering legal services, including AI-powered software. These agreements are often called end-user license agreements, or EULAs, and can take many forms. Although many people casually click through terms and conditions when accessing websites and apps for personal use, lawyers can't afford to be so casual when client confidentiality is at risk.

Other software vendors' data collection depends on the type of license. For example, Microsoft generally does not collect data if the user is working with an enterprise license purchased by the employer. But if that user opens a document on a personal device, such as a personal laptop or even on a company cell phone, Microsoft may collect data. A simple answer to some confidentiality concerns is the use of virtual private networks (VPNs), but a VPN provides no protection against EULA terms. As for law students, if they handle confidential information while working as a clerk, extern, or intern, they must ask their employer about guidelines for using non-work accounts, such as the Westlaw or LexisNexis accounts provided by their law schools.

One outcome is certain: If a lawyer ignores confidentiality concerns when using technology, they eventually will discover that a software vendor has gathered and used a client's confidential data. Innocence will not be bliss for long. This discussion is not meant to alarm lawyers. But it is meant to raise the confidentiality issue in every lawyer's consciousness.

3. *Detecting bias*

AI systems are human creations, trained on vast amounts of human data. Humans carry implicit biases, which AI systems can inherit from the data on which they are trained. Their output then reflects these biases, which may disproportionately harm certain groups. The challenge for the lawyer in the AI world is dealing with biases that may be difficult to detect and control.

Bias is not new, even in the legal publishing industry. When publishing the Supreme Court's long-repudiated opinion in *Korematsu v. United States*,[25] Westlaw chose to use the plaintiff's Japanese name (Toyosaburo Korematsu) instead of his American name (Fred Korematsu). The corrected version currently available on Westlaw uses the name "Fred Toyosaburo Korematsu"

25. 323 U.S. 214 (1944).

and includes this statement: "Editor's Note: The case title and text within the opinion were amended to correctly reflect the proper name of one or more parties."[26] This type of bias will find its way into output from AI systems. Lawyers must take care to detect these biases and refrain from amplifying them in their own writing.

Likewise, using historical data to train AI may perpetuate historical biases based on race, gender, sexual orientation, and other characteristics. An example involving Amazon and experimental AI may serve as a warning. Here, Amazon had sought to pioneer the use of AI to assist in the hiring process.[27] Amazon trained its system using historical hiring data that reflected a history of gender bias against women applicants. As a result, Amazon's AI system made recommendations that perpetuated this historical gender bias. Although Amazon scrapped the system before using it, others have replicated these bias-based results in AI systems.[28]

Removing bias from historical data has proved an elusive task. The bias is baked into the millions, even billions, of data points the AI system uses to train its LLM, and the links are invisible.[29] As one employer noted, AI systems treated applicants named Jared who played lacrosse more favorably than any other applicant because the data in the LLM linked the name Jared and participation in lacrosse to predicted job success.[30] Another source of potential bias is the growing use of AI algorithms in criminal sentencing and predictive policing. Invisible biases may perpetuate racial or socioeconomic inequality in the justice system.

The presence of potential bias does not mean a lawyer should not use AI systems when appropriate. But the potential for bias is one reason why a lawyer must develop competence before using AI-generated outputs. Any time

26. Likewise, Westlaw omitted the first name of the defendant Gordon Kiyoshi Hirabayashi in *Hirabayashi v. United States*, 320 U.S. 81 (1943). Though Westlaw today includes Mr. Hirabayashi's first name, Westlaw doesn't note the change as it does in the *Korematsu* case.

27. Jeffrey Dastin, *Insight—Amazon Scraps Secret AI Recruiting Tool That Showed Bias Against Women*, REUTERS (Oct. 10, 2018), https://www.reuters.com/article/world/insight-amazon-scraps-secret-ai-recruiting-tool-that-showed-bias-against-women-idUSKCN-1MK0AG.

28. Zhisheng Chen, *Ethics and Discrimination in Artificial Intelligence-Enabled Recruitment Practices*, 10 HUMANS. & SOC. SCIS. COMMS. 567 (2023), https://www.nature.com/articles/s41599-023-02079-x.

29. *See id.*

30. *See* Mark Lemley, *Discrimination and the Human Algorithm, Symposium on Orly Lobel's "The Equality Machine,"* YALE J. REGUL. (Mar. 18, 2023), https://www.yalejreg.com/nc/discrimination-and-the-human-algorithm-by-mark-lemley/.

a lawyer uses an AI system, the lawyer must vigilantly look for potential bias lurking in the background and consider how it might impact legal outcomes.

Ultimately, when it comes to AI, lawyers should use it knowingly and cautiously. Lawyers should experiment with it, as long as the experimentation does not put confidential information at risk of disclosure. And lawyers should look for ways to use it to improve efficiency while minimizing the associated risks.

D. *Best practices when using AI in appellate practice*

Although using AI does carry a risk, lawyers shouldn't overlook the benefits. Generative AI works by predicting text through its rapid analysis of patterns in data. For instance, Meta AI can scan volumes of text, seemingly in an instant, to predict which word most often follows another word. When Meta AI was asked which words most commonly follow the term "heretofore," it generated this response:

> In legal writing, the three words that most often follow the word "heretofore" are:
>
> - granted (e.g., "heretofore granted")
> - made (e.g., "heretofore made")
> - entered (e.g., "heretofore entered")
>
> "Heretofore" is an archaic adverb that means "up to this point in time" or "previously." It's often used in legal documents to refer to actions, agreements, or decisions made before the current point in time.

This predictive text function of generative AI makes it well suited to assist lawyers in many technical aspects of their writing, including:

- Checking for spelling, punctuation, and grammatical errors
- Coming up with alternative ways to phrase a sentence, including generating lists of synonyms
- Changing the tone of a legal document, such as by making it more or less formal
- Reviewing a passage to check for consistency in word choice, formatting, and style

On the flip side, predictive text models don't fare well in performing legal research or analyzing legal issues. At least for now, AI-assisted legal research and drafting often results in "hallucinations," where the system fabricates legal authorities, including party names, case law citations, and summaries.

Because AI models are trained on recognizing patterns rather than understanding legal principles, they may generate plausible-sounding but entirely fictional case law. When it comes to legal analysis, AI systems often have trouble sorting relevant information from irrelevant information, leading to misapplication of the law to the facts. Moreover, its reliance on pattern recognition can oversimplify complex issues, overlooking subtleties and context. These shortcomings further emphasize the importance of human oversight when it comes to using AI to assist in the practice of law.

If you decide to use AI to help with legal drafting, you can take steps not only to ensure accuracy but also to make AI-assisted writing sound more natural. Text generated by AI tends to sound formulaic. The pattern-recognition features of AI systems lead to repetition of certain sentence structures, words, and phrases. Therefore, be sure to review and edit AI-generated text before incorporating it into your legal writing. Check not only for accuracy but for tone and word choice as well. Vary sentence structure and read the text aloud, adjusting as needed.

Finally, be aware that some courts require lawyers to disclose their use of generative AI when drafting court documents. Several federal courts have issued standing orders to disclose AI use, although the practice isn't widespread as of this chapter's writing.[31] For example, on March 1, 2024, Judge Stanley Blumenfeld, Jr., of the U.S. District Court for the Central District of California issued this standing order regarding AI:

> **Artificial Intelligence.** Any party who uses generative artificial intelligence (such as ChatGPT, Harvey, CoCounsel, or Google Bard) to generate any portion of a brief, pleading, or other filing must attach to the filing a separate declaration disclosing the use of artificial intelligence and certifying that the filer has reviewed the source material and verified that the artificially generated content is accurate and complies with the filer's Rule 11 obligations.[32]

As the use of generative AI in legal drafting becomes more accepted, and as the technology improves to become more reliable, these types of orders may fall by the wayside. For the time being, however, they serve as another reminder of Chapter 7's admonishment to always check local court rules before filing a brief.

---

31. *See Tracking Federal Judge Orders on Artificial Intelligence*, LAW360 PULSE, https://www.law360.com/pulse/ai-tracker (last visited Sept. 9, 2024).

32. *Standing Order for Civil Cases Assigned to Judge Stanley Blumenfeld, Jr.*, U.S. DIST. COURT, C.D. CAL. (Mar. 1, 2024), https://s3.documentcloud.org/documents/24747791/blumenfeld_ai-order.pdf.

VI. Conclusion

The integration of legal technology into appellate practice presents both opportunities and challenges for lawyers. As discussed in this chapter, the ethical, thoughtful, and strategic use of legal technology can enhance the quality of appellate advocacy. By understanding new technology while remaining mindful of its limitations, lawyers can more effectively and efficiently represent their clients.

Moreover, appellate lawyers who keep up with evolving legal technology can enhance their marketability. In a rapidly changing world, employers and clients will seek out lawyers who can adapt and innovate. This chapter has provided you with concepts and guidelines to incorporate technology into your legal practice. We encourage you to stay up-to-date and embrace the inevitable changes that will come your way.

Discussion Questions

1. How can generative artificial intelligence assist with legal research in appellate practice? What are the potential pitfalls?
2. What parts of the brief writing process do you think could be automated, and what parts require a human touch?
3. Aside from what this chapter has discussed, how might the use of generative AI and other advanced technologies might raise new ethical considerations for appellate lawyers?
4. How do you think legal technology will continue to evolve and impact appellate practice in the next ten to twenty years?
5. What skills and competencies will appellate lawyers need to develop to stay ahead of the technology curve?

Chapter 13

Appellate Advocacy in Other Contexts: Moot Court, Clerkships, and Pro Bono Advocacy

In this chapter, you will learn how to use your appellate advocacy skills in contexts outside of traditional appellate litigation. Specifically, you'll learn how to:

- Succeed in moot court competitions
- Prepare for judicial clerkships
- Participate in pro bono appellate programs

I. Introduction

Thus far, this book has focused on helping you hone your advocacy skills in the context of traditional appellate litigation. Outside of this traditional context, your appellate advocacy skills are highly transferable to other situations you may encounter as a law student or lawyer. This chapter will explore how these skills can be applied in three distinct settings: law school moot court programs, judicial clerkships, and pro bono appellate initiatives. By recognizing the value of appellate expertise in these contexts, you can enhance your professional development and increase access to justice.

II. Moot court programs

Moot court programs have a rich history. In their modern form, moot court competitions in U.S. law schools date back to at least the early twentieth century.[1] Since then, moot court has evolved into a staple of legal education, with numerous competitions and programs worldwide. By participating in moot court, law students can develop essential skills in research, writing, oral advocacy, teamwork, and time management. Serving on a moot court team can also build camaraderie and boost a law school's reputation.

This chapter focuses on succeeding in moot court competitions, which present a unique blend of academic rigor and competitive pressure. While moot court shares many similarities with real-world appellate advocacy, the competition aspect introduces different types of challenges. The guidance provided in this chapter will benefit students seeking to improve their moot court performance.

In addition to providing guidance for student competitors, this chapter also addresses the crucial role of coaches in moot court success. Effective coaching is essential to helping students navigate the demands of competition and develop their skills. This section offers practical advice for coaches to create a supportive and productive team environment, provide constructive feedback, and foster student growth.

A. Succeeding in moot court competitions

In a moot court competition, student teams represent fictional appellants/petitioners and appellees/respondents in hypothetical appeals. In a typical competition, teams have a specific time period after the problem is released during which to draft and submit briefs. Between the brief deadline and the actual competition, teams will have some time to rehearse their oral arguments. At the actual competition, teams will compete head-to-head in oral argument rounds. A team's performance is based on a combination of the score assigned to its briefs and the score assigned by the judges to its oral arguments.

Beyond these basics, moot court competitions can vary greatly. A typical moot court competition focuses on a specific area of law, such as national security, civil rights, or disability law. Other competitions focus on a particu-

1. *See History of the Ames Moot Court Competition*, HARVARD LAW SCHOOL, https://hls.harvard.edu/ames-moot-court/history-of-the-ames-moot-court-competition/ (last visited Sept. 29, 2024).

lar forum, like the International Criminal Court, or a specific type of dispute resolution, like arbitration or mediation. Some competitions provide a closed-universe problem (no outside research), while others are open. Each competition will have specific rule sets regarding eligibility, scoring, outside assistance, and tournament style (e.g., round robin, single elimination).

Although moot court competitions assess many of the skills that law students use both in the classroom and in practice, performing well in a competition requires different strategies than either classwork or actual legal work require. This section presumes that you have the basic research, writing, and oral advocacy skills to do well in moot court. The advice below focuses on how to excel as a competitor.

1. *Preparation is key*

If your goal is to win a particular competition, you should start preparing up to a year in advance. Let's say your goal is to compete in a particular competition during your 3L year. During your 2L year, help your school's team in its preparations for your target competition. Examine the problem and the competition's rule set to get a feel for the nuances of grading and judging. If possible, travel with the team to the competition as an assistant coach and (if allowed) observe your team's oral argument rounds. Pay attention to the type of feedback the judges provide in their comments and scoresheets. Watch the semifinal and final rounds to see how the winning teams perform.

Even if you are unable to participate in a prior year's tournament, you should still prepare early in the competition cycle. Start by becoming familiar with your law school's moot court structure. Is it a faculty-led program? A student-run board? Are students responsible for raising their own funds, or does the school provide funding? Does the school have to pre-approve the competitions? Does the school or university require special approval for travel, especially international travel?

Once you have ironed out the logistics, your team should register for the competition. Ensure you have assembled a solid team (or teams) of eligible students. The team should have a mix of students (1L if allowed, 2L, and 3L) to allow for year-to-year continuity. Identify a head coach, either in the faculty or the legal community. Some competitions require teams to have coaches. Determine if you can bring your coach to the tournament and work on associated funding issues. Designate a team captain as the point of contact for all competition-related communications.

After the competition releases the problem to students, you may not be allowed to seek outside help during the brief-writing period. If that's the case, then solicit brief-writing advice before the problem is released. Consider meeting with a professor or writing specialist for feedback, and study any feedback from past tournaments you've participated in. Review appellate advocacy texts (like this one) to brush up on your skills.

Remember that being thoroughly prepared includes the logistics of getting to and from the tournament. If your competition is outside your local area, make travel arrangements well in advance. If you wait until the last minute, airfares may be prohibitively high and preferred hotels may be sold out. For international travel, ensure you've met all passport and visa requirements. When you pack your wardrobe and supplies, plan as if you'll go all the way to the final round. If applicable, iron out any details related to disability accommodations.

2. *Know the rules and strategize*

As soon as they're available, read the competition rules thoroughly. Ensure you understand all the rules, and contact the organizers to clear up any ambiguities, if needed. Update your personal calendar with relevant dates and deadlines. Ensure you understand rules related to coaching and outside assistance. Carefully review information related to the number of teams your school can send, how the organizers select which side each team briefs and argues, the judging criteria for briefs and oral arguments, and the method by which teams advance to the finals. If possible, find out whether the competition will be judged by professors, local attorneys, practicing judges, or a mix.

3. *Write a winning brief*

For the most part, the writing advice contained in this book applies to writing a moot court brief. You'll want to write in a simple, straightforward manner, using persuasive writing and storytelling techniques. Format your brief cleanly, using white space and distinct headings. Ensure your Argument is organized logically. Select a basic and easily discerned organizational paradigm, like CREAC, for each individual argument.

In some ways, however, writing a winning competition brief differs from writing a winning brief in real-world appellate practice. The law students or lawyers who are reading and scoring your brief are looking for ways to distinguish yours from the many others that look quite similar. Consequently, superficial errors, like typos or formatting issues, are low-hanging fruit for judges looking for quick point deductions. Although formatting a brief professionally is always important, in moot court competitions it can be critical to success. You don't want to leave easy points on the table. Review Chapter 7 for additional guidance on formatting briefs.

Keep in mind as well that the students or lawyers who are scoring your brief are volunteers and likely squeezing in your brief between other responsibilities, like work and school. Thus, reducing cognitive load is critical. A clean brief that's easy to read will be received favorably. Review Chapters 8 and 9 for a discussion of efficient writing and the psychology of persuasion.

4. Rehearse early and often

After your team has turned in its brief, you should shift your attention to rehearsing oral arguments. Often, your team will have to argue both sides, regardless of which side you represented in writing the brief. Thus, frequent and consistent rehearsals are fundamental to performing well on competition day.

In the week or two leading up to the competition, you'll want to schedule dress-rehearsal-type arguments in front of high-quality judges. Ideally, the judges for these sessions will be a mix of lawyers with practice area expertise, appellate judges, and upper-class students with moot court experience. If you feel intimidated about contacting local judges and lawyers to help you practice, work with your law school's alumni relations/development office. The office can help you identify local alumni who are willing to support students from their alma mater. Your professors may also be able to help you identify potential volunteer judges (or serve as judges themselves). Reaching out to these alumni to schedule practice sessions can also provide you with an organic networking opportunity.

Once you have some volunteer judges locked in, provide them with the moot court problem, a copy of your brief, and some potential questions to ask during oral argument. Working with your team to come up with potential questions is a terrific way to prepare, and your volunteer judges will appreciate the help. Also keep in mind that your practice sessions can take place in person or virtually. Holding a virtual rehearsal is probably the most convenient option, but if your competition requires in-person argument, you'll want to schedule at least one in-person practice in the week or two before the competition.

Working backwards, you should also schedule some lower-stakes rehearsals about three to four weeks before the tournament. These practice sessions can take place with your teammates or other law students. In fact, rehearsing with fellow students who know nothing about your competition can be quite beneficial. They can provide a perspective similar to the volunteer judges you'll encounter at the competition who often are not terribly familiar with the problem. The "uneducated" feedback you'll receive, albeit frustrating, will approximate some of the feedback you're likely to encounter at the competition.

5. *Dazzle the judges*

In a real-world oral argument, the panel of appellate judges may be assessing your performance to a certain degree, but more likely they're directing their energy toward eliciting information to help them make an important, perhaps precedent-setting, decision. At a moot court competition, the judges have no decision to make other than how to rank your performance. Thus, the somewhat unfortunate truth is that moot court oral arguments often emphasize style over substance. To be certain, the best teams will demonstrate their command of both the facts and law. But as with the briefs, the judges are also looking for the low-hanging style points. This means that appearance and delivery take on an outsize significance in moot court.

With this in mind, consider how you can align your presentation skills with the expectations of moot court judges. Confident posture, purposeful hand gestures, appropriate volume, even pace, and an assured demeanor can go far. Indeed, a polished presentation can create a halo effect. A few lapses in the substance of your argument may be overlooked if your delivery is on point.

Another tip is to come up with a catchy theme that you clearly articulate during your argument. Although real-world arguments often resist simplistic framings, moot court arguments can benefit greatly from a well-defined theme. Remember that the moot court judges must turn in score sheets almost immediately after the round concludes. As a result, oral argument scores are highly influenced by first impressions. A memorable theme articulated in the opening of your argument can help unify your message and convey the perception that you're prepared, polished, and in command.

And as hard as it can be sometimes, embrace feedback and use it to improve performance. In most competitions, judges will provide immediate feedback at the end of a round. Listen carefully for important clues regarding their likes and dislikes. In some tournaments, you'll see the same judges in future rounds. However, be cautious when adjusting your strategy based on individual feedback, especially if the feedback focuses on presentation style or delivery. Such comments can be biased, reflecting personal preferences rather than objective improvements. Unless feedback clearly identifies a detrimental habit (e.g., distracting pen-clicking), avoid altering your approach based on a single judge's opinion.

6. *Enjoy the ride*

As clichéd as it may sound, don't forget to have fun. At its core, a moot court competition is both a game and an adventure. Although the pressure may feel intense in the moment, the lasting benefit comes from the opportunities to sharpen your skills, explore new places, forge lasting bonds with classmates, and connect with peers from other schools. If your competition takes you out of your state or country, carve out some time for sightseeing. Regardless of how your team performs, plan a celebratory dinner to mark the occasion. You'll eventually forget the finer points of your competition performance, but the fond memories and warm feelings can last a lifetime.

Success in moot court competitions requires hard work, a thick skin, and a learning mindset. By developing your appellate skills and following the strategies above, you should be in a good place to perform well.

B. Coaching a moot court team

Whether you're a practicing lawyer or an upper-level student, opportunities abound to serve as a moot court coach. Almost invariably, moot court coaches are volunteers, and teams are always looking for good coaches. Serving as a coach allows you to play a vital role in developing law students and guiding them through the rigors of competition. This section provides advice on how to be an effective and supportive moot court coach.

1. *Establish clear expectations*

Once you're on board as the team coach, schedule a team meeting as soon as possible to set expectations. You'll want to let the students know how to contact you and whether you have any preferences regarding communication (e.g., no text messages). During this meeting, you can also help the team set internal deadlines for writing the brief and scheduling practice arguments. Ask the students if they have any specific goals for the competition or any particular skills they would like to develop throughout the process. You can also help the team divide up responsibilities and roles. Above all, encourage the team to communicate openly with you.

2. *Empower student leadership*

All sorts of obstacles can arise while preparing for a competition, ranging from law school logistics to issues with the competition's organizers. As a coach, you may be tempted at times to take the reins. To the extent possible, resist this temptation and let the students take the lead. Moot court competitions can help students develop skills beyond appellate advocacy. Competitions can provide opportunities to work on time management, professional communication, and self-efficacy. Encourage students to solve their own problems but be available as a sounding board. Step in only when necessary, and always with the goal of supporting and empowering your team.

3. *Understand the pressures students face*

In any given semester, a law student may be taking classes, working as an extern, serving as an officer for one or more student organizations, and taking care of family members. Balancing moot court obligations with these other priorities can be daunting. If you find that your team members are falling behind in their moot court prep, understand that they're most likely dealing with other priorities. In your role as the coach, you can gently encourage the team to stay on track while also expressing understanding for their busy law school lives.

4. *Provide effective on-site coaching*

When coaching at the actual competition, consider your responsibilities carefully. You may be traveling a great distance, staying at a hotel in an unfamiliar city, and coordinating other logistics. While some coaches prefer a hands-on approach, accompanying students and sharing meals, others focus solely on competition activities, allowing students to travel and socialize independently. Unless the law school requires you to chaperone the team, your approach is up to you. Remember, however, that the team will look up to you as a role model and take cues from your behavior.

During the competition, strike a balance between constructive feedback and encouragement. If you're allowed to observe the students during their oral argument rounds, be mindful when it comes to critiquing their performance. Avoid focusing on performance aspects that cannot be changed immediately, as this may cause more harm than good. In addition, encourage students to treat other teams with courtesy and respect. As a coach, you set the tone, so be sure to model the behavior you expect from your team and interact respectfully with other coaches.

5. *Encourage the team to reflect*

Regardless of how the team performs, be sure to schedule a post-competition meeting or activity to debrief and strategize. Consider treating the team to coffee or lunch as a gesture of appreciation for their efforts. During this meeting, take the time to celebrate the team's achievements and highlight individual strengths. Open the floor for a candid discussion to identify areas for improvement and gather feedback. Encourage students to share their experiences, insights, and suggestions for future growth. Above all, let the students know that you're proud of their hard work and dedication.

This post-competition meeting also serves as a valuable opportunity for the team to unwind and bond. By reflecting on their experience, the team can gain valuable insights and develop strategies for future competitions. This meeting can also help you wrap up the coaching experience on a high note for everyone involved.

By following these strategies, you can create a positive and productive coaching experience and help your moot court team develop their advocacy skills. Moreover, your impact as a coach can extend beyond the competition. As a mentor and role model, you can foster students' professional development. Providing a good moot court experience can also inspire your students to serve as coaches in the future.

III. Preparing for appellate court clerkships

From the first day of law school orientation, if not earlier, law students hear about exalted, but elusive, judicial clerkships. Many first-generation law students have never heard of judicial clerkships. Even for students who know what a judicial clerkship is, they do not fully understand what these jobs entail and why they should pursue one.

Every year, most, if not all, law schools track and tout the number of their graduates who secure judicial clerkships. Judicial clerkships generally are the gold standard of post-graduation jobs, requiring a law degree and lasting at least a year.

Despite the aura surrounding judicial clerkships, law schools, courts, and judicial officers do not do a good job of selling students on these incredible and important jobs. Too often, whether directly or indirectly, law students hear they are not ideal "law clerk" applicants. Please do not take that message to heart. There is no ideal law clerk applicant.

The only way to ensure you will not get a judicial clerkship is by not applying in the first place. One of the authors, a first-generation law student himself, nearly did just that, believing that others far more worthy would snag those coveted clerkships. After all, judicial clerkships seem so out of reach — indeed, just 3 to 5 percent of recent law graduates begin their legal careers working as a law clerk. And many in that 3 to 5 percent were not "ideal candidates," but they were the right candidates for the right judicial officer. If you are interested, do not write yourself out of your own life story. Believe in yourself and apply. This author did, and it was life changing.

A. The basics of the job

So, now you know you should consider clerking but still have no real idea about what the job entails. Let's explore.

Appellate and trial courts have law clerks, as do different jurisdictions, including federal, state, and local courts. Most judicial clerkships are for one or two years. But some judicial officers choose to have permanent clerks who work with the same judicial officer for longer periods of time.[2]

Law clerks are often called elbow clerks because they sit side-by-side with the judicial officer, working on cases directly. Each clerk's specific duties will vary depending on the judicial officer, even on the same court. Even so, most law clerks conduct legal research, prepare case summaries, advise the judge on legal matters, and draft rulings. A law clerk generally will work alone on an appeal, though the law clerk likely will confer with the judge, other law clerks, and staff attorneys. In that regard, most law clerks find the experience to be rewarding and collegial.

Judicial officers take pride in being accurate. Law clerks help them be that. Law clerks spend much of their day reading briefs and studying records. The law clerks must focus on the details. Certainly, judicial officers will review the briefs and the record, but because of the number of cases they handle, judicial officers must rely on the law clerks to know the record cold. Most of the rest of a law clerk's day is spent researching the law and writing up that research, either in the form of a memorandum or draft decision. Law clerks spend little time in the courtroom itself except to observe the occasional oral arguments on their assigned cases.

The benefits of clerking include learning the law and legal analysis from members of the judiciary, interacting and building relationships with judicial officers and other law clerks, and making a meaningful contribution to the court. Working in a judicial clerkship instead of jumping directly into practice offers other benefits:

- The ability to hone legal research and writing skills: Law clerks generally conduct in-depth research on legal issues related to the cases before the court and often draft bench memoranda, legal opinions, and rulings.

---

2. Most courts also have staff attorneys who work on cases, though they generally work for the entire court instead of being assigned to a specific judicial officer. Some recent graduates and law clerks will find opportunities as a staff attorney. The duties of law clerks and staff attorneys can differ dramatically depending on the court. Often staff attorneys focus on a very narrow area of the law, such as habeas proceedings or unemployment benefits cases.

- The opportunity to advise the judicial officer: Law clerks provide valuable insight to help the judicial officer decide complex legal issues. This advisory role is crucial, especially in high volume courts with significant caseloads.
- Exposure to the judicial process: Law clerks get the comparatively rare opportunity to peek behind the curtain and gain understanding of how courts and judges operate. They experience court proceedings and discussions on case law and court strategy.
- Career development: Many law clerks find that their clerkships can help launch their careers in a thoughtful and purposeful way. Clerkships can have a long-term impact, especially for those hoping to pursue a career in litigation, academia, or the judiciary.

Judicial clerkships also provide a transition from law school to practicing law in a relatively safe and nurturing environment: The law clerk works under the watchful eye of a seasoned lawyer turned judicial officer. Most judicial officers take an interest in their law clerks' careers. And many law clerks find that their judicial officer becomes a lifelong mentor. For these reasons, judicial clerkships historically were coveted. In recent years, they have been losing some of their luster, especially as the cost of law school skyrockets, private law firm salaries soar, and salaries for government-employed law clerks remain comparatively low. Those who secure a clerkship at the U.S. Supreme Court may see law firms competing to hire them by offering large six-figure sign-on bonuses, and some federal circuit court clerkships may open up similar, though not as lucrative, opportunities. But for most, a judicial clerkship is a lower-paying, temporary job that offers significant rewards not immediately but rather over time. And for most, it's worth it.

B. Due diligence

Applicants who are considering a clerkship should do their due diligence. Two temptations arise during the application process: (1) taking the "holy grail" approach, applying for the most prestigious clerkships to build the resume, or (2) taking the "shotgun" approach, applying everywhere to improve the odds. Applicants should avoid these temptations. Instead, applicants should ensure the specific court and judge will provide the experience the applicant seeks. Sometimes the "holy grail" clerkship will do just that, but not always. Applicants ultimately should make wise decisions about where to clerk, just like they would regarding any other important career decision.

To that end, before beginning the application process, applicants should consider what they hope to get out of a clerkship. If the applicant is hoping to work draft rulings and opinions, then the applicant should make sure the court and the judicial officer have law clerks do just that. Many do, but others do not. Instead, some courts and judicial officers have law clerks create bench memoranda. In short, clerkship experiences vary greatly. Applicants need to consider their own needs when applying to help ensure that both they and the judicial officer have a positive experience if the applicant is hired.

Due diligence means that applicants must assess the differences between the ways the various courts and judges work with law clerks. Many offer unique opportunities. For example, at the intermediate appellate level, the Arizona Court of Appeals, Division One, allows staff attorneys, law clerks, and externs to participate when the panel conferences cases. They present cases to the panel and answer questions. They get to hear the panel members' thoughts on the drafts and the analysis. Few courts offer this opportunity. An applicant who wants to gain insight into judicial decision-making may find a clerkship at Division One more valuable than a more prestigious clerkship at a different court. If the applicant is looking for more hands-on learning at the trial-court level, the applicant should look to the federal district courts and state trial courts. Indeed, working with a respected state court judicial officer in the jurisdiction where the applicant intends to practice may provide a far more valuable experience than a more prestigious clerkship in a distant location.

Once the applicant has a good understanding of their own goals, the applicant can begin researching specific courts and judicial officers. Applicants should talk with folks in the law school's placement office. Often, other students and alumni have worked with the various courts and judicial officers and so have acquired valuable insights, and many are willing to talk with current students about their experiences. Courts themselves recognize the need to improve their recruiting efforts, and many go to nearby law schools to meet with interested students. And many are using remote recruiting programs to reach students from more distant schools. Take advantage of these programs.

Participating in a judicial externship while in law school is another way to gain valuable insight. Externships give law students a first-hand view of the court's day-to-day operations. They allow law students to build relationships with current law clerks and staff attorneys who may prove to be invaluable resources. And plenty of externships serve as feeder opportunities. For these reasons, a law student must bring their best self to their externship. For those who cannot afford to take a year or two to serve as a law clerk, a judicial externship can offer some of the same benefits as a law clerkship. Some even refer to the externship experience as a pre-graduation clerkship opportunity.

C. A personalized cover letter

Today, too many view the cover letter as a fungible document. It is not.

Form letters abound. Too many applicants skip inclusion of the judicial officer's name so as to avoid the need for updates. Those generic letters offer no specific reason for wanting to work with that judicial officer on that court. To the reviewing judicial officer, judicial assistant, and current law clerks, such letters are a sure sign of a shotgun approach. In that regard, many cover letters are a lost opportunity to get the judicial officer's attention, especially for the less-than-ideal applicant. Some form language in a cover letter is okay, but the cover letter must answer these three questions: (1) why me, the applicant; (2) why you, the judicial officer; and (3) why now?

The cover letter is an opportunity to infuse life into an otherwise cold resume and transcript. If, as an applicant, you are interested in working with a specific judicial officer and on a specific court, the cover letter should say so. For example, an applicant who is interested in Indian law should consider federal courts within the Ninth and Tenth Circuits where much of that law is made, and the cover letter can make that point. If the applicant is interested in experiencing conferences at the Arizona Court of Appeals, Division One, the cover letter should talk about the applicant's interest. If the applicant is applying to a judicial officer because of the judicial officer's work in a particular area, such as tax law or criminal prosecution, say so in the letter and say why.

The cover letter also is an opportunity to give the judicial officer insight into the applicant. It is the chance to "draw the sting" of any potential perceived flaw in the resume. Jumping to the most common flaw, 90 percent of all law students are not in the top 10 percent of their class. And a significant percentage of law clerks are part of that larger 90 percent. Indeed, a significant percentage of the judicial officers hiring law clerks also were not in the top 10 percent of their class. Address that type of issue. If the first semester has pulled down the applicant's grade point average but they have improved that grade point average ever since, say so, and then turn it into a positive by highlighting the improvement: highlight higher grades, perhaps in legal writing or appellate practice, for example. In short, use the cover letter to succinctly tell your story.

For the sake of due diligence, applicants should research the judicial officers they are applying to. Today, applicants have access to more information about judicial officers than at any other point in history. Many have their biographies posted online, and a growing number have a social media presence. Applicants can easily find a judicial officer's noteworthy decisions, and they can assess a judicial officer's writing style and approach to legal reasoning. All this information gives the applicant a better understanding of who the judicial officer is and how the judicial officer thinks, and it will likely give the applicant insight into what should be in a cover letter to get that judicial officer's attention.

Once the applicant has a better understanding of the specific judicial officer, the cover letter should flow more naturally. It should leave the judicial officer looking forward to meeting the applicant. And it will make it more likely that the applicant will get an interview.

D. An informative and readable resume

Three common mistakes arise in resumes: (1) the resume is too long; (2) the resume is too hard to read; and (3) the resume offers no insight into the applicant. So here are seven golden rules to follow to help you avoid these mistakes.

One, unless the applicant had a career before law school, the resume should be just one page. If the applicant had a career before law school, the resume ideally should be just one page, but absolutely no more than two pages.

Two, the font should be large enough to ensure readability. Too many think the solution to a one-page resume is a smaller font. It is not. Judges are used to reading legal filings in a certain font and font size. Applicants should look to the local court rules to decide what to use for their resume. Adhering to the local court rules regarding font can make the resume feel more familiar to the judicial officer and others who may read it. (This advice also applies to the cover letter.)

Three, the resume should use standard margins. Narrow margins are not an appropriate substitute for brevity and careful editing. Judicial officers know that. A well-crafted, to-the-point resume shows the judicial officer the applicant is discerning and cares about writing.

Four, the resume should have plenty of white space. White space makes it easier to read and provides room for notes.

Five, the resume should be easily readable on paper and on the screen. Many aspire to the paperless office, but not all are successful. Additionally, not everyone who will read the resume and other materials will use the same format, so, if possible, the resume should be in a format that cannot be modified (such as a PDF).

Six, the applicant should edit the resume to ensure it does not contain extraneous information. For example, if the applicant worked for a firm where they reviewed documents for privilege, say so (including the type of privilege), but do not go into a step-by-step explanation of the review process.

Seven, personalize the resume if possible. Applicants should look for commonalities with the judge and tag them in the resume. Again, a little research on the judge can do wonders. But be sincere—for example, rescuing dogs should not be on the resume unless it is part of who the applicant is. Judicial officers can suss out those things pretty quickly.

E. A useful writing sample

To be effective, a writing sample should be clear and concise. It should not be a document that others have edited. Law review articles are interesting and may have a place on the resume, but for the judicial officer, they provide little insight into the applicant's actual writing ability.

To begin, the applicant must consider what restrictions the judicial officer has placed on the writing sample, such as page or word limits. And, just as with the cover letter and resume, the formatting matters. With word processing, applicants no longer need to literally cut and paste a photocopy from a larger document, which means they can edit the work to meet the judicial officer's requirements. If the writing sample is part of a larger work, put the provided portion into context.

In selecting the writing sample, avoid overly complex writings. The goal is to showcase the applicant's writing for the judicial officers, the judicial assistants, and the law clerks. The sample should demonstrate the applicant's ability to winnow down the issues, just like an appellate lawyer would do. The sample should move through the analysis thoughtfully and thoroughly. The writing should be crisp and engaging. Even dry legal topics can be engaging if the work is well written.

The writing sample also should show the applicant's best work. By the time law students are applying for judicial clerkships, they will have had the opportunity to draft more than just a law review article or a first-year memorandum. Those other documents are more helpful.

In editing your writing sample, look at the judicial officer's published work. Often, the applicant can identify certain style markers. The applicant should consider making conforming edits to their sample. For example, if the judge uses the serial comma, then use the serial comma in the writing sample. Look at the judge's paragraph structure. If the judge uses mostly short paragraphs or three or four sentences, then the writing sample should do the same. Making these changes does not require the applicant to entirely give up the applicant's own style, but it does demonstrate the applicant's ability to write like the judge. Many judges expect clerks to learn to write in that judge's voice, and so demonstrating this ability during the application process can open the door to an interview.

F. The interview

Most qualified (even if not ideal) applicants will get at least a few interviews. Interviews are almost always stressful. Preparing for the interview can reduce the stress and increase the likelihood of success.

First, consider asking the judge's judicial assistant or current clerk if the judge has any particular expectations for the interview. Doing so shows a sincere interest in the judge, respect for the judge's role, and the applicant's desire to be prepared. Judicial staff often are willing to give some general insight. Also, reach out to others who have interviewed with the judge as they often can provide more detailed insight. The school's career services office may be able to help identify some of these folks.

Second, review the cover letter, resume, and writing sample. Be prepared to talk about anything mentioned in them. One of the authors once asked about an acronym on an applicant's resume. The applicant did not know what it stood for. That fact alone was not fatal to the applicant, but it suggested that the applicant had not looked at the resume for a while.

Third, the applicant should go into the interview with a positive attitude. A judge is setting aside the time to meet and talk with the applicant, which means that the judge has decided that the applicant is able to do the job; otherwise, the judge would not have scheduled an interview. At the interview stage, the judge wants to get to know the applicant. What an amazing thing for a law student to have a judge be interested in them. The goal is to give the judge insight into who the applicant is, not who the applicant wishes they were. Successful applicants find a way to just be themselves during this process. Most applicants can accept when a judge decides to go with someone else; the applicants who struggle the most after an interview are those who presented as the person that they thought the judge wanted to meet.

Fourth, have an elevator-speech conclusion. The judge may or may not ask if the applicant has anything else to add. That is okay. That speech can follow a judge's simply thanking the applicant for coming. The applicant can respond with a sincere thank you and follow it with the pitch very naturally.

Fifth, have some questions ready. They should not be employment-focused questions, such as start dates and salary. The questions should be focused on the judge and making sure the judge has all the information needed to make their decision. A good wrap up question is "What can I tell you about myself that we have not covered?" or "As you're making your decision, what else would you like to know about me?" It shows courage and openness. And it invites the judge to touch on something that might have been overlooked.

Sixth, be prepared to meet and interact with the judge's staff. Often, a judge's staff also interview the applicants. Though this phase can be more casual, it is not hanging-out-with-friends casual. Be professional and genuinely curious about their experiences. Ask them what an applicant can do to be most prepared to clerk for the judge. And treat everyone with respect and dignity. Say hello and thank you. When the applicant sends a thank you note or email to the judge, they should also send one to each staff person involved in the process.

Again, if a judge extended an interview, the applicant is well on the way to getting the job. And even if it does not work out, the applicant still has made a solid connection in the legal community. And the story may just be beginning. Judges interview more applicants than they can hire. So even if one judge does not extend an offer, it does not mean the applicant did not impress the judge. And judges trade recommendations when an applicant impresses them. Every year, law clerks get hired from this secondary market.

IV. Pro bono appeals

Appellate practice can be gratifying on many levels. Lawyers often enjoy the intellectual challenge, the blend of written and oral advocacy, and the ability to shape legal precedent. However, a career as an appellate lawyer isn't always easy to come by, especially for recent law graduates. Nevertheless, lawyers and law students can gain valuable appellate experience by representing appellate clients on a pro bono basis.

Various methods exist to find pro bono clients. An interested lawyer could contact local legal services organizations, nonprofits like the American Civil Liberties Union, or the courts directly. This method works well for lawyers who already have some appellate experience. For less experienced lawyers (and law students), working with a structured pro bono appellate program can be a better alternative.

Pro bono appellate programs play an important role in increasing access to justice for individuals and organizations who can't afford legal representation. Moreover, reducing the number of self-represented litigants can increase judicial efficiency, as proceedings typically go more smoothly when all parties are represented by counsel. Pro bono programs also strengthen the legal community by building partnerships among courts, lawyers, firms, and law schools.

Furthermore, pro bono appellate programs can help lawyers and students enter into appellate practice. In a typical program, cases are carefully screened and volunteers are provided assistance and oversight in drafting the brief and preparing for oral argument. Some programs also provide malpractice insurance coverage to their volunteers. In this manner, pro bono programs can mitigate some of the risks of undertaking a new area of practice.

Many appellate courts, both state and federal, administer their own pro bono programs. For example, the U.S. Court of Appeals for the Ninth Circuit has had a pro bono program since 1993.[3] Per the court, the program "has grown from 12 cases per year to approximately 160."[4] Court staff review pending cases involving self-represented litigants and select cases that "would benefit from briefing and argument by counsel."[5] Moreover, the court ensures that almost every pro bono case will include oral argument.[6] During the appeal, the court's pro bono coordinator assists volunteer lawyers with logistical issues and cost reimbursement.[7]

Law students can participate in the Ninth Circuit's pro bono program through their law schools' clinical program, if applicable. For instance, Pepperdine Caruso School of Law's Ninth Circuit Appellate Advocacy Clinic draws its caseload from the court's pro bono program.[8] Students work in teams of two under the supervision of clinical faculty to draft a brief and participate in oral argument.

---

3. *Pro Bono Program*, U.S. Courts for the Ninth Circuit, https://www.ca9.uscourts.gov/probono/ (last visited Sept. 29, 2024).

4. *Id.*

5. U.S. Court of Appeals for the Ninth Circuit, Pro Bono Program Handbook 1 (2019), https://cdn.ca9.uscourts.gov/datastore/uploads/probono/Pro%20Bono%20Program%20Handbook.pdf.

6. *Id.*

7. *Id.* at 3.

8. *Ninth Circuit Appellate Advocacy Clinic*, Pepperdine Caruso School of Law, https://law.pepperdine.edu/experiential-learning/clinical-education/clinics/ninth-circuit-appellate-advocacy/ (last visited Sept. 29, 2024).

Lawyers and students can also seek out nonprofit organizations that administer pro bono appellate programs. One of the authors has worked with the Veterans Consortium Pro Bono Program to represent veterans with cases pending at the U.S. Court of Appeals for Veterans Claims.[9] These cases typically involve a full or partial denial of the veteran's claim for benefits, such as disability compensation or education benefits. All volunteers must undergo in-depth training on veterans law prior to undertaking an appeal. Volunteers then work with a mentor attorney to obtain the record, contact the client, and identify appellate arguments. Although most cases do not include oral argument, this program nonetheless helps in developing client counseling and written advocacy skills.

The Ninth Circuit program and the Veterans Consortium are just two examples of the many programs available throughout the United States. Your jurisdiction likely provides similar opportunities for volunteer lawyers. Participating in these programs will allow you to improve the administration of justice while working on your own writing and advocacy skills. Moreover, pro bono work allows you to fulfill your professional obligation "to provide legal services to those unable to pay."[10]

V. Conclusion

In this chapter, we explored how to apply appellate advocacy skills beyond traditional appellate litigation. By leveraging these skills in moot court competitions, judicial clerkships, and pro bono programs, law students and lawyers can enhance their professional development while contributing to the legal community. We encourage you to consider other contexts in which you can make a positive impact by applying what you've learned through your study of appellate advocacy.

---

9. *The Veterans Consortium Pro Bono Program*, The Veterans Consortium, https://www.vetsprobono.org/ (last visited Sept. 29, 2024).

10. Model Rules of Pro. Conduct r. 6.1 (Am. Bar Ass'n 1983).

Discussion Questions

1. What are your strengths and weaknesses in appellate advocacy, and how can you leverage or improve them in moot court, clerkships, or pro bono work?
2. Reflect on your past experiences in law school or legal settings. How have you already applied appellate advocacy skills in unexpected ways?
3. What are your career goals, and how can developing appellate advocacy skills in alternative contexts help you achieve them?
4. How do you see yourself using appellate advocacy skills to make a positive impact in the legal profession or your community? Consider areas both within and outside the practice of law.
5. What skills or knowledge do you need to develop further to feel confident about applying your appellate advocacy skills in alternative contexts?

Appendices

Appendix A

Sample Appellate Brief Editing Checklist

Formatting According to Court Rules

- Have I used the correct font and spacing throughout the brief?
- Are the margins and indentation correct?
- Are headings and subheadings clearly labeled and consistent?
- Have I included all required components of the appellate brief?
- Have I properly formatted the cover/case caption page, tables, and certificates?
- Have I used the appropriate legal citation format consistently and correctly?

Argument and Analysis

- Have I clearly stated the issues in a persuasive manner?
- Is my argument logical and well-supported?
- Have I effectively used legal authorities and case law precedent?
- Have I used an analytical paradigm to organize my argument?
- Have I accurately structured the type(s) of legal reasoning I'm using in my brief (e.g., rule-based, analogical, statutory construction)?
- Have I addressed weaknesses and counter-arguments?

Clarity and Conciseness

- Have I avoided using jargon and legalese?
- Is my language simple and straightforward?
- Are my paragraphs and sections concise and focused?
- Are my headings clear and persuasive?
- Have I avoided wordiness by checking for the following:
  - Nominalizations
  - Passive voice
  - Expletives
  - Redundant words and phrases

Writing Style

- Is my writing natural and conversational?
- Have I used persuasive writing techniques effectively?
- Have I used transition words, phrases, and sentences effectively?
- Is my language professional and respectful?
- Have I avoided bias and inflammatory language?

Mechanics and Grammar

- Have I written concisely by avoiding passive voice, expletives, and nominalizations?
- Have I proofread carefully to correct any grammatical, punctuation, or spelling errors?
- Have I used editing and proofreading technology to check my work?
- Have I listened to my brief aloud to identify unnatural language, wordy sentences, or other errors?

Final Check

- Have I checked the relevant court rules (including local rules) to ensure compliance?
- Have I reviewed the brief for accuracy and completeness?
- Is my formatting and style consistent throughout?
- Have I verified my citations and authorities?
- Have I proofread for errors and typos?

Appendix B

Sample Oral Argument Checklist

Overall Preparation

- I have carefully reviewed the briefs, record on appeal, and any motions.
- I have checked to see whether the authorities cited in the brief are still good law, and whether the law has changed since the briefs were filed.
- I have reviewed the court's rules and procedures for oral argument.
- I have identified which judges will hear my argument and considered their perspectives.

Argument Preparation

- I have identified the key points I want to address in my argument.
- I have organized my argument logically and prepared an outline.
- I have anticipated potential questions and prepared responses.
- If applicable, I have planned for a concise and impactful rebuttal.
- I have practiced my delivery and timing, preferably in a moot court session with live feedback.

Organizing Materials

- I have organized my materials into a few, easily accessible folders or binders:

- Argument outline and key points
- Case summaries and key quotes
- Record excerpts and key documents
- Relevant case law and statutes
- Notes on anticipated questions and responses

- I have used tabs, dividers, and clear headings to facilitate quick access.
- I have highlighted key points and phrases for easy reference.
- I am using a small notebook or pad for quick notes during argument.

Delivery

- I have researched the venue and courtroom technology in advance.
- I have practiced speaking at a comfortable pace and volume.
- I have prepared a clear and organized introduction, including a roadmap.
- I have practiced answering questions directly and concisely.
- I will refrain from arguing with the judges or opposing counsel.
- I will show respect and professionalism throughout.

Additional Tips

- Listen carefully to the judges' questions and respond thoughtfully.
- Stay calm and composed, even under pressure.
- Use clear and concise language, avoiding jargon and legalese.
- Be prepared to concede or distinguish unfavorable authorities.
- Show respect for the court, opposing counsel, and the legal process.

Appendix C

Other Suggested Texts

Texts about Writing Style

- William Strunk Jr. and E.B. White, The Elements of Style (4th ed., Longman, 2000)
- Bryan A. Garner, Garner's Redbook: A Manual on Legal Style (3rd ed., West Academic, 2013)
- Richard C. Wydick, Plain English for Lawyers (5th ed., Carolina Academic Press, 2005)

Texts about Persuasion

- Robert Cialdini, Influence: The Psychology of Persuasion (Harper Business, 2009)
- Daniel Kahneman, Thinking, Fast and Slow (Farrar, Straus and Giroux, 2011)

Texts about Appellate Practice

- Edward A. Carnes, et al., Appellate Practice Handbook (LexisNexis, 2017)
- Gregory S. Cook, et al., Appellate Litigation (ALI-ABA, 2018)
- David R. Fine, Appellate Advocacy: Principles and Practice (West Academic, 2019)

Other Appellate Advocacy Books

- Ruggero J. Aldisert, Winning on Appeal: Better Briefs and Oral Argument (2nd ed., NITA, 2017)
- Deborah J. Merritt, et al., Learning from Good Briefs: What Makes Them Good, and How They Can Inform Your Writing (West Academic, 2019)
- Bryan Garner, The Winning Brief: 100 Tips for Persuasive Briefing in Trial and Appellate Courts (3d ed., Oxford Univ. Press, 2014)
- Antonin Scalia & Bryan A. Garner, Making Your Case: The Art of Persuading Judges (West Group 2008)

Index

R

S

T

V

W